THE MAGIC OF
YOUR TABLE SAW

THE MAGIC OF YOUR TABLE SAW

John A. Corinchock

Reston Publishing Company, Inc.
A Prentice-Hall Company
Reston, Virginia

Library of Congress Cataloging in Publication Data

Corinchock, John A.

  The magic of your table saw.

  1. Saws.   2. Woodwork.   I. Title.

  TT186.C67   6841.083   80-27394

  Includes Index

  ISBN 0-937558-03-6

DeWalt Catalog No. 35600-15

WARNING: MANY ILLUSTRATIONS IN THIS BOOK AND OTHERS OF ITS KIND SHOW THE SAW IN USE WITH THE BLADE GUARD REMOVED. THIS IS DONE SOLELY IN THE INTEREST OF CLARITY IN THE ILLUSTRATIONS AND SHOULD NEVER BE CONSIDERED AS A NORMAL WORKING PROCEDURE.

This handbook provides basic information relating to table saws. It is not intended to replace instructions or precautions given by the maker or vendor of any table saw that you may consider using. Additionally, while this handbook contains many safety tips, it is not possible to provide precautions for all possible hazards that might result. Standard and accepted safety procedures should be applied at all times.

© 1980 by
Black & Decker (U.S.) Inc.
701 East Joppa Road
Towson, Md. 21204

Text prepared and book designed by Robert Scharff & Associates, Ltd.

10 9 8 7 6 5 4 3 2 1

Printed in the United States of America

Table of Contents

Introduction to the table saw—choosing the right saw—table saw size—table saw capacity—cutting unit parts—cutting controls—special upper-cutting action—power drive arrangements—the rip fence—auxiliary rip fence facing—the miter gauge—the miter gauge lock down screw—the kerf guide—how to mark the kerf guide—table saw motors—wiring requirements—blade guards—swing-away blade guards—how to move the swing-away type blade guard—kerf splitters—aligning the kerf splitter—antikick-back pawls—on-off switches—key locking feature—the overload protector and its function—choosing table saw accessories.

Why saw kerf clearance is important—how kerf clearance is achieved—wood cutting blades—crosscut blades—rip saw blades—types of combination blades—the planer combination blade—plywood blades—carbide tipped blades—choosing the right carbide tipped blade for the job—metal cutting blades—replacing a saw blade—abrasive cutoff wheels—standard dado heads—the parts of a standard dado head and their installation—Quick-set dado heads—setting the Quick-set dado head—molding shaper heads—mounting the molding cutterhead—using "hold-downs"—other table saw accessories—miter gauge clamp—stop rods—miter square for making right angle cuts—hold-down fingers—safety accessories—shop vacuum.

Following manufacturer's instructions for assembly—ideal locations for your table saw—lighting and ventilation—making the proper electrical connections—using "slow-blow" fuses—the dangers of voltage variations—having the electrical system serviced—proper grounding procedures—grounding plugs and adapters—using the proper gauge extension cords—installing a saw blade—why alignment is so important—the basics of table saw alignment—the types of faulty alignment—blade-table alignment or heel adjustment—squaring the miter gauge—operation of the rip fence clamp handle—adjusting the rip fence clamp handle—adjusting the table saw guide rails—aligning the rip fence—setting the rip fence pointer—bevel adjustments—vertical or 0° bevel stops—45° bevel stop—adjusting the drive belt tension—aligning the blade guard and splitter—a final word about adjustments.

Preface

Accurate, straight-line sawing is essential in nearly all woodworking projects. The table saw is a power tool that accomplishes this job quickly and efficiently. The saw's very design lends itself to accuracy. Its miter gauge and rip fence guide the work, reducing the chance of human error. The bevel angle and miter controls can be set precisely. Accessories such as dado and molding cutters give the tool the versatility to perform all types of woodworking tasks.

The table saw has a number of guards and safety devices which should be kept in place and used whenever possible. In many illustrations in this book, the guards have been removed. This is solely for the sake of clarity and should never be regarded as normal operating procedure. No matter how well any power tool is designed for performance and safety, the final responsibility for safe operation lies with the operator. Chapter 4 deals with safety. Read and learn it well. It is the most important chapter in the book. Remember, any operation you do not feel comfortable or confident doing is a dangerous one.

That is why it is important for anyone new to the art of woodworking on the table saw to start at Chapter 1 and learn the basics. Jumping into one of the more involved projects detailed in the latter chapters before doing this invites poor results and possibly hazardous situations.

Any woodworking project is an investment on the part of the builder. He or she invests time, energy, and money. The rewards can be great, both personally and financially. But there is nothing satisfying about a wood joint that does not fit snugly or a miter that is cut improperly. Doing the job right the first time leads to true woodworking magic on the table saw. It is the sincere hope of everyone involved with this book that it will be of aid to any homecraftsperson —beginner or advanced.

I would like to thank all my colleagues at Robert Scharff and Associates for their fine work in editing, designing, and illustrating this book. Thanks to Robert Middleton for constructing the woodworking jigs shown throughout the book. Finally, a sincere thank you to Carlton F. Moe for his technical assistance and advice in bringing this book to its completion.

John A. Corinchock

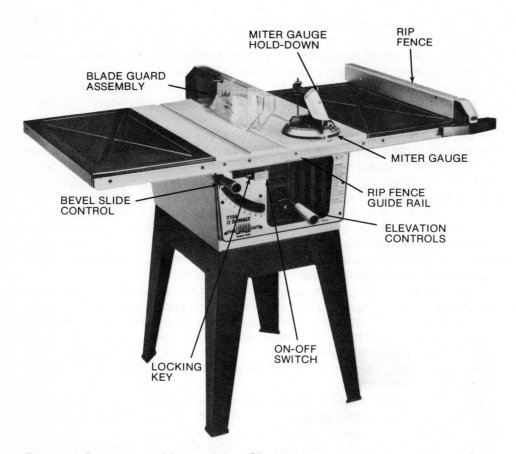

MITER GAUGE
HOLD-DOWN

RIP
FENCE

BLADE GUARD
ASSEMBLY

MITER GAUGE

BEVEL SLIDE
CONTROL

RIP FENCE
GUIDE RAIL

ELEVATION
CONTROLS

LOCKING
KEY

ON-OFF
SWITCH

Figure 1-1: Basic parts and features of a 10" table saw.

Chapter 1
Know Your
Table Saw

The table saw forms the cornerstone of every good workshop. Sometimes called the bench, variety, or stationary circular saw, this power tool can perform a wide range of sawing operations from the simplest straight cut to the most beautiful and intricate molding work. The true value of a table saw becomes apparent when you consider that sawing takes place in over 80% of all woodworking operations.

The table saw is a simple tool, both in its design and operation (Figure 1-1). When properly adjusted, the saw's rip fence and miter gauge assure accurate straight line cutting by reducing the chance of human error to a minimum. That's the magic of a table saw. All you do is set the saw and guide the work. The saw does the rest, crosscutting exact lengths and square corners and quickly ripping smooth and exact widths (Figure 1-2). What's more, basic crosscuts and rip cuts are easy once the operator understands the correct running and safety procedures. Other more involved operations can be mastered with a bit of practice and patience. Six basic cuts—the crosscut, the bevel crosscut, rip, bevel rip, miter, and bevel miter—form the basis for all woodworking. Every other cut, no matter how intricate, is a combination of these six cuts. The combinations are almost endless (Figure 1-3). Plus, with accessories such as dado and molding cutterheads, as well as abrasive cutoff wheels, the magic of the table saw extends even further.

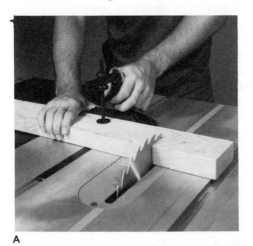

A   B

Figure 1-2: The two most common methods of guiding work: (A) Miter gauge and (B) rip fence.

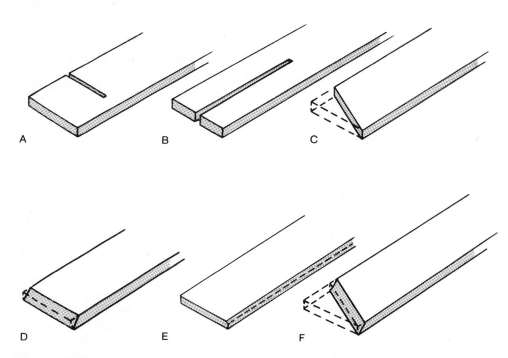

Figure 1-3: The six basic cuts used in woodworking: (A) Crosscut; (B) rip; (C) miter; (D) bevel crosscut; (E) bevel rip; and (F) bevel miter.

If you already own a table saw, but only use it for the basic woodworking cuts, you probably realize the tremendous potential of this precision cutting tool. This book will help you harness that potential and use it for any number of woodworking jobs. Besides covering all the basic and advanced wood cuts, there are chapters on wood joint design, furniture construction, and finishing work using the table saw. There are also chapters detailing installation and adjustment, safety, care and maintenance, as well as a special section filled with valuable home shop information.

If you are planning to buy or have just purchased a table saw, learn the basics well before attempting more complex cuts. Although the table saw is one of the safer power tools ever built, there is always the possibility of hazards whenever a power tool is not handled properly. Consider any safety features or accessories which will make the type of work you plan to do both safer and easier. Finally, always keep your saw in good working order and follow any specific instructions or precautions described in your owner's manual.

Table Saw Size. The size of a table saw is determined by the diameter of the largest saw blade that the saw will accommodate. A saw which can be fitted with a blade up to a maximum of 10" in diameter is known as a 10" table saw.

Table Saw Capacity. Table saw capacity is determined approximately by blade size. For instance, with the blade set at a 90° angle, a 10" saw can successfully cut through wood up to 3-1/2" thick; a 12" saw can handle boards up to 4-1/8" thick. **Note:** See Chapter 5 for additional information concerning the cutting capacity of Uppercut™ saws.

Cutting Unit Parts and Controls. The focal point of any table saw is where the action takes place, at the saw blade itself. The saw blade is mounted on a threaded shaft known as an arbor. The standard diameter for most table saw arbors is 5/8″. A portion of the blade projects up through the table insert of the saw. The table saw will come equipped with a standard table insert suitable for use with all regular and carbide-tipped saw blades within the saw's capacity. A special, wider insert is necessary when cutting with dado and molding cutterheads (Figure 1-4).

Figure 1-4: Two types of table inserts: (left) Standard insert; (right) special wider insert for dado and molding operations.

The arbor on which the blade is mounted can be tilted with a simple adjustment of the tilt control. The control shown in Figure 1-5 is a calibrated slide mechanism which allows for quick, easy bevel settings. The knob swings up and down in an arc and can be locked at any desired angle. A counterbalance offsets the weight of the motor and transmission, assuring a smooth, accurate sliding action. The tilt scale, located beneath the control, can be easily read and indicates the exact angle setting. Adjusting the tilt control mechanism is discussed in detail in Chapter 3.

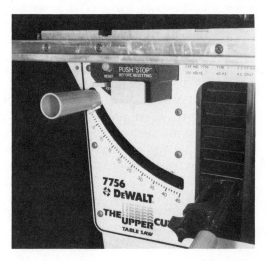

Figure 1-5: Sliding tilt control for setting saw blade bevel.

A second, separate control sets the blade elevation or depth-of-cut (Figure 1-6). Actually, there are two elevation controls. The large handle is for quick coarse settings. A slight turn to the left unlocks this handle, which can then be either lifted up or pushed down until the proper blade elevation is reached. Turning the handle back to the right locks the blade at this setting. The small knob to the left of the coarse elevation control is used for fine elevation adjustment after the rough setting has been locked into place. The total elevation travel of the fine adjustment knob is about 1-1/4", so its major function is to assure precise elevation settings. The elevation unit on this table saw is balanced in such a way that the blade will automatically lower itself below the table top after being unlocked. This saves both time and labor.

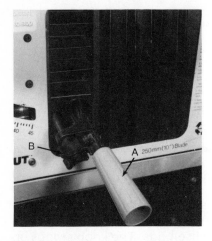

Figure 1-6: The two elevation controls: (A) The coarse slide control; (B) the fine elevation knob.

Special Uppercutting Action. The table saw illustrated throughout this book features a new type of crosscutting action called uppercutting. With an Uppercut™ table saw it is possible for the operator to crosscut finished stock up to 8" wide without sliding it into a cranked-up blade. On these models the blade remains below table level until the piece to be cut is firmly clamped or otherwise held down in place. The saw blade is then started and raised into the workpiece by pushing down on the elevation control handle (Figure 1-7). It is also possible to lock the blade in place for conventional crosscutting, ripping, or angle cuts.

The uppercut feature provides an additional element of safety since the hands need not be placed near a rotating blade. Accuracy is also increased. Uppercutting is discussed in detail in Chapter 5.

Power Drive Arrangements. The arbor is turned by the saw's motor in one of two ways, either a direct-drive arrangement or a belt and pulley system. Most modern table saws are driven by belt and pulley systems which have certain advantages over the direct-drive arrangement (Figure 1-8). One such advantage is the increased maximum cutting thickness of the saw. With belt and pulley saws it is not necessary to position the motor directly under the table as is the case with direct-drive models. The only space needed is for the drive pulley. This extra space allows for the higher positioning of the arbor which results in a greater percentage of the saw blade projecting above the table top.

Figure 1-7: The uppercut feature in action.

Figure 1-8: Saw motor, drive pulley, and saw arbor as seen from beneath the saw.

Another point in favor of belt and pulley arrangements is the reduced coasting time of the blade after it has been turned off. It is also easier to change the motor of a belt-driven saw. While motor failure is not common in well cared for saws, it may become necessary to change motors if you relocate the saw in another shop having a different current supply.

Rip Fences. Both the rip fence and the miter gauge serve to accurately guide the workpiece past the saw blade. The metal rip fence is used in all ripping operations. It is mounted on slides or slots built into the sides of the table top. The front slot is calibrated to show the exact distance the fence is located from the saw blade. To move the fence, raise the clamp handle (Figure 1-9) and with one hand move the fence to the desired position. Grasp the rip fence over the adjusting screws (Figure 1-10) and exert pressure to the rear as you move the fence sideways. This will hold the T-bar snugly against the guide rail and keep the fence absolutely parallel to the saw blade. Push the clamp handle down to lock the fence in position.

Figure 1-9: Raising the rip fence clamp handle.

Figure 1-10: Correct method of moving the rip fence.

Notice that holes in the rip fence allow for the easy attachment of auxiliary wood facing. Such auxiliary facing should be used when cutting with the dado or molding cutterhead, or whenever the operation calls for additional fence support. A smooth, straight board about 3/4" thick and the same size as the fence works well in most cases. Attach the wood fence with 2" round headed wood screws or a bolt and wing nut arrangement (Figure 1-11).

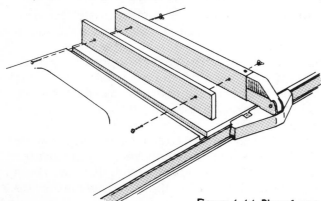

Figure 1-11: Plans for an auxiliary wood fence.

The rip fence must always be aligned parallel with the miter gauge slots of the table. Proper alignment cannot be overstressed. It assures good smooth cutting, reduces the possibility of dangerous kickbacks, and decreases unnecessary strain on the blade, drive train, and motor. Adjusting the rip fence is described in Chapter 3.

Miter Gauges. In all crosscutting operations, the miter gauge is used as the guiding device. The miter gauge slides in slots milled into the table top. There are two guiding slots, one to the right of the saw blade and one to the left. Although the right slot is used most often, the gauge can be set in either slot. The miter gauge can be set at any angle between 0° and 60°. Some gauges have positive stops at 0° and 45°, two of the most often used settings (Figure 1-12).

Figure 1-12: Making an angle cut with the miter gauge.

Although the degree marks are fairly accurate, it is best to make a test cut on a piece of scrap board when doing very precise work. Check this against a known standard before making the actual cut. Most miter gauges are designed for the easy attachment of auxiliary wood facing. Such facing may be necessary when working with longer pieces.

The miter gauge of saws equipped with the uppercutting feature discussed earlier in this chapter has a lock screw in its miter bar (Figure 1-13). When screwed down, the lock screw expands the miter bar slightly so it holds tightly in the table slot. The locking miter bar is used when making repetitive cuts with the uppercut feature. This assures the gauge will not move and makes it easy to do a large number of cuts quickly.

Figure 1-13: Tightening the miter gauge lock down screw.

Kerf Guides. The "kerf" is the slot formed by the saw blade as it cuts through the workpiece (Figure 1-14). Its width depends on such things as the saw blade's type, thickness (gauge), and its teeth arrangement. The kerf guide, on the other hand, performs a number of useful functions when cutting with the saw. Usually molded in a color which contrasts with the table top, the kerf guide acts as a reminder that everything in this area is in the path of the blade or cutting tool. Keep everything that you don't want to cut away from this path. This includes your hands.

Figure 1-14: Arrows point to the kerf made by the saw blade.

The kerf guide also serves as an aid when aligning workpieces with the saw blade. Its matte finish easily takes pencil marks which will show exactly where the material will meet the blade.

To accurately mark the guide, first cut off a board with the blade vertical (0° bevel). Turn off the saw, but keep the wood held tightly against the miter gauge (Figure 1-15A). By holding a soft lead pencil against the edge of the wood, you can mark the path of the blade edge by moving the wood and miter gauge along the slot. Periodically you should re-mark the line as it gets worn away. You should also re-mark the line after changing blades. Now when you are ready to cut materials, line up your mark on the workpiece with the line on the kerf guide and you'll be sure of accurate cuts without guesswork or trial and error (Figure 1-15B).

A   B

Figure 1-15: Correctly marking the kerf guide.

SAW MOTORS AND POWER SUPPLIES. Table saws are available with motors of various sizes and power ratings, so obviously the blade speed will vary from one saw to the next. However, the speed at which the saw operates when cutting is not overly critical. For example, the full load speed of a 10″ table saw equipped with a 60 cycle AC motor will be around 3450 rpm, but this can vary from one saw model to the next. Saws larger than this will quite naturally run at a slower arbor speed unless their motor is considerably larger.

Wiring Requirements. It is important to check the wiring of the shop where you plan to use the table saw. It is obvious that the saw motor cannot produce any more power than it receives from the power line running into the workshop. Be sure that your power fully agrees with the nameplate marking on the table saw. For example, volts 50/60 Hz means use alternating current **only**. Voltage variations of more than 10% will cause overheating and a loss of power.

Power lines which were designed to supply power to lights only will not sufficiently fulfill the needs of a power tool. A line that properly supplies one major power tool may not be adequate for several plus a number of light fixtures. Take into account that wire which is heavy enough to carry sufficient current a short distance will be too light for a greater distance. If you have any doubts whatsoever as to whether or not your power lines are adequate for the tools in your workshop, have the line checked by a qualified electrician. The best possible setup for any shop is a circuit for your table saw and other power tools that is independent of the lighting circuit. Complete electrical installation instructions are given in the following chapter.

SAFETY FEATURES. Modern table saws are designed for maximum safety during operation. The blade guard, antikickback fingers, and the splitter or spreader are the three most common safety features offered as standard equipment on most table saws. Electrical overload protectors and safety on-off switches are two other examples of highly practical safety devices.

Blade Guards. The blade guard performs several important safety functions. Its main job is to keep the hands and fingers of the operator away from the side of the moving blade. The guard also helps deflect flying wood chips away from the operator, which otherwise may create a hazard to the eyes. The blade guard should be in place for all through-cutting operations. A through-cutting operation, as the name implies, is one in which the saw blade cuts completely through the entire thickness of the workpiece. In a blind cutting operation, on the other hand, the saw blade does not project above the top face of the workpiece. A partial kerf or groove is cut into the underside of the workpiece.

Many different types of blade guards have been developed by saw manufacturers. Perhaps the most popular are those made of high-impact, see-through plastic. They provide maximum visibility as well as safety. The swing-away type blade guard (Figure 1-16) is a great time saver. This guard does not have to be removed, but can be lifted or pivoted completely behind the saw for easy tool or blade changes.

To move the guard out of the way for measuring cuts or changing blades, merely pick up the clear plastic portion and raise it up and back to rest tilted backwards. Before cutting, swing the guard back into position over the blade. To move the guard and splitter off the table top surface for non-through-cutting,

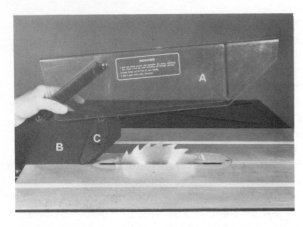

Figure 1-16: The (A) blade guard, (B) kerf splitter, and (C) antikick-back pawls of the table saw.

pull the release pin in the guard bracket (Figure 1-17) and swing the entire assembly back and down out of the way (Figure 1-18). When finished, always return the guard back to its correct position on the table top. Swing the complete assembly up and forward. The release pin will snap into the locked position automatically. Do not use the saw without proper guarding. (MANY ILLUSTRATIONS IN THIS BOOK AND OTHERS OF ITS KIND SHOW THE SAW IN USE WITH THE BLADE GUARD REMOVED. THIS IS DONE SOLELY IN THE INTEREST OF CLARITY IN THE ILLUSTRATIONS AND SHOULD NEVER BE CONSIDERED AS A NORMAL WORKING PROCEDURE.)

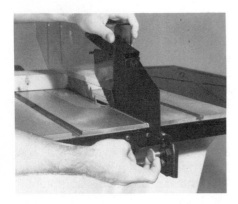

Figure 1-17: Releasing the pin of the guard assembly.

Figure 1-18: Guard assembly in swung away position.

Kerf Splitters. A splitter or spreader is a valuable aid in helping to prevent kickback. Kickback occurs when the woodpiece being cut binds on the saw blade. The splitter, a piece of metal located directly behind the saw blade, supports the blade guard and helps keep the saw kerf (or saw cut) open and moving through the blade smoothly. The splitter is especially valuable when making ripping cuts and should always be used in any operation of this kind.

Proper alignment of the splitter is quite important. When assembling the blade guard unit, use a straightedge to align the saw blade and splitter. Center the kerf splitter in the width of the saw cut.

Antikickback Pawls. The spring loaded antikickback pawls help hold the cut wood in place in the event of kickback. Check the antikickback device periodically and replace any worn or damaged pawls.

On-Off Switches. The on-off switch shown in Figure 1-19 has a removable key locking feature to prevent unauthorized and quite possibly hazardous use of the machine by children and others. The key must be in place before the saw will operate. The saw switch is pulled out to start the motor and pushed in to stop it. This type of switch is an added safety feature. If any trouble arises, this push-in switch can be quickly shut off with a simple bump of the operator's hip.

Do not cycle the motor switch on and off rapidly, as this may cause the arbor nut to loosen. If this does happen, turn the saw off and allow the blade to come to a complete stop. Tighten the arbor nut securely.

Figure 1-19: Removing the locking key of the on-off switch. The overload reset button is located above the key slot.

Never leave the saw when the power is on, and never leave the saw until the cutting tool has come to a complete stop after the switch has been turned off. Remove the key to lock the switch. It may be removed whether the switch knob is in the "on" or "off" position. If the key is removed while the switch is off, the switch may not be turned on. If the key is removed while the switch is on, the switch may be turned off, but may not be turned on again without first inserting the key.

Overload Protector. The saw's overload protector (Figure 1-19) guards against damage to the motor during times of extreme overload. The button located above the locking key must be pushed to the reset position before the saw will start again. There should be an audible "click" when this is done. If there is not, allow the motor to cool further until you do hear a "click" when the reset button is pushed. Always set the saw's on-off switch to the "off" position before pushing the overload reset button. If the switch is on, the motor will start when the reset button is pressed.

OTHER FEATURES. Table saw manufacturers offer a broad variety of accessories that can expand the saw's versatility and make complex cuts quick and easy. Other accessories or jigs can be constructed in your workshop at minimum cost. Choose or build any table saw accessory very carefully. It should be especially designed to fit your saw model. Operating the saw with mismatched accessories can be hazardous. Check your owner's manual or ask your saw dealer to find out exactly what is best for your machine. A number of the most popular and helpful table saw accessories are described in Chapter 2. Others are described throughout the book in those sections pertaining to their specific use.

Chapter 2
Saw Blades and
Table Saw Accessories

The proper selection and use of saw blades and accessories can make cutting on a table saw a great deal easier and more effective. To accomplish this, however, you must have some knowledge of the saw blades and table saw accessories available.

SAW BLADES. The purpose of the saw blade on a table saw, of course, is to cut various materials. But, regardless of the material being severed, the saw blade must cut a kerf slightly wider than its own body in order to prevent binding and overheating. This clearance is achieved in one of four different ways:

1. By setting or bending the ends of the teeth, alternating right and left so the kerf is wider than the thickness of the blade. Called a **flatground blade** (Figure 2-1A), the set of each tooth must be the same.

2. By grinding or tapering the steel between the teeth and the hub so as to leave the ends of the teeth at the original thickness of the blade. Called a **hollow-ground or taper-ground blade** (Figure 2-1B), this design produces a very smooth cut.

3. By grinding a limited amount of steel around the blade's perimeter so that the rim is thinner than the body of the blade (Figure 2-1C). A **thin-rim blade** produces a very smooth cut, but it must never be used on cuts deep enough to put the full gauge of the blade in the kerf—usually 1-1/2" regardless of blade size.

4. By brazing or swedging teeth that are slightly wider than the body of the blade. Most carbide-tipped blades are **swedge blades** (Figure 2-1D).

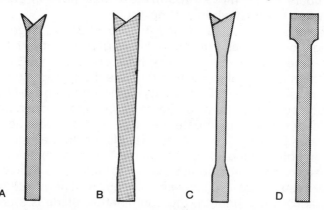

Figure 2-1: Four classes of blades: (A) Flatground blade; (B) hollow- and taper-ground blades; (C) thin-rimmed blade; and (D) swedge blade.

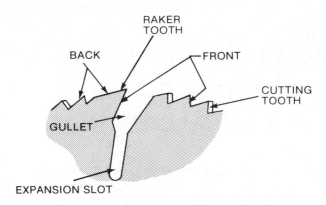

Figure 2-2: Parts of typical saw blades.

While all wood cutting saw blades belong to one of these four categories, the type of work a saw blade will do is determined by the size and shape of its blade teeth and gullets (Figure 2-2). Several kinds of common saw blades and the jobs they can perform are described below.

Wood Cutting Blades. Unfortunately, because of the nature of wood and the variety of materials that the craftsperson works with, there is no one blade that can perform all cuts perfectly. For instance, the combination type blade is designed to do both crosscutting and ripping, but is not the best blade you can obtain for either type of cut.

Most wood cutting blades are usually classified as to the task they perform.

Crosscut Blade—This flatground blade (Figure 2-3A) is designed for cutting across the grain of either hard- or softwood, as well as plywood, veneers, or other composition materials. While this blade can also be used for mitering, it shouldn't be used for ripping. As with all flatground blades, the teeth are set alternately so that they are slightly wider than the blade body in order to prevent binding and overheating. The small teeth are filed with a bevel on both the face and back to a sharp point. This shape permits the teeth to cleanly sever the wood fibers as they move through the wood. The small gullets of this blade produce a fine sawdust when cutting.

Rip Saw Blade—The rip saw blade (Figure 2-3B) has large teeth somewhat resembling those of a hand rip saw. It is designed to cut with the grain only on both hard- and softwoods; don't use it for crosscutting. Being a flatground blade, its teeth are set alternately, but unlike the crosscut type, they are filed straight across (no bevel). This straight filing forms chisel-like cutting edges which gouge out lengths of wood fibers during ripping operations. The gullets are also deeper to accommodate the larger chips produced.

Combination Blades—There are several blades on the market that do a fast, clean job on both ripping and crosscutting. The most common type—**the chisel-tooth flatground combination blade**—has teeth like a rip saw, but the design of the hook is such that it will crosscut equally well (Figure 2-3C). While its cut is not extraordinarily smooth, the combination blade is a good all-purpose blade, especially suited for construction work. Most table saws come equipped with a chisel-tooth combination as standard equipment.

Another popular flatground combination blade is the **novelty tooth type** (Figure 2-3D). Peak performance with this blade—often called a master combination—is assured in both ripping and crosscutting because it has extra large gullets to carry through the sawdust without binding. That is, this type of combination blade is divided into segments of either two or four cutter teeth and raker teeth with a deep gullet separating each segment. The two cutter teeth design rips a little easier than the four cutter teeth design, but the cut is not quite as smooth and the tendency for splintering is greater. Still, both types of novelty blades deliver a smoother cut than the standard combination blade.

Figure 2-3: Typical saw blades: (A) Crosscut blade; (B) rip saw blade; (C) chisel-tooth combination blade; and (D) novelty tooth combination blade.

The **planer combination** is a precision-ground blade that fills the need for a single saw which can perform the functions of ripping, cutting off, and mitering in all solid woods. Often called a **miter blade,** it is best used in cabinet work, furniture making, etc. Planer blades cut plywood beautifully, but they dull quickly because of the glue in the plywood. Planer saw blades generally have four cutting teeth and a single raker. These teeth have no set. Planer blades are tapered or hollow-ground so that they are thinner at the hub than they are at the rim (Figure 2-4A). Many table saw users make the mistake of treating the planer blade as a general purpose blade and expect it to do exactly the same work as a combination rip and crosscut blade, which it won't do. There is a definite limit to the thickness of the material that can be cut with the planer combination blade. If the user persists in overloading his blade, the result will invariably be burned and dulled teeth and resharpening expense. So if you want to keep a planer blade in good condition, treat it like the fine tool it is, and don't use it for heavy, coarse work.

Other types of combination blades are designed to perform specific woodworking jobs. The **hard-tip combination blade,** for example, quickly and accurately cuts hardwoods and plastics. The blade's skip-tooth design makes it an excellent blade for the cutting of lightweight aluminum extrusions and other soft, nonferrous metals provided plenty of lubrication is used. Its flame-hardened, quenched teeth stay sharp longer, but don't cut quite as smoothly as other combination blades.

Plywood Blade—This fine-tooth saw blade with either hollow-ground or thin-rimmed taper design (Figure 2-4B) cuts with a minimum of splintering in plywood, paneling, veneers, and thin laminated materials. It also makes smooth crosscuts and miters. Since many blades of this type are made specifically for cutting plywood that is 3/4" or less in thickness, it should never be used on cuts deep enough to put the full gauge of the blade in the kerf.

A   B

Figure 2-4: (A) Planer blade and (B) plywood blade. Arrow shows difference in the extent of grinding between a hollow-ground planer blade and thin-rim plywood blade.

Carbide-Tipped Blades. Tungsten carbide is the hardest man-made metal in existence. Its major role in the manufacture of circular saw blades is wear resistance. Carbide-tipped blades stay sharp much longer than conventional steel blades under comparable conditions. They are also capable of cutting a wider variety of materials—wood, plastic, plywood, cement-asbestos board, composition board, rubber, and many types of nonferrous metals such as aluminum, brass, and copper.

Once used primarily in industrial applications, carbide-tipped blades are rapidly becoming popular with serious do-it-yourselfers. Even though their initial cost is higher, the long life of carbide-tipped blades makes them a higher utility value to anyone who does heavy-duty volume sawing. They also save time by reducing the need to change saw blades to suit the job requirement. All carbide blades can be considered combination blades; that is, they can be used to rip, crosscut, and cut off.

The teeth of most carbide-tipped blades are brazed, allowing resharpening or replacement. If dulled or damaged, the blade should be reconditioned by a professional saw sharpener or by the manufacturer. The carbide teeth have no "set." In most styles, the tips are wider than the body to provide tooth clearance. This clearance is obtained in thin rim blades by grinding the blade body on a taper immediately behind the teeth resulting in extremely smooth cutting. Tips are ground (Figure 2-5) according to the primary use of the blade.

Square Top Grind—A heavy-duty, well supported cutting edge that resists shock better than other grind styles. Recommended for rough, heavy-duty cutting where a smooth finish is not required.

Alternate Top Bevel Grind—Results in a keener, smoother cutting edge. Cuts faster and with less resistance, leaving a smoother finish than square top grind.

Triple Chip Grind—A special tooth design for proper chip formation and cutting edge protection for sawing nonferrous metals and other hard materials.

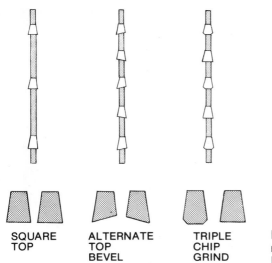

SQUARE
TOP

ALTERNATE
TOP
BEVEL

TRIPLE
CHIP
GRIND

Figure 2-5: Three popular tooth arrangements used with carbide-tipped
blades.

Although carbides are very versatile, best results are obtained when the
proper blade for the job is selected (Figure 2-6). For instance, the 8-tooth,
square-top, carbide-tipped blade is specifically designed for cutting tough-to-
cut materials such as wallboard, asbestos-cement siding, asbestos, and laminated plastic. It will also work where speed and finish are not critical. A 28-
tooth alternate ground, carbide tooth blade is designed for all types of wood,
plywood, veneers, and similar prefinished materials. On the other hand, a 100-
tooth thin rim produces a very thin kerf and is recommended for cabinet and
finishing work with both hard- and softwoods. While the novelty-tooth combination carbide blade with four alternating bevel ground cutting teeth and
raker tooth pattern is excellent for hard- and softwoods, particleboard, and
plywood, the 60-tooth triple-chip ground blade is best for cutting all types of
aluminum extrusions, tubing, and sheets, as well as other nonferrous metal
such as brass, copper, magnesium, and lead. Keep in mind that as a general
rule, the more cutting teeth on the saw blade, the smoother the finish cut.

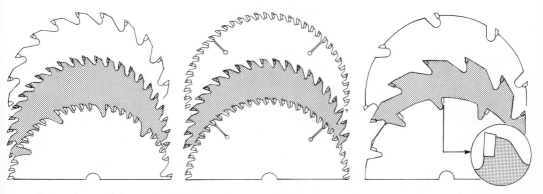

Figure 2-6: Various tooth combinations for carbide-tipped blades.

Metal Cutting Blades. There are two basic types of metal cutting blades (Figure 2-7): the nonferrous metal blade and the friction blade. The former's taper-ground teeth are shaped and set specifically for smooth, free cutting of all metals except iron and steel. Friction blades, as their name implies, cut by friction action. They are designed for cutting corrugated or sheet roofing, black iron, furnace pipe, or thin bar. Friction blades cut faster with less filings than abrasive blades and they do not require sharpening.

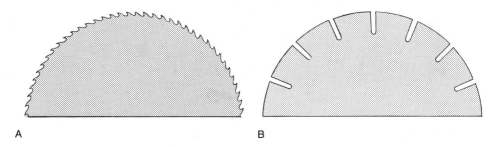

A   B

Figure 2-7: Two types of metal cutting blades: (A) Nonferrous metal blade and (B) friction blade.

Replacing a Saw Blade. Before installing or replacing a table saw blade, make sure that the power cord is removed from the power source. While you should always follow your saw owner's manual, the following will give some idea of how it is accomplished. Start by removing the two flathead screws which hold the table top insert in place and lift out the insert (Figure 2-8) from the table. If there is a blade already installed on the arbor, place a block of soft wood to keep it from turning. Then, using a properly sized wrench, loosen the arbor nut (Figure 2-9) by turning it in a counterclockwise direction when looking at the end of the arbor shaft. (Some table saws have a setup where two wrenches must be employed to remove the arbor nut.) After the nut has been removed, carefully remove the blade from the arbor.

Figure 2-8: Removing the table insert.

Figure 2-9: Removing the blade.

Place the new saw blade on the arbor so that the directional arrow (and teeth) will be pointing toward the front of the saw. Tighten the arbor securely and replace the table top insert. (Never operate the saw without an insert plate.) Rotate the blade by hand to make certain that it is running free and clear before plugging in the power cord. Be sure the switch is OFF.

To cut properly, saw blades must be kept sharp and well maintained. Complete information on the care of saw blades can be found in Chapter 14.

OTHER CUTTING TOOLS. In addition to saw blades, other cutting tools used on the table saw include abrasive cutoff wheels, dado heads, and straight and shaped molding cutters.

Abrasive Cutoff Wheels. There are two basic types of abrasive cutoff wheels (Figure 2-10). One is aluminum oxide, which is used to cut ferrous metals (steel, cast iron, stainless steel) and hardened nonferrous metals (hard brass, aluminum, bronze). The other is silicon carbide for use on nonmetallic materials, such as stone, concrete, cinder block, limestone, corrugated plastic, sandstone, gypsum wallboard, soft brick, ceramics, brick tile, asbestos-cement boards, plasterboard, carbon, brake linings, insulation boards, and soft nonferrous metals. This type will also do a good job on the softer metals such as aluminum, and is sometimes recommended for cutting small-diameter steel rods.

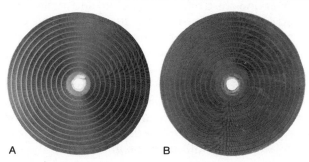

A   B

Figure 2-10: Two types of abrasive cutoff wheels: (A) Aluminum oxide and (B) silicon carbide.

While abrasive wheels for use on the table saw arbor can be obtained in several diameters, thicknesses, and grades, an 8″ diameter, 3/32″-thick, reinforced resin-bonded grade is the most satisfactory average home shop use. (Nonreinforced wheels tend to be brittle and should never be used.) As with saw blades, don't run the cutoff wheel faster than the manufacturer's recommended maximum speeds.

The abrasive wheel is mounted on the saw arbor in the same manner as a saw blade. Information on how to use abrasive cutoff wheels can be found in Chapter 13.

Dado Heads. The dado head is one of the most valuable cutting tools available to the table saw owner. It can cut grooves, rabbets, mortises, tenons, etc., in thicknesses from 1/8″ to 13/16″ in a single pass. In other words, the dado head cuts down the time consumed in making many wood joints. There are two basic types of dado heads: the standard, or conventional, and "Quick-set" types.

Standard Dado Heads—Actually, there are basically two types of dado heads, the flatground and the hollow-ground. While the latter is more expensive, it produces a much smoother cut and should be used in high-quality work. Either type consists of two outside saws (Figure 2-11), each about 1/8″ thick, whose teeth are not given any set, and inside saws, or "chippers" one 1/4″, two 1/8″ (some heads include two additional 1/8″ chippers instead of the 1/4″ one), and one 1/16″ thick (thickness at the hub). The cutting portions of the chippers are wider than the hub to overlap the adjacent cutter or saw. When assembling a cutter head, arrange the two outside saws so that the large raker teeth on one are opposite the small cutting teeth on the other. This produces a smoother cutting and easier running head. Also, be sure the wide cutting portion of the chippers are placed in the gullets of the outside saws, not against the teeth, so that the head cuts cleanly and chips have room to come out. Stagger the inside cutters so their teeth don't come together. For example, if three cutters are used, they should be set 60° apart.

Never use the chipper blades without the two outside saws. For example, to cut a dado 1/2″ wide, use the two outside saws, each 1/8″ in width, plus a single 1/4″ or two 1/8″ chippers. Actually, any width dado head can be used—the size is limited only by the length of the motor arbor. However, most dado head sets have only enough blades to make cuts up to 13/16″ wide.

When the width of the finished cut is to be wider than the dado head, make two successive cuts. If more than one cut is required they must overlap a bit at the center. If the width of the dado is more than twice the capacity of the cutter head, set the head for slightly over one-third of the dado width and make three overlapping cuts. If needed, you can control the exact width of the groove with paper washers. These washers, 3 to 4″ in diameter, can be placed between the blades and chippers. You can increase the width even more with cardboard (up to 1/16″ thick) instead of paper.

The standard dado head (Figure 2-12) is installed on the motor shaft in the same manner as a saw blade. The blade guard, splitter, and antikickback device can't be used when employing the dado and should be removed from the saw. Also, the standard table insert must be replaced with a dado insert which has a slot wide enough to accommodate a full-width dado head.

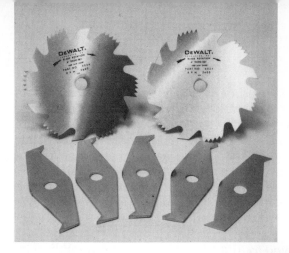

Figure 2-11: Typical flatground standard dado head.

Figure 2-12: Installing a standard dado head on a saw arbor.

Quick-Set Dado Heads—This adjustable dadoing tool, shown in Figure 2-13, works by means of a flat core studded with tool-steel cutters that are mounted between matched, tapered outside plates. It doesn't work with chippers simply because rotating the outside plates puts the cutting knives on a particular width-of-cut path. In other words, the knives are "spread" from the minimum cut of 1/4" to the maximum cut of 13/16".

Figure 2-13: Two styles of Quick-set dadoes.

To set a Quick-set dado, loosen the arbor nut. **Caution:** Be sure that the tool is unplugged before performing this operation. Turn the tool until you see the black arrow. Hold the blades and center disk stationary with one hand (Figure 2-14A) and rotate the outside plates with the other hand, until the arrow points to the desired width. Tighten the arbor nut. If you want to cut a groove for a very tight fit of a board, such as a shelf, make a trial cut on scrap material. Then, if you want to make the cut slightly wider or narrower, loosen the arbor nut and move the arrow slightly toward the next larger or smaller number, whichever way you want to change the width. Always be sure to tighten the arbor nut before starting the table saw.

The Quick-set dado is assembled for right-hand (clockwise) rotation, with the flat side of the tool against the shoulder of the arbor (Figure 2-14B). Be sure that the insides of the plate are clean of sawdust, otherwise the blades won't cut true to size. Also, occasionally clean the cutters with a saw blade gum solvent.

The design of the Quick-set and standard dado heads' cutting teeth permits sawing with the grain, across the grain, or at an angle.

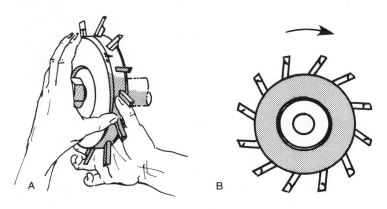

Figure 2-14: Setting a Quick-set dado.

Molding Shaper Head. A molding cutterhead with shaper knives (Figure 2-15) makes it possible to cut a wide variety of straight moldings or shapes on the table saw. The cutterhead is mounted to the saw's arbor in place of an ordinary saw blade. It is necessary to remove the standard table insert and replace it with a dado insert which has an opening large enough to accommodate the molding head and cutters.

In many cases, it is also necessary to use special auxiliary wood facing on the rip fence. To construct this special fence (Figure 2-16), first make two 1" thick facings to fit your rip fence. Straight-grained hardwood is best. Clamp one facing to the fence on top of a 1" thick scrap board. Then, use a set of planer and jointer cutters in the head to cut a semicircular notch in the bottom edge of the facing for cutter clearance. Prepare the other facing in like manner and mount the two facings on opposite sides of your fence with countersunk bolts and nuts.

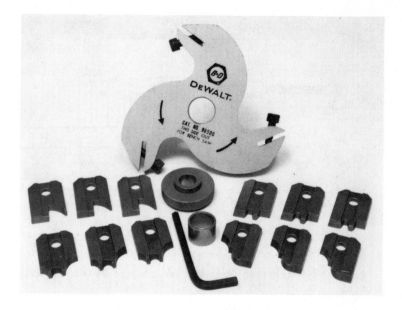

Figure 2-15: Typical molding shaper head.

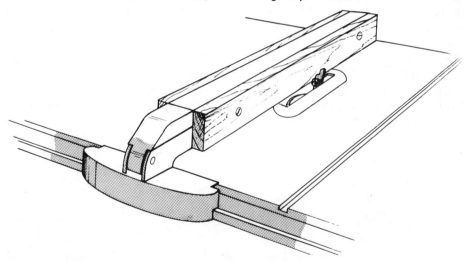

Figure 2-16: Construction of the special fence used for shaping operations. Details on the actual construction can be found in Chapter 9.

Any device which holds the work against the fence or saw table is called a "hold-down." The hold-down and guide illustrated in Figure 2-17 is an example. This shows an adjustable hold-down device for the various widths and thicknesses of material which supports the work at all times against the impact of the cutter. Some form of hold-down should be used wherever possible.

The wide variety of knives or cutter shapes made to fit these molding cutter-heads gives the operator an almost unlimited number of molding shape possibilities from which to choose (see Chapter 9).

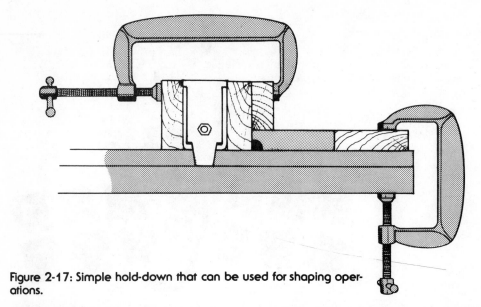

Figure 2-17: Simple hold-down that can be used for shaping operations.

OTHER ACCESSORIES AND JIGS. Operational safety and cutting accuracy should be the main concerns of every table saw owner. Modern table saws are designed with these two factors in mind. They provide a fast, accurate and safe means of cutting and working with wood, plastics, and nonferrous metals. In addition to the alignment and safety features built into every saw, a large number of accessories and jigs are used in woodworking jobs. These accessories and jigs further increase working safety and cutting ease. Numerous accessories and jigs are shown throughout this book, most of which you can make. In this chapter, we'll concern ourselves with those you can purchase. Some, such as the taper jig (Figure 2-18), can be either purchased or made.

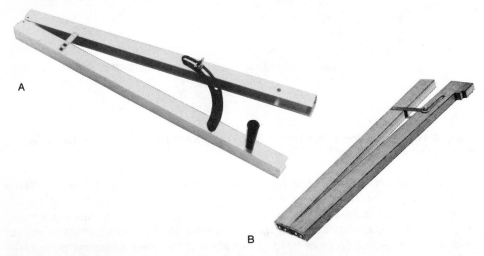

A

B

Figure 2-18: (A) Commercial metal taper jig that can be used for plotting and sawing single or double tapers on a table saw. The jig can be adjusted for tapers up to 15° (3" per foot). (B) A wooden taper jig can be made as described in Chapter 5.

Miter Gauge Clamp. This clamp arrangement—which is standard equipment on some saws, an accessory on others—is helpful when crosscutting or mitering (Figure 2-19). With it, work can be clamped tightly and securely to the miter gauge, thus completely eliminating any tendency for the work to creep toward or away from the saw blade. The clamp setup also makes crosscutting and mitering safer since the hands needn't come near the blade. In addition, when you crosscut longer material, the clamps will hold the work on the miter gauge, which frees your left hand to support the workpiece.

Figure 2-19: Miter gauge clamp in use.

Miter Gauge Stop Rod. Fitted to the miter gauge, this accessory (Figure 2-20) holds short workpieces to prevent their creeping and also positions them for cutting off to a predetermined length. The stop rod is fitted into the miter gauge on the side away from the saw blade.

Miter Square. This clamping and guiding device (Figure 2-21) is designed with the specific purpose of making right-angle saw cuts a "can't miss" operation. The accurate construction of such practical items as picture frames, door frames, window frames, and furniture moldings becomes a simple task. And, one of the most convenient features of this miter square is that both left- and right-hand miter cuts can be made without having to make minor angle adjustments for the two different miters. The quick clamping jaws hold both flat or irregularly shaped pieces firmly in place, and the length gauge assures accuracy when cutting pieces to similar lengths.

Figure 2-20: Miter gauge stop rod in use.

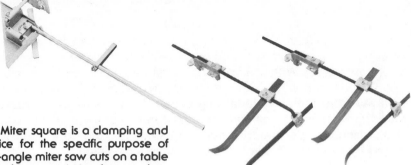

Figure 2-21: Miter square is a clamping and guiding device for the specific purpose of making right-angle miter saw cuts on a table saw, for such things as picture frames, door frames, window frames, furniture moldings, etc. One of the most outstanding features of the miter square is that right- and left-hand miter cuts can be made without having to make minor angle adjustments for the two different miters.

Figure 2-22: Hold-down fingers keep work in place during operations in which it may be difficult to manually hold and guide work.

Hold-Down Fingers. The hold-down fingers, such as those shown in Figure 2-22, provide dependable accuracy and increased safety during ripping type cuts, molding operations, and dadoing jobs. The hold-down components—the four spring steel "fingers" or guides, their clamps, and the two "L" shaped steel bars with securing clamps—are designed to assemble easily to a simple wood auxiliary fence constructed by the operator. The four spring fingers adjust to any setting and hold the workpiece firmly against the table surface and fence as the cut is being made.

Other Valuable Accessories. Safety goggles (Figure 2-23A) or safety protective spectacles (Figure 2-23B) should be worn when performing any operation on the table saw. If any degree of dirt and sawdust is raised, be sure to wear a dust mask (Figure 2-23C). To reduce the effect of loud saw noises on your hearing, you may wish to wear ear plugs (Figure 2-23D).

Another important safety accessory is a shop vacuum cleaner (Figure 2-24). It will help to keep your table saw and shop free of sawdust and other debris. This versatile tool can also be used for other clean-up jobs around your home.

Figure 2-24: Shop vacuum cleaner at work.

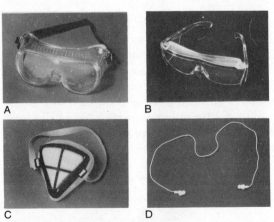

Figure 2-23: Important safety equipment: (A) Safety goggles; (B) protective spectacles; (C) dust mask; and (D) ear plugs.

Chapter 3
Installation
and Adjustment

Before beginning any woodworking or cutting operation, take the time to properly install and adjust your table saw. Check to see that the power supply is adequate and properly connected. Follow the manufacturer's specific instructions when assembling the saw. Some manufacturers simplify the setting up operation by assembling and testing the machine at the factory. The saw is then partially knocked down for shipment to you. After final assembly, make any adjustments to the table, miter gauge, or rip fence that are necessary. These adjustments should be checked periodically to assure accuracy.

LOCATING THE TABLE SAW. The table saw should be installed in a location that provides adequate space for the handling of work materials. The optimum location for cabinet type saws is in the center of the workshop. This will provide for the maximum amount of space on both sides as well as the front and back of the saw. The ripping and crosscutting of long pieces of stock or large panels require this good amount of working room for maximum safety. The proper table height should always be below waist level.

Sufficient lighting and ventilation are two other factors that should be carefully considered when locating the table saw. Although most operations can be performed on both sides of the saw blade, most operators prefer one side over the other for one reason or another. When at all possible, position the table saw so that the lighting favors this preferred side. In any case, never operate the saw without a clear view of what you are doing.

Good ventilation is a factor often overlooked in even the most carefully planned work areas. Yet all sawing operations, especially those done on plastics or masonry with abrasive cutoff wheels, produce dust and other particles that can irritate the eyes, nose, and throat. While protective gear should always be worn, proper ventilation can minimize such problems.

Electrical Connections. As previously mentioned in Chapter 1, the proper electrical supply and connections are essential to safe, efficient cutting. The wire from the power source to the machine must be of the proper size in order to obtain the maximum operating efficiency from the saw motor. Before plugging the cord into the power outlet, recheck the saw's nameplate to be absolutely sure the motor's voltage needs match those supplied by your power source. (Remember: Volts 50/60 Hz means alternating current only.)

The electrical line should also be fused with a 20-ampere fuse. If a 20-ampere fuse blows during that fraction of a second when the motor is switched on, do not replace it with a fuse of a higher rating. Replace it with a 20-ampere fuse of the "slow-blow" or delay type which, because of its special fusible link, will withstand the momentary overload and still deliver the proper protection at all other times.

If the motor is plugged into a circuit that is already overloaded, quite naturally the line will not supply enough current for the saw's needs. The result will be a voltage drop that will cause the motor to overheat as it struggles to carry the cutting load. Voltage variations of 10% or more can seriously harm your table saw motor. Many times a perfectly good motor is condemned for not producing sufficient power, when the electrical system is to blame. That is why it is advisable to have a completely separate line for your workshop. This line should be made of at least 10-gauge wire.

If the table saw motor is running hot or is short of power, have your local power company check your voltage. First, check it with no load and then with a load. Without a load, the voltage reading should be approximately equal to the motor's rating. Under a full load, the line voltage should drop no more than 5%.

It is recommended that you never disassemble your table saw or attempt to do any rewiring in the electrical system. Such repairs should be performed by your table saw dealer or qualified professionals. Should you be determined to make a repair yourself, remember that the green colored wire is the "grounding" wire. Never connect this green wire to a "live" terminal.

Grounding. In the event of a malfunction or breakdown, grounding provides a path of least resistance for electric current to reduce the risk of electrical shock. Therefore, the table saw should always be properly grounded while in use. The saw illustrated throughout this book is equipped with an electric cord having an equipment-grounding conductor and a grounding plug. The plug must be plugged into a matching outlet that is properly installed and grounded in accordance with all local codes and ordinances. Do not modify the plug provided—if it will not fit the outlet, have the proper outlet installed by a qualified electrician. Improper connection of the equipment-grounding conductor can result in a risk of electrical shock. The conductor with insulation having an outer surface that is green with or without yellow stripes is the equipment-grounding conductor. If repair or replacement of the electric cord or plug is necessary, do not connect the equipment-grounding conductor to a live terminal. Check with a qualified electrician or service technician if the grounding instructions are not completely understood or if in doubt as to whether the tool is properly grounded.

Grounded, cord-connected tools intended for use on a supply circuit having a nominal rating less than 150 volts—This tool is intended for use on a circuit that has an outlet such as the one illustrated in Figure 3-1A. It also has a grounding plug such as that shown in the same illustration. A temporary adapter (Figures 3-1B and C) may be used to connect this plug to a two-pole receptacle (Figure 3-1B) if a properly grounded outlet is not available. The temporary adapter should be used only until a properly grounded outlet can be installed by a qualified electrician. (These adapters are not for use in Canada.) When using an adapter, connect the extending green wire to the outlet-plate retaining screw, provided the outlet itself is properly grounded. The green wire can also be connected to any other permanent ground, such as a water or electric-conduit pipe.

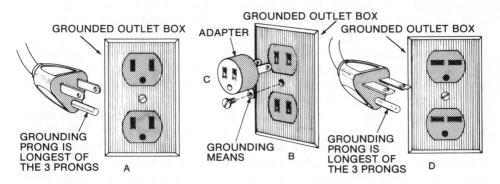

Figure 3-1: Types of power outlets, grounding plugs, and adapters.

Grounded, cord-connected tools intended for use on a supply circuit having a nominal rating between 150-250 volts, inclusive— This tool is intended for use on a circuit having an outlet and a grounding plug such as those illustrated in Figure 3-1D. Make sure the tool is connected to an outlet having the same configuration as the plug. No adapter is available or should be used with this tool. If the tool must be reconnected for use on a different type of electric circuit, the reconnection should be made by qualified service personnel; and after reconnection, the tool should comply with all local codes and ordinances.

Extension Cords. If you plan on operating the table saw at a considerable distance from the power source, use a three-conductor, grounding-type extension cord. Be sure the extension cord is of adequate size to assure safe operation and to prevent power loss and motor overheating. Immediately replace or repair any damaged cord. The table shown here will help you determine the minimum size wire required for your needs.

Ext. Cable Length	Wire Size (A.W.G.)	
	(120 Volts)	**(220/240 Volts)**
50'	#14	#18
75'	#12	#16
150'	#10	#14
200'	# 8	#12
300'	# 6	#10
500'	# 4	# 8

INSTALLING OR CHANGING SAW BLADES. Before installing or replacing any saw blade, make sure the saw is disconnected from its power source. Raise the blade guard out of the way. Remove the screws that hold the table insert in place and lift out the insert. Place the blade in a vertical position (0° bevel). Raising the saw arbor to its maximum elevation will make working on the saw much easier.

To remove a blade from the saw's arbor, first insert the hex wrench provided with the saw into the end of the saw arbor. This keeps the saw blade from turning. (A block of softwood placed against the front of the blade is also good for this purpose.) Loosen the blade nut by turning it with the standard wrench provided. Turn the nut in a counterclockwise direction as you look in from the end of the saw arbor (Figure 3-2). After the arbor nut is unfastened, remove both the flange and the blade from the saw arbor.

If you are installing a blade on the arbor for the first time, refer to your owner's manual for the proper order in which to place the parts on the arbor shaft. Handle the saw blade carefully, installing it on the arbor so the teeth of the blade above the top of the table are pointing down at the front of the table, as shown in Figure 3-3. Replace the arbor flange and the blade nut. Overtightening of the blade nut is not necessary since the nut becomes self-tightening during operation. Replace the table top insert. Never run the table saw without the insert in place. Turn the blade by hand to make certain it is running free and clear on the arbor.

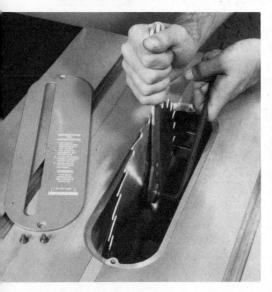

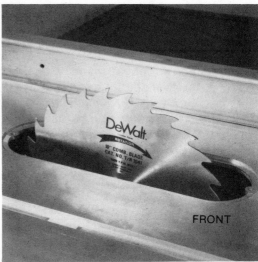

Figure 3-2: Installing a blade in the saw arbor.

Figure 3-3: The proper direction of rotation. Teeth should point down at the front of the table.

ADJUSTMENT AND ALIGNMENT. To get the most out of your table saw, it is essential to keep it properly adjusted and aligned at all times. This will guarantee the saw's maximum performance.

While the table saw manufacturers thoroughly test, inspect, and accurately align their saws before they leave the factory, there are a number of factors which can throw the saw out of line.

All moving parts will wear, and the abrasive action of the dust and dirt produced during cutting operations can add to this process. Rough handling during transportation can knock saw components out of alignment. Adjustment and realignment will be necessary to maintain the saw's accuracy. The saw should be checked initially and periodically adjusted.

Table saw alignment is quite a simple matter. The following three points sum up all there is to know about the subject:

1. The table grooves or slots in which the miter gauge bar slides, the rip fence, and the saw blade must all be parallel to one another.

2. The rip fence, the saw blade, and the miter gauge head must all be perpendicular to the table surface.

3. When the miter gauge is set at 0°, it must rest at a right angle to the saw blade and rip fence.

This is one area where all operators, from beginner to master woodworker, are on equal ground. There is no reason why the saw of a novice cannot be set up as accurately as that of an old pro. The beginner's initial problem may be the inability to analyze the reasons behind poor cutting results. Figure 3-4 shows the six types of faulty alignment, their symptoms, and remedies.

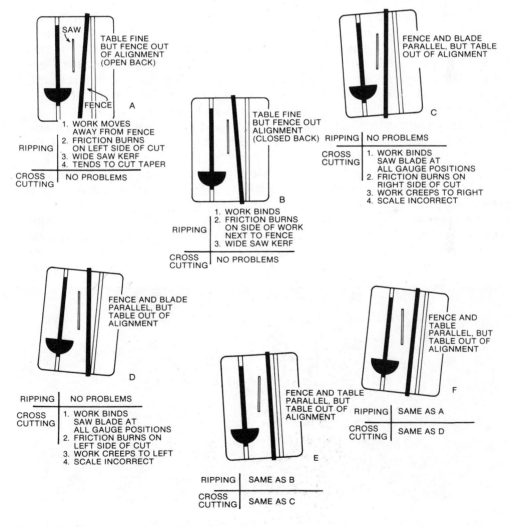

Figure 3-4: The six types of improper alignment.

There are also checks you can make while working which will supply you with a constant stream of information concerning the tool's accuracy. The simplest and one of the best checks is to apply a square to a ripped edge or crosscut. If the square indicates that the cut isn't up to standard, check into the reasons why. Before doing any type of work on the saw, turn the power shift to "off" and disconnect the saw from its power supply.

Blade-Table Alignment or Heel Adjustment. The importance of precise blade-table alignment cannot be overemphasized. Proper rip fence and miter gauge alignment cannot be achieved unless the tabletop is correctly squared with the saw blade. In other words, the miter gauge slots must run parallel to the saw blade. If they do not, the blade will bend at the end of the cut. This condition of misalignment is known as "heel." Table saw manufacturers pay close attention to "heel" adjustments, but over a period of time, readjustment will probably become necessary.

To check the blade-table alignment, raise the saw blade to its maximum elevation, and raise or remove the blade guard. Take a crayon and mark one of the saw blade teeth that is set (bent) to the left as you stand at the front of the saw. Turn the blade until the marked tooth is even with the surface of the table. Place the head of a combination square in the left miter gauge slot, holding it snugly against the slot's right side (Figure 3-5A). Adjust the blade of the combination square so it just touches the tip of the marked tooth.

Move the square along the miter slot until it is at the rear of the saw blade. Rotate the saw blade until the marked tooth is even with the table at the table insert's rear end. The tooth should again contact the combination square (Figure 3-5B). If the degree of contact is the same in both the front and rear positions, the saw blade is parallel to the miter gauge slots and no adjustment is necessary.

It is also possible to check blade-table alignment by precisely measuring the distance from the marked tooth to the edge of the miter gauge slot. Measure at a right angle to the saw blade. When the table is in proper alignment, both the front and rear measurements will be the same.

A   B

Figure 3-5: Check the blade-table alignment with a combination square.

If the marked tooth fails to contact the combination square (the measured distance is greater) after the tooth is rotated to the rear position, it is necessary to move the rear carriage mount of the table saw to the left. When it is apparent that the marked tooth has moved toward the square (the measured distance is less), the rear carriage mount should be moved to the right.

Loosen the two bolts holding the **rear** carriage mount to the tabletop (Figure 3-6). (**Note**: Do **not** loosen the bolts in the **front** carriage mount at this time.) With a mallet or soft-faced hammer, tap the rear carriage mount lightly in the correct direction until the "heel" is removed. Use one of the two methods described above to check the alignment. If it is correct, retighten the carriage mount bolts. Now move the blade through the whole bevel angle range to assure that there is no binding. If the system does not slide freely, the **front** carriage mount is probably not square to the carriage after the adjustment.

The rear of the front carriage mount should ride square against the front face of the carriage (Figure 3-7). If it does not, loosen the right screw of the front carriage mount and tap the carriage mount to the front or rear as required. (DO NOT LOOSEN THE LEFT CARRIAGE MOUNT SCREW.) Heel adjustment is much more difficult when all four of the carriage mount bolts have been loosened. This is because the counterbalance exerts a sideways force of 30 pounds on the system which is difficult to overcome manually. Tighten all bolts when the adjustments have been made.

Figure 3-6: Arrows point to the rear carriage mount screws.

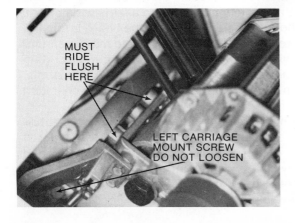

MUST
RIDE
FLUSH
HERE

LEFT CARRIAGE
MOUNT SCREW
DO NOT LOOSEN

Figure 3-7: The correct position for the front carriage mount.

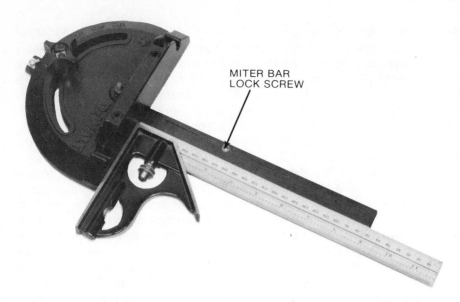

MITER BAR
LOCK SCREW

Figure 3-8: Checking the miter gauge for squareness.

Figure 3-9: Adjusting the miter pointer to 0°.

Miter Gauge Adjustment. Periodically check the miter gauge for squareness. Use a square to assure accuracy (Figure 3-8). Adjust the miter gauge to a 0° setting, and place the square against the face of the miter gauge and along one of the miter gauge slots. Another method of checking for proper alignment is to lock the gauge in the 0° setting and make a test cut on a fairly wide board. After the cut is made, check the board for squareness. If the board is square, the miter pointer can be adjusted to 0° (Figure 3-9). It is best to make a similar check at the 45° mark. However, when making this angled test cut, be certain that the board does not creep along the miter gauge and throw off the angle. Table alignment or heel adjustments should always be made before checking the miter gauge alignment.

The miter gauge should move smoothly in the miter gauge slot. When lubrication becomes necessary, a small amount of silicone compound or powdered graphite sprinkled into the slot will do the job nicely. Move the gauge back and forth in the slot until it moves easily. The slide bar and slot should also be periodically cleaned and waxed. Inspect both the gauge and slot for any slight burrs, and remove them with a fine file.

Adjustments to the Rip Fence Clamp Handle and Guide Rails. The rip fence has been designed for easy one-hand operation (Figure 3-10). The procedure for proper operation and clamp adjustment is as follows: Lift up on the clamp handle. This releases the clamping action. Hook the rear clamp over the end of the tabletop and support bar. Then, lower the front of the rip fence into the guide rail. The lock at the rear should extend over the tabletop and support bar (Figure 3-11). Push down on the clamp handle to activate the clamp. If the clamp is too tight, the nut at the rear of the clamp should be backed off until the lock is loose. With the lock loose and the handle closed, tighten the clamp nut until the lock bar just touches the support bar. (The T-bar should be pushed toward the rear.) Then, tighten the clamp nut two turns. This should provide adequate clamping; however, you may adjust it for more or less pressure if you desire. Keep in mind that too little clamping pressure may allow the rip fence to move during ripping and too much clamping pressure may cause undue stress on the clamp components.

With the rip fence clamp tension properly set, it is now possible to adjust the guide rails. Adjust the right-hand guide rail first, then the left rail.

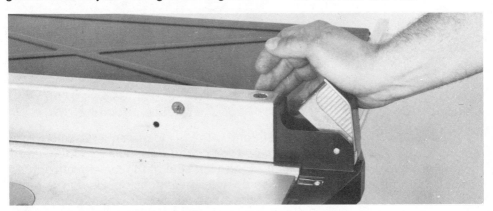

Figure 3-10: Rip fence clamp handle in released position.

ADJUSTING NUT

Figure 3-11: Proper placement of the rear rip fence clamp on the support base.

Set the rip fence T-bar on the right guide rail as far to the left as you can without covering up the left mounting screw (Figure 3-12). Do not lock the rip fence in place. Place a dime or a washer of the same thickness between the rip fence and the tabletop. Adjust the rail so that the bottom of the T-bar just rests in the channel. Now, snug up the left mounting screw. Move the fence and the dime as far to the right as you can, keeping them on the tabletop, not the extension, and without covering the right screw which mounts the rail to the tabletop. Again, position the rail so that the bottom of the T-bar just rests in the channel, and tighten the screw. Now, recheck the position of the left end of the right rail and tighten the left screw.

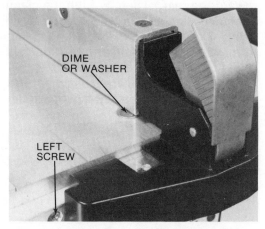

Figure 3-12: Adjusting the right-hand guide rail.

Adjusting the left guide rail is best done with the aid of a small C-clamp or a locking jaw pliers (Figure 3-13). Place the left and right rails together where they meet. Place the rip fence as far to the left side of the table extension as possible without covering the left screw into the extension. Using the dime again as a spacer, set the position of the guide rail as before. Snug up the left screw first, then snug up the right screw. Remove the clamp and double check the position of the guide rail all along the tabletop surface. Set the height of the table extension in the same manner as you have just done for the tabletop. Be sure that the table extensions do not extend above the tabletop surface. Tighten all guide rail and support bar screws.

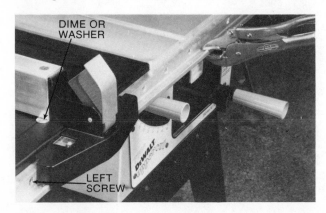

Figure 3-13: Adjusting the left-hand guide rail.

Aligning the Rip Fence on the Table. The saw's tabletop has been made with a great deal of precision, so it is usually possible to use the tabletop as an aid in aligning the rip fence parallel with the blade. Set the rip fence alongside of either the right or left miter gauge slot, and lock the fence in place. It should be exactly even with the edge of the miter gauge slot, as shown in Figure 3-14. When the rip fence is parallel with one miter gauge slot, it is automatically parallel with the second slot, because both of the grooves are milled simultaneously during the manufacturing of the tabletop.

If the rip fence does not rest parallel to the miter slot, adjustment is necessary. There are two rip fence adjustment screws, one on each side of the fence. When it becomes necessary to move the far end of the fence to the right, loosen the right side screw a few turns. Tighten the left side screw until the fence moves as far to the right as necessary, then retighten the right screw. If you wish to move the far end of the fence to the left, loosen the left side screw, tighten the right screw to make the adjustment, and retighten the left.

After the initial adjustments have been made, locate the fence along the miter slot and recheck for alignment. Make any readjustment necessary. Always be sure that the fence is not tilted toward the blade. This will cause the workpiece to pinch or bind on the blade during ripping operations. This can overload the motor, increase the possibility of dangerous kickbacks, and generally produce a poor quality cut.

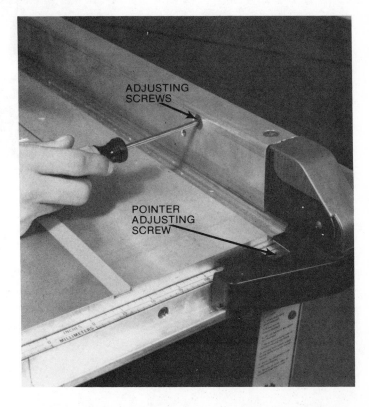

Figure 3-14: Aligning the rip fence with the miter gauge slot.

The see-through pointer on the rip fence indicates the width of the rip cut. The pointer should be checked periodically to assure that it is set at zero when the fence is located next to the blade. Due to the set of teeth, hollow-ground, etc., the rip pointer should always be adjusted after changing blades. Loosen the screw, slide the pointer to the correct position, and retighten the screw (Figure 3-15).

Bevel Adjustments. The 0° and 45° bevel angle stops are preset at the factory, but these stops may need periodic adjustment. These two stop screws are located in the forward carriage mount. They are adjusted with a hex wrench provided by the saw's manufacturer (Figure 3-16).

Figure 3-15: Setting the rip fence pointer.

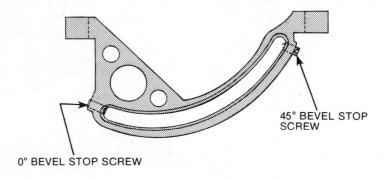

45° BEVEL STOP SCREW

0° BEVEL STOP SCREW

Figure 3-16: Location of the 0° bevel and 45° bevel stop screws.

Vertical or 0° Bevel Stop—To make the adjustment, raise the blade to maximum height and set it on the 0° stop. Place a square on the tabletop and against the flat portion of the blade (Figure 3-17). Do not rest the square against the saw teeth. If a gap exists between the blade and the square near the tabletop, loosen the left-hand stop screw and adjust the bevel control slide handle (or crank) until the gap disappears. Turn the stop screw back in until it contacts the guide pin. Adjust the blade to an angle of 5 or 10°, then turn it back to 0° and recheck the alignment using the square.

If the gap is between the square and the top of the blade, use the bevel control handle or crank to move the blade flush to the square. As before, turn in the stop screw so it barely contacts the guide pin and recheck the alignment.

45° Bevel Stop—To adjust at the 45° stop, an adjustable square or any other known 45° angle is required. Set the bevel control on the 45° stop and check the blade position with the 45° standard (Figure 3-18). When adjustment is necessary, use the right-hand adjustment screw in the forward carriage mount. Turning the screw in will tilt the top of the blade to the right. To tilt the top of the blade to the left, back the screw out a few revolutions and use the bevel control handle or crank to move the blade into the exact 45° angle shown by the standard. After making the adjustment, turn the screw in so it just touches the guide pin and recheck your work.

Periodically, and certainly when bevel adjustments are made, the bevel pointer should be readjusted. Simply loosen the hold-down screw, slide the pointer to the proper position, and retighten the screw.

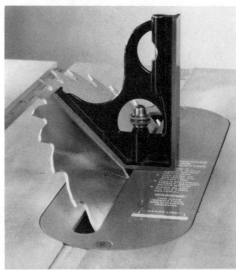

Figure 3-18: Checking the 45° bevel setting.

Figure 3-17: Checking vertical blade alignment.

Belt Tension Adjustment. The drive belt tension of belt and pulley type table saws should not require frequent adjustment. If it becomes necessary to alter the tension setting, loosen the three bolts that hold the motor to the elevating arm. Insert the flat blade of a screwdriver between the motor housing and the elevating arm, as shown in Figure 3-19. Spread the two apart until the desired belt tension is achieved. (An 11-ounce force yields a 1/8" deflection in the center of the span.) After making the adjustment, securely tighten the bolts. If they are too loose, the belt tension will be lost when the motor is started up. Do not force the bolts tight. This could result in stripping the threads.

Aligning the Blade Guard and Splitter. For the safe operation of the table saw, the blade guard and splitter must be properly assembled and aligned. Follow the assembly instructions given in your owner's manual.

After the unit is in place on the saw, raise the blade to its maximum elevation and lock it in place. Use a straightedge to align the blade and splitter (Figure 3-20). Center the splitter in the kerf (the width of a saw cut). Then, tighten the screws which hold the splitter to the guard bracket.

A Final Word About Adjustments. How often your table saw will be in need of adjustment depends on how much the saw is used and what type of operations are performed on it. Saws used in production work and those used largely for ripping operations deserve particular attention. In any case, properly set up the saw, and keep it that way. Remember, a table saw will only cut as smoothly and as accurately as you allow it.

Figure 3-19: Adjusting drive belt tension.

Figure 3-20: Aligning the blade guard and splitter.

Chapter 4
Safety and
Your Table Saw

This chapter is the most important one in the book. While it may be the most boring to read, the safe operation of the table saw and any of its attachments should be the first consideration of the saw operator. Both safety and successful woodworking depend on the operator's complete knowledge of the saw's components and the ability to execute the proper cutting methods. The table saw is an easy tool to use, but as mentioned earlier, there is a certain amount of hazard involved when working with any type of power tool. Exercise caution, and respect the saw's power and capabilities at all times. This will considerably reduce the possibility of personal injury. Failure to do so can result in a serious accident. The following precautions will give the beginner a solid safety outline, but they can't cover the wide range of possible situations that can occur when using the table saw. So it is extremely important that the operator remain alert and think ahead whenever using the saw. A periodic review of this list is a good idea for even the most experienced operator.

1. Very carefully read the owner's manual supplied with your saw. Know the saw completely. Learn its applications and limitations. Familiarize yourself with its specific safety features (Figure 4-1).

2. Tighten all clamps and levers prior to starting the machine. Don't attempt to adjust the saw while it is running. To avoid accidental starting, disconnect the saw from its power source when making adjustments or changing accessories such as saw blades or molding cutters.

3. Keep all cutting tools clean and sharp for quality work and safest operation. Don't use saw blades of larger diameters than those recommended for the tool.

Figure 4-1: Safety features to look for.

4. Dress for safety. No loose, long sleeves, neckties, gloves, or other dangling apparel should be worn that could be caught up by the cutting tool or workpiece. All jewelry—including rings and wrist watches—should be removed. Wear nonslip footwear, preferably with steel toes.

5. Protect your eyes and ears. Wear safety glasses or goggles. Ordinary eyeglasses are only shatter-resistant and are not considered safety glasses. A face shield or safety mask is recommended when the cutting is extremely dusty. Wear earplugs or earmuffs when using the saw for extended periods of time.

6. Be sure to properly ground the machine to protect the operator from electrical shock. Never use the saw in a dangerous environment, such as a damp or wet location, or expose it to rain. Keep the workshop clean and the floor in good condition. Litter can cause slipping or tripping, and this invites accidents.

7. Work in well-lighted areas only. It is best that the table saw have its own light, preferably adjustable, so that shadow-free illumination can be provided for any operation.

8. Always be sure that any loose tools and adjusting wrenches are removed from the machine before turning it on. To reduce the chances of an accidental start, be certain that the on-off switch is in the "off" position before plugging in the saw.

Always use the blade guard, splitter, and antikickback fingers on all through-sawing operations. Through-sawing operations are those where the saw blade cuts completely through the workpieces, as in ripping and crosscutting. If the guard is removed for a special operation, replace it afterwards. **Note:** MOST PHOTOGRAPHS IN THIS BOOK DO NOT SHOW THE BLADE GUARD, SPLITTER, AND ANTI-KICKBACK DEVICE IN PLACE; THIS IS BECAUSE THE OPERATIONS CAN BE SEEN CLEARLY WITHOUT IT.

9. Keep your hands clear of the blade. Don't allow your hands to get closer than 6" from the blade, and never hold them directly in line with the blade when feeding a workpiece. In fact, never stand or have any part of your body in line with the path of the cutting tool.

10. Hold the workpiece firmly against the table, miter gauge, rip fence, or other guiding device. Secure work with clamps (Figure 4-2) or a vise whenever it is practical. It's much safer and it frees both hands to operate the tool. Also, provide support for the rear or sides of the workpiece when cutting extra long or wide stock.

11. Always keep each hand in such a position that if by any chance it should suddenly be pushed or carried forward, it will pass safely by one side of the blade. When using the miter gauge (Figure 4-3), keep both hands at the outer side (not the blade side). When using the rip fence, keep both hands at a safe distance from the blade. When ripping narrow stock, use a push stick to move the workpiece past the blade. Push the material between the saw blade and the fence completely past the saw blade (Figure 4-4).

12. Don't attempt to guide a long board for ripping with the miter gauge; use the fence, instead. **Never** use the fence as a second guide or as a length stop when using the miter gauge.

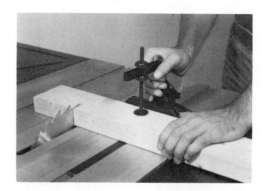

Figure 4-2: Whenever possible, use clamps to hold the workpiece.

Figure 4-3: Proper way to cut with a miter gauge.

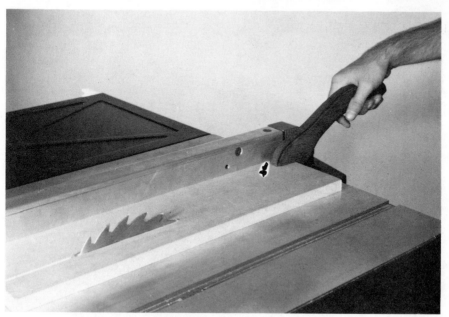

Figure 4-4: Use a push stick when ripping narrow stock.

13. Feed workpieces into the blade or cutter against the rotation of the blade or cutter. Don't overload or force the saw to cut. The need for forcing usually indicates that the cutting tool is dull, that you're cutting too deeply, or the fence is misaligned. Many very deep or oversized cuts must be accomplished by making repeat passes. Only run the saw at the rate for which it was designed to operate.

14. Always complete the "pass." For example, when crosscutting, a board will be severed when the blade has passed through it (Figure 4-5). Never reach over or behind the cutting tool with either hand, no matter what reason, until the blade or cutter has fully stopped.

15. Don't attempt to perform any "freehand" operations. Operating the saw "freehand" means using only the hands to support and guide the workpiece. The miter gauge or rip fence should always be used to guide the workpiece past the blade.

16. Don't take your eyes off the workpiece while cutting. Talking to anyone while running the saw will impair the proper concentration needed for safe operation.

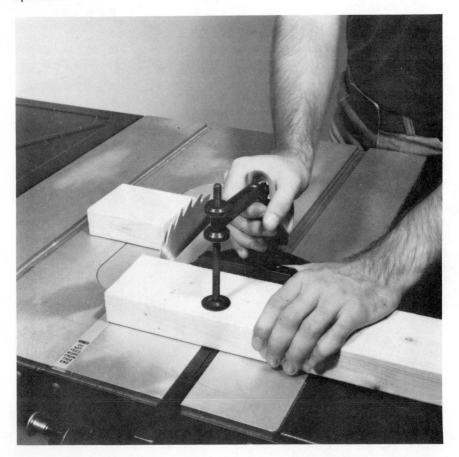

Figure 4-5: Always complete a "pass."

17. Before attempting to free a stalled saw blade, always disconnect the machine from the power source.

18. Keep all children and visitors at a safe distance from the operating saw. Make your workshop as child-proof as possible by removing the table saw lock key. Also, you can padlock your workshop to prevent entry, or you may want to install a lockable master switch that controls all electricals in the area.

19. Only use recommended accessories with your table saw. Consult your owner's manual. The use of incorrect accessories may lead to serious injury. Also, mount any accessory by carefully following the instructions that come with the tool.

20. Don't overreach. Keep the proper footing and balance at all times. Avoid awkward cutting operations and hand positions. A sudden slip could cause your hand to slide into the moving saw blade or cutter.

21. Look for damaged parts before beginning any sawing operation. Check the alignment of moving parts and the mounting arrangements of cutting tools; and look for any binding or excessive friction between moving parts, or other problems which can affect the safe operation of the saw. Replace damaged parts or have them properly repaired.

22. Never run the table saw while under the influence of drugs, alcohol, or any medication which may make you drowsy. Don't work when you are tired. Alertness is the most important factor when operating any power tool.

23. Don't stand on the table saw. Serious injury could occur if the tool is tipped or if the cutting tool is accidentally contacted. Don't store materials above or near the tool such that it is necessary to stand on the tool to reach them.

24. Never leave the tool running unattended. Turn the power off and remove the key (Figure 4-6). Don't leave the saw until the blade comes to a complete stop.

Figure 4-6: Remove the key before leaving the saw.

Kickback Precautions. Kickback is one of the most dangerous and most common of all table saw hazards. Kickback occurs when the saw blade binds in the workpiece. This can throw the workpiece back at the operator with great force. As mentioned in the general safety rules, a piece of stock left on the table that slides into the running saw blade can also be thrown with considerable force. Once you know the possible causes of kickback, you can take the steps necessary to prevent it. A few of the most common causes are:

1. When a saw blade is dull, has too little set, or is mounted backwards;
2. When the splitter guard and antikickback fingers are not used;
3. When crosscutting against the rip fence;
4. When a small piece of wood falls on a revolving blade;
5. When failing to complete a pass before releasing your hold on the workpiece;
6. When cutting "freehand" without the use of any guiding device such as the miter gauge or rip fence;
7. When sawing badly warped stock;
8. When ripping stock with large or loose, unsound knots; and
9. When rip fence is misaligned.

Chapter 5
Crosscutting and
Ripping Operations

Mastering the basic saw cuts is the first step in becoming an accomplished woodworker. As it was stated at the beginning of this book, there are only six basic saw cuts in woodworking: the crosscut, rip, bevel crosscut, bevel rip, miter, and bevel miter. Any cut made on the table saw will either be one of these cuts or a combination of several. Of these six cuts, the crosscut and rip are the most fundamental operations. When you consider that roughly 90% of all cutting operations involve crosscutting or ripping of one type or another, the importance of making these cuts smoothly and effectively becomes obvious.

Keep in mind that the saw guard and all other safety devices should always be used during all through-sawing operations. In many of the photographs shown in this book, the guard has been removed for the sake of clarity. USE ALL SAFETY DEVICES AND GUARDS RECOMMENDED BY THE MANUFACTURER. Remember, too, that the saw teeth above the surface of the table rotate in the direction of the operator, so they will enter the top of the woodpiece first. It is therefore necessary to place the workpiece on the saw table finished side up. This is true of plain plywood, veneers, and any of the laminated plywood materials (Figure 5-1). When cutting a piece which has both sides finished, a fine-tooth blade with a minimum set or a hollow-ground saw blade with the teeth widely set will give the best results.

Always keep in mind that every cut will produce a saw kerf. A saw kerf is the slot normally formed by the saw blade (Figure 5-2). The width of the saw kerf can vary depending on the style, the gauge, and the amount of set on the teeth of the saw blade. Whatever the kerf size, it should always be kept on the waste side of the cut.

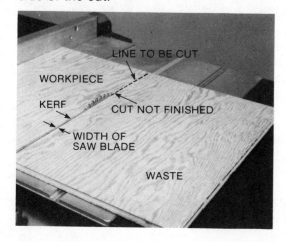

Figure 5-1: Cut workpieces with the finished side up.

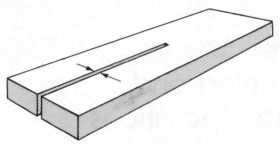

Figure 5-2: The "kerf" is that slot normally formed by the saw blade (arrows). Its width will differ depending on the type, gauge, and amount of set.

CROSSCUTTING. Simple crosscutting is performed by placing the good edge of the workpiece against the miter gauge and advancing both the workpiece and miter gauge past the saw blade. Straight crosscutting is making a cut across the grain of a piece of wood at a 90° angle to the edge against the miter gauge face (Figure 5-3). All crosscuts are made across the narrow dimensions of the stock. The miter gauge is used when making all crosscuts and may be positioned on either side of the saw blade. For straight crosscuts, the miter gauge is set at 0° and locked in place.

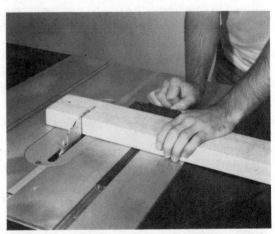

Figure 5-3: Straight crosscutting. Hold the work as shown here.

Draw a line on the stock at the cutoff point. It should be long enough to be used for sighting. A mark drawn on the table insert or kerf guide in line with the saw blade is a useful aid in the positioning of the work against the miter gauge (see Chapter 1). Slide the work to the side as necessary to line up the cutoff mark with the saw blade. When the scrap piece is at the left, align the cutoff mark with the right side of the blade. This will assure that the kerf will be in the scrap. If the scrap piece is at the right, align the cutoff mark with the left side of the blade. If the miter gauge is positioned in the left-hand slot, hold the miter gauge handle with the right hand and use the left hand to hold the material. When the miter gauge is located in the right-hand slot in the table, reverse these hand positions. Keep both hands on the same side of the saw blade. Placing them on opposite sides of the saw blade may cause the blade to bind in the cut and result in a dangerous kickback. Set the blade so the blade gullet is just above the stock (Figure 5-4).

Figure 5-4: The saw blade should project so that the blade gullet is just above the stock.

After rechecking for correct positioning, start the cut slowly, holding the workpiece firmly against the miter gauge and table. Do not pause while making the cut, but never force the work against the blade. Hold the supported piece, not the piece to be cut off. This is one of the general rules of all table saw operations. While some feathering of the cut (Figure 5-5) is inevitable, it can be minimized by simply slowing up the cutting speed.

The cut is not complete until the work has passed the blade. Always remember this: Although the pass is complete when the work has been advanced past the blade, the operation is finished when the work and the miter gauge have been returned to the starting point.

Shift the workpiece off to the side somewhat so there is no possibility of it catching the saw blade as you bring it back to the starting point.

Do not use the free hand to pick up a cutoff while the blade is still turning. The hand holding the miter gauge could slip into the blade. If the free hand should bump the cutoff into the turning blade, the cutoff could be thrown back against the operator with considerable force. It is also possible that the action of the blade on the cutoff might cause the free hand to be thrown into the saw blade. So, never pick a free piece up off the table while the blade is turning unless it is a long one, which eliminates the possibility of either hand coming into contact with the blade. It only takes a few seconds for the blade to stop turning after the switch has been turned off. Wait and be safe. At no time whatsoever should the rip fence be used as a cutoff gauge when crosscutting.

Figure 5-5: Feathering can be reduced by slowing down the cutting speed.

59

This basic procedure can vary due to the size of the work or the specific type of cut made; however, the important factors—slow feed, good hand position, and proper support—should not change. Always provide for these factors. For example, when deciding which side of the miter gauge slot to employ, take into consideration which one will offer the most support.

Miter Gauge Hold-Down Clamp—Some manufacturers produce miter gauges equipped with a hold-down clamp as standard equipment (Figure 5-6). Others offer them as an option. This device acts as a safeguard against both wobbling and creeping, which can quickly ruin the precision of the cut. The hold-down device clamps the woodpiece securely against the miter gauge and makes it possible for the operator to keep his hands at a safe distance from the saw blade.

Figure 5-6: The miter gauge hold-down attachment provides additional support for both straight and mitered cuts.

The Uppercutting Feature—Uppercutting saws, as mentioned in Chapter 1, crosscut woodpieces up to 8″ wide and 1-1/2″ thick from the underside. The stock is held or clamped securely in position and the saw blade is raised up and through the work from its position under the table. This uppercutting action is a very convenient feature, but as with any cutting operation, caution must be exercised during its use. Proceed as follows:

First, lower the saw blade beneath the level of the table and lock it in place. Next, position the workpiece. To assure proper positioning, a special start line is marked on the table insert (Figure 5-7). The edge of the workpiece closest to the operator should be placed on this start line. This placement assures that the forward edge of the blade is being used to make the cut. This produces cutting forces which exert downward pressure to help hold the workpiece on the table. If only the rear edge of the blade is used for cutting, the cutting forces will be upward and will try to lift the workpiece up and off of the table. The start line shown in these illustrations is based on 90° crosscutting. Figure 5-8 indicates where the start line should be placed for both 10″ and 9″ blades. Do not use the uppercut with blades smaller than 9″ in diameter.

After the woodpiece has been properly positioned and secured, start the saw motor and unlock the elevation handle. Simply push the handle down to bring the saw blade up and through the wood. After the cut has been made, raise the elevation handle to lower the saw blade back down under the table, and turn off the motor. As always, wait until the blade has stopped turning before touching the workpiece.

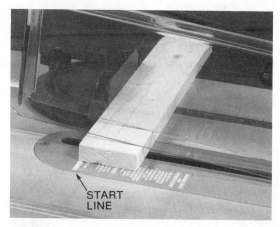

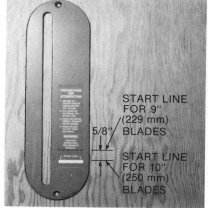

Figure 5-7: Position the workpiece on the start line when uppercutting.

Figure 5-8: Starting lines for both 10" and 9" blades.

While this uppercutting feature has a good number of uses, there are several things the operator should always keep in mind. This cutting action should be used only for crosscutting operations, and even then only for those cuts which require a single uppercutting stroke of the saw blade. Do not use the uppercut feature for any of the ripping or shaping operations discussed later in this book or any other book of its kind. These operations require some fairly high cutting forces, as well as the placement of both hands on the workpiece. In attempting to perform these procedures with the uppercut feature, the operator would most definitely lose some of the working control necessary for the safe operation of the saw.

Adhere to the saw's limitations. It is possible to through cut materials up to 8" in width and 1-1/2" in thickness in a single stroke. If there is any doubt as to whether one stroke will accomplish the job, turn the saw's ignition switch to the off position, raise the blade guard, and place the workpiece alongside the blade when it is set at its full elevation (Figure 5-9). If, for any reason, this uppercutting technique is used on materials which will not be cut through in a single elevating pass, align the workpiece so that the edge farthest from you will be cut through and the edge closest will not (Figure 5-10). In this way the blade can then be locked into its elevated position and the piece pushed through the blade to complete the cut.

However, this procedure is not recommended as a general cutting practice. Always use the saw's miter gauge to position the workpiece and hold it firmly in place when not using a securing clamp. The blade guard and all other safety features should be used during this and all other through cutting operations. Lift the blade guard and position the material in the desired cutting location. It is also often possible to simply slide the material in place from the front of the guard.

Using Auxiliary Miter Gauge Facing. Longer pieces have a tendency to wobble during crosscutting operations. To prevent this from happening, the miter gauge is often fitted with a larger auxiliary face. To be effective, this face board should be at least 1" higher than the maximum depth of the cut and should

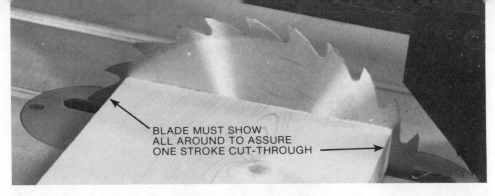

Figure 5-9: Blade must show all around to assure one stroke cut-through.

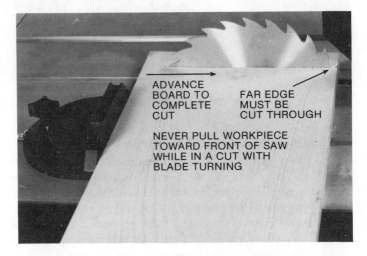

ADVANCE BOARD TO COMPLETE CUT

FAR EDGE MUST BE CUT THROUGH

NEVER PULL WORKPIECE TOWARD FRONT OF SAW WHILE IN A CUT WITH BLADE TURNING

Figure 5-10: Uppercutting oversized pieces.

extend at least 12" or more on either side of the miter gauge. Holes already provided in the miter gauge make fastening this larger fence with wood screws an easy job (Figure 5-11). A scale built into the face of the auxiliary fence is a useful item (Figure 5-12). A piece of sandpaper or abrasive cloth can also be glued to either the gauge or auxiliary face to give it more gripping power (Figure 5-13). This will help prevent creeping during crosscut operations. Use rubber cement so that the sandpaper or abrasive cloth can easily be removed and replaced when it loses its effectiveness.

Figure 5-11: Attaching auxiliary miter gauge facing.

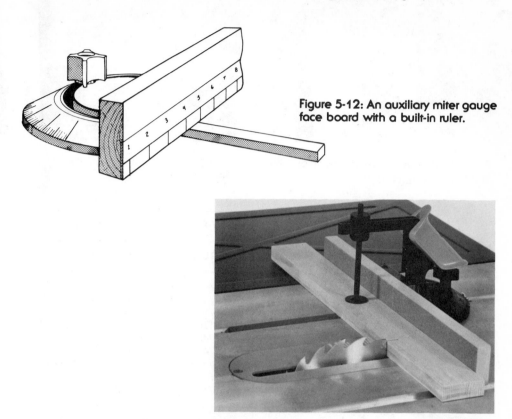

Figure 5-12: An auxiliary miter gauge face board with a built-in ruler.

Figure 5-13: An auxiliary miter gauge face board with an abrasive cloth facing.

When using extension facing, never use your hand to push against the free end of the work. This practice can pinch the kerf closed, causing the workpiece to bind on the blade. The result would be a dangerous kickback. Follow the basic crosscutting procedure outlined earlier in this chapter. If you have a free hand, use it only as a guide or to provide additional support.

At times it is advisable to design a special miter gauge face for use in certain types of cutting. Kerf cutting for the bending of wood, and cutting grooves for finger lap or box joints are two examples discussed later in this book.

Roller Supports. The overhanging ends of extremely long pieces of work will tend to drop down during crosscutting operations. This makes proper support essential. Employing a sawhorse (Figure 5-14) or a roller support (Figure 5-15) is one of the best ways to deal with this problem. The support is set up parallel to the saw table and the work rides along on hardwood rollers which turn on dowel pins. Plans for the support shown here are given in Figure 5-16.

Reversing the Miter Gauge to Cut Wide Pieces. At times, the stock width results in the miter gauge starting position being located off the table surface. When this is the case, reverse the miter gauge in the table slot and use it as shown in Figure 5-17. One hand pulls the miter gauge firmly against the forward edge of the workpiece, while the second hand pushes against the opposite edge. When using the miter gauge in this position, it is necessary to support the work throughout the entire cutting operation.

Figure 5-14: A sawhorse makes an excellent support for long lengths.

Figure 5-15: Crosscutting with the aid of the roller support.

PARTS CHART FOR CROSSCUT SUPPORT			
PIECE	**THICK**	**WIDTH**	**LENGTH**
A	3/4	2-7/8	22-1/2
B	3/4	3/4	2-7/8
C	5/8	1-7/8 DIA.	—
D	1/2 DIA.	—	2-1/4
E	3/4	3-5/8	27
F	3/4	1-3/4	30
G	3/4	3-5/8	29
H	1-5/8	3-5/8	20
I	3/4	3-3/4	20

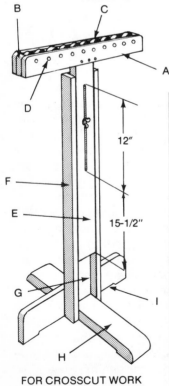

FOR CROSSCUT WORK

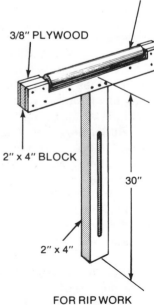

FOR RIP WORK

Figure 5-16: Plans for the roller support.

Figure 5-17: Using the miter gauge backwards to cut wide pieces.

Methods of Crosscutting to Length. Although it can be used to square off the end of a piece of stock, crosscutting is usually employed to size work to exact dimensions. Sometimes duplicate pieces are required. In either case, it is often wise to rig up some sort of mechanical setup to assure cutting accuracy.

Using Clearance or Stop Blocks—When a number of short pieces must be cut to the same length, attaching a clearance block to the saw's rip fence is one way to do the job quickly and easily (Figure 5-18).

Another similar setup using stop blocks is shown in Figure 5-19. When the stop block is clamped to the table in this manner, hold the stock against the miter gauge as the cut is being made. Be absolutely sure to use a clearance block when employing this setup. Failure to use the clearance block will most definitely result in kickback. The blade guard and the splitter guard should be in position whenever these cuts are made. This will prevent the back teeth from picking up a cut-off piece and throwing it forward. A simple adjustable clearance block is shown in Figure 5-20.

Figure 5-18: Using the clearance block.

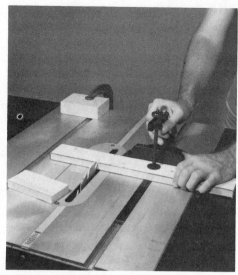

Figure 5-19: Another way of employing stop blocks.

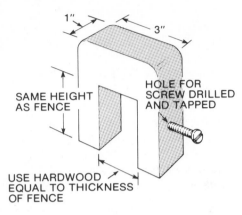

1"   3"

SAME HEIGHT
AS FENCE

HOLE FOR
SCREW DRILLED
AND TAPPED

USE HARDWOOD
EQUAL TO THICKNESS
OF FENCE

Figure 5-20: An adjustable stop block and how it is made.

Using Stop Rods—A stop rod is a handy accessory for the crosscutting of longer workpieces. Move the rip fence out of the way and use the miter gauge as the guiding device. Square one end of all the pieces that are to be cut and attach the stop rod to the miter gauge as shown in Figure 5-21. Measure the distance from the end of the stop rod to one of the saw teeth that is set to the left (Figure 5-22). Position the squared end of the piece against the stop rod and proceed to make the cut.

Figure 5-21: Using stop rods to crosscut to length.

Figure 5-22: Determine length of work by measuring from rod to point of one tooth set in its direction.

Using Auxiliary Facing With Stop Blocks—Another method of cutting longer pieces to exact lengths is to use auxiliary miter gauge facing with stop blocks (Figure 5-23). Make the auxiliary fence long enough on both sides so it will not tip the miter gauge out of position. Screw, nail, or clamp the stop block to the auxiliary face board at the desired length. The rip fence is always removed from the table for this type of cut. Remember, never use the rip fence for spacing crosscuts of any kind, unless it is equipped with a suitable stop block arrangement.

When the job calls for the cutting of a large number of pieces to the same length, a production setup using two miter gauges can be employed. The miter gauge on the right side of the saw blade is used to cut the left end of the workpiece square. The miter gauge on the left side, equipped with a stop block attached to a wooden auxiliary fence, cuts the opposite end to the exact length.

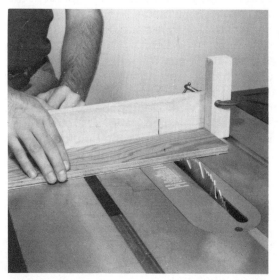

Figure 5-23: A stop clamped to auxiliary wood facing.

Figure 5-24: A simple rip cut.

RIPPING. A lengthwise cut made along the grain of the workpiece is known as a rip cut (Figure 5-24). Do not use the uppercut feature with a table saw so equipped when ripping. During a ripping cut, one edge of the work rides against the saw's guide fence (also known as the rip fence) while the flat side of the board rests on the level table surface. Therefore, make sure that one edge of the piece is straight so it can ride against the fence and one surface is flat and smooth for easy sliding on the table surface. Boards with bent or curved edges can cause the saw blade to stick or bind, kicking the piece back in the direction of the operator. Unevenly edged pieces can also buckle or twist on the saw blade. If your hands are near the saw blade when the kickback or buckling occurs, there is a danger that one or both hands may be jerked loose and thrown into the blade. To help prevent kickbacks and buckles, make sure the saw blade is sharp and has a good set, and that the workpiece has reasonably true surfaces to help guide it along the rip fence and support it without rocking.

Figure 5-25: Blade guard, splitter, and antikickback fingers should always be used for ripping.

All ripping operations should be made with the blade guard in position on the saw. The guard should have antikickback pawls and a splitter to prevent the saw kerf from closing in on and binding the saw blade (Figure 5-25).

Badly warped boards shouldn't be ripped, as they are sure to bind during the cut. Also large, loose, unsound knots in the wood can present a hazard. If a knot is jarred loose just after it has been cut, it can fly out in the direction of the operator with considerable force. So, before starting the ripping operation, knock out any loose knots from the material with a hammer.

Using the Rip Fence. The rip fence is used for all ripping, bevel ripping, resawing, and rabbeting operations. Modified ripping operations, such as taper ripping and wedge cutting, also employ the rip fence as the guiding device. When using the rip fence, always observe the following safety precautions:

1. Do not use the uppercut for ripping.

2. Always use a push stick or block to move the piece past the saw blade if the operation calls for placing either hand closer than 4″ from the blade or whenever the procedure calls for their use.

3. Never make these cuts freehand (without using the rip fence or auxiliary devices when required) because the blade could bind in the cut and cause a kickback.

4. Always securely lock the rip fence when in use.

5. Remove the miter gauge from the table.

6. Make sure the blade guard is installed for all through-sawing type cuts. Replace the guard immediately following completion of resawing, rabbeting, dadoing, or molding operations.

Frequently check the action of the antikickback pawls by passing the workpiece alongside of the spreader while the saw is off.

Pull the workpiece toward you. If the pawls do not dig into the workpiece and hold it, the pawls must be replaced.

7. Have the blade extend above the top of the workpiece so that the gullet is clear of the top. Additional blade exposure would increase the hazard potential.

8. Do not stand directly in front of the blade in case of a kickback. Stand to either side of the blade.

9. Keep your hand clear of the blade and out of the path of the blade.

10. If the blade stalls or stops while cutting, turn the switch off before attempting to free the blade.

11. Do not reach over or behind the blade to pull the workpiece through the cut, to support long or heavy workpieces, to remove small cut-off pieces of material, or for any other reason.

12. Do not pick up small pieces of cut-off material from the table. Remove them by pushing them off the table with a long stick. Otherwise, they could be thrown back at you by the rear of the blade. Always use caution.

13. Do not remove small pieces of cut-off material that may become trapped inside the blade guard while the saw is running. This could endanger your hands or cause a kickback.

Turn the saw off. After the blade has stopped turning, lift the guard and remove the pieces.

Refer to Chapter 4 for further information concerning table saw safety.

Setting the Rip Fence. To set the rip fence for the proper width-of-cut, hold a rule at a right angle to it or set a square against it and measure the distance from the fence to the blade (Figure 5-26). An alternate method is to mark the piece to be ripped in the desired position and then adjust the rip fence until the mark is in alignment with the saw blade. If the teeth of the blade have a set to them, check this measurement against one that points toward the fence. Remember to take into consideration the width of the saw kerf and position the piece so the kerf will be on the waste side of the cutoff line.

The Basic Rip Cut. It is possible to locate the rip fence on either the right or the left side of the saw blade. The instructions given below are based on right side location. If, for any reason, you prefer to use the rip fence on the left side of the saw blade, correct these instructions accordingly.

Start the motor and wait until the saw blade reaches its full speed. Slowly advance the workpiece, holding it down and against the guide fence. As always, never stand in the line of the saw blade when making the cut.

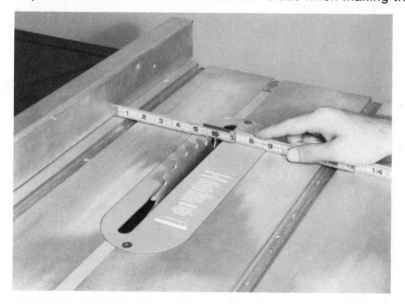

Figure 5-26: Measuring the distance from the rip fence to the blade when setting the fence for rip cuts.

Using the correct hand positions to hold the work while the cut is being made is of the utmost importance. Hold the work with both hands (Figure 5-27A). Use the left hand to hold the work firmly against the guide fence. Hook the fingers of the right hand over the fence as shown and use this hand to feed the workpiece into the blade (Figure 5-27B). As you feed the piece forward with your right hand, keep the left hand in its original position, holding the piece securely against the guide fence throughout the pass. But **do not** continue with the left hand beyond the front edge of the blade. Instead, feed with the right hand until the work is past the saw blade and the antikickback fingers. After the work has passed this point, the right hand can be removed and the work will either stay on the table and tilt up slightly to be caught by the rear end of the guard, or it will slide off the table to the floor (Figure 5-27C). Alternately, the feed can continue to the end of the table. When this is the case, the work can then be lifted and brought back along the outside of the guide fence. Allow the waste stock to remain on the table and do not touch it until the saw blade has come to a complete stop. When ripping short pieces, push the workpiece past the saw blade until the overhang at the rear of the table causes the back edge of the workpiece to tilt up into the palm of your hand. There is no return in ripping.

A

B

C

Figure 5-27: The proper hand positions for the rip cut: (A) Both hands can be used to start the cut. (B) Hook the last two fingers of your right hand over the rip fence. Use the first two fingers of that hand to snug the work against the fence. (C) The completion of the cut.

Ripping Wide Stock. Stock which measures at least 4″ between the blade and the rip fence is classified as wide. For best results, adjust the blade height so the gullet is just above the thickness of the stock. At this height, the blade will give a very smooth cut. It may seem more logical to use the maximum blade height setting. And it is true that at this setting the blade cuts faster, with the least friction on the rim of the blade. The chances of burning the workpiece are also reduced. But, this maximum setting may cause excessive chipping of the wood and the greatest amount of hand exposure to the whirling blade. So, it is generally recommended that the blade projection be no more than 1/4″ above the top of the stock.

Ripping Narrow Stock. When the workpiece to be ripped is less than 4″ wide, a push stick should be used to complete the feed. When completing the feed with a push stick, wait until the stock is over the front edge of the table. Then, pick up the push stick in your right hand as shown in Figure 5-28, and continue to apply pressure with the stick until the cut is completed. Move the piece completely beyond the blade. Never reach over the saw itself to pick up the stock. This is true even when the blade guard is in place.

Push Sticks and Push Blocks. For easier, safer work, it is best to have several different designs of push sticks available when doing ripping work. A number of the most common designs are shown in Figure 5-29. Always keep in mind that the push stick must be thinner than the width of the stock that is being cut. If it is too wide, it will not clear the area between the guard and the guide fence. An even more dangerous situation will exist if the saw blade cuts into the end of the push stick. The force of the blade may flip the push stick out of your hand and cause your hand to drop into the saw blade. Or, the workpiece may kick back.

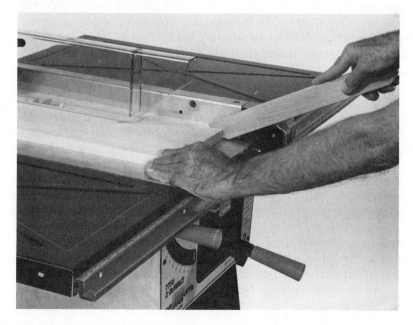

Figure 5-28: Using a push stick when cutting narrow stock.

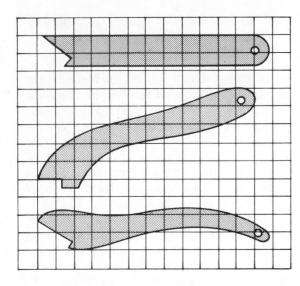

Figure 5-29: Some common push stick designs. Each square equals 1".

A push block, as shown in Figure 5-30, allows the operator to apply even pressure throughout the cut. The notched stick setup shown in Figure 5-31 is a good hold-down method when working with small pieces. When using this setup, however, make sure that the stick is cut short of the fence so the push board will clear the fence at the end of the cut.

Ripping Extremely Narrow Materials. When ripping material under 2" in width, an ordinary push stick may interfere with the blade guard. In these cases, a flat push board is a valuable accessory. When using a push board for these types of operations, the width of the pusher must be added to the width of the rip when positioning the fence. Use the setup shown in Figure 5-32 when the stock to be cut is no longer than the distance from the front of the table to the center of the saw blade. When the workpiece is longer than this, begin the ripping operation with the push board positioned upside-down as shown in Figure 5-33. Feed the stock with the left hand until it reaches the front of the table. Release the feed pressure and turn the push board over as you firmly hold the workpiece in position. Now you can finish the cut using the procedure described above for the shorter workpiece.

Sometimes when ripping very thin material, it is advisable to make a special insert. The standard equipment insert is made of 11 gauge steel which is approximately 1/8" thick. Use a piece of 1/8" aluminum or steel cut to the same size as the standard insert (Figure 5-34). This type of insert will give the workpiece support on either side of the blade and prevent the narrow strip from being pulled down due to the cutting action of the blade. Measure from the edge of the insert opening in the tabletop to the blade and layout slot to be cut. Use a drill or jig saw with a metal cutting blade to cut the slot, then file the edges smooth.

Ripping Long Stock. When ripping long stock, the workpiece often begins to sag down behind the table. To prevent this from happening, some sort of outfeed is needed to support the stock. Often, another power tool (such as the drill press) or bench, set at the proper height, will do nicely. The most recommended outfeed support table is the homemade roller table mentioned earlier in this chapter.

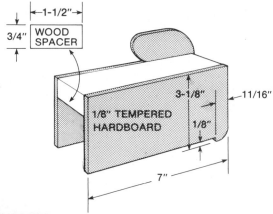

Figure 5-30: (Above) An easy-to-make push block. (left) Using the push block to rip narrow stock.

Figure 5-31: Notched stick hold-down jig.

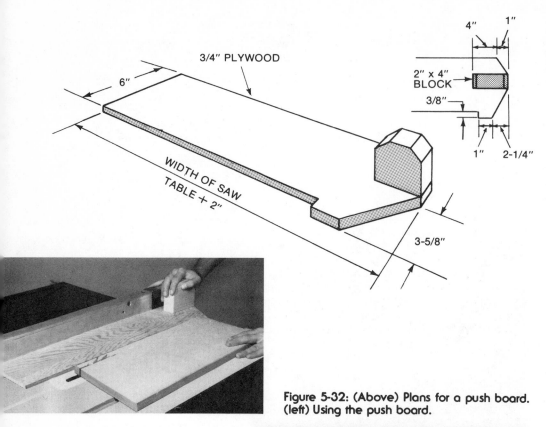

4"
1"

2" x 4"
BLOCK

3/8"

1"
2-1/4"

3/4" PLYWOOD

6"

WIDTH OF SAW
TABLE + 2"

3-5/8"

Figure 5-32: (Above) Plans for a push board. (left) Using the push board.

Figure 5-33: Another way of positioning the push board.

Figure 5-34: Special insert method of ripping narrow material.

Another way of ripping longer pieces of stock is to saw through them a little more than half their total length. Then, turn off the saw, draw the material back out of the saw, and turn it over end to end. Start the saw once more and complete the cut from the other end.

Ripping Thin Stock. One of the problems that must be dealt with when cutting thin stock, such as paneling, is the tendency of the stock to catch between the bottom of the rip fence and the table surface. The best way to prevent this from happening is to attach an auxiliary wood fence to the saw's metal fence (Figure 5-35). To do so, follow these instructions:

1. Cut approximately a 3/4" thick piece of wood to the length and height of your saw's guide fence.

2. Attach this wood strip to the guide fence with wood screws. Insert the screws through the holes already provided in the guide fence.

3. Make certain that the auxiliary wood fence fits flush against the table surface so that a thin piece of stock cannot fit beneath it.

The best blade for the cutting of plywood paneling is a combination or plywood blade without too much set. The blade should protrude above the plywood to a height equal to the height of the blade teeth. Remember to place the plywood on the table with the good side up.

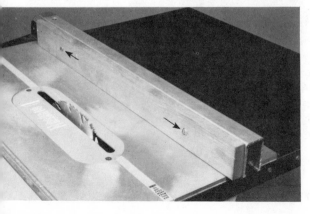

Figure 5-35: The auxiliary rip fence in position on the saw.

Ripping Very Thin Stock. Use a combination planer blade for the best results when cutting very thin stock. But before making the cut, a 3/8" plywood auxiliary table fence, such as the one shown, should be clamped over the regular table (Figure 5-36). After this has been done, turn the power on and raise the blade slowly, cutting through the auxiliary plywood table fence. The thin stock can then be placed on the table against the fence. Hold the piece firmly in place and feed it into the blade with a thicker piece. As shown, this auxiliary table can be used for other types of cutting operations as well (Figure 5-37).

Resawing. The process of ripping a thick board to make a thin board is known as resawing. When the work does not exceed the capacity of the saw, the job can be treated as any other ripping operation. But before beginning this cut, it is necessary to construct a special jig known as a "fingerboard" or "featherboard" jig. A featherboard is a board cut off at an angle of 60°. At the cut end, a series of parallel cuts are then made part way into the board, as shown in Figure 5-38.

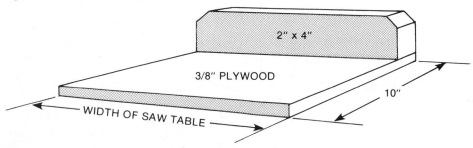

Figure 5-36: An auxiliary wood table fence.

Figure 5-37: One use for the auxiliary wood table fence.

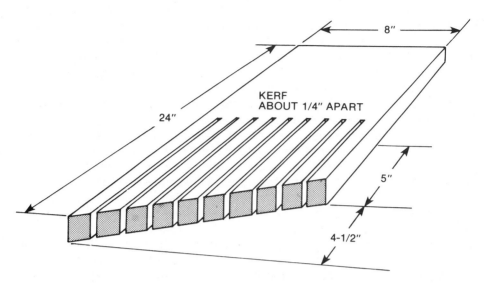

Figure 5-38: Common featherboard (sometimes called fingerboards).

This featherboard is then clamped to the in-feed side of the saw table in such a way that it bears against the workpiece to be resawed. Its long edge should be opposite the front end of the saw (Figure 5-39). The featherboard firmly holds the stock against the ripping fence, and its fingers prevent the piece from being thrown back toward the operator. If the featherboard were clamped too far away from the operator, it would bear against the saw cut and pinch the blade.

As mentioned above, the board can be resawed in a single pass if the board thickness is within the maximum capacity of the saw. When it is thicker than the capacity, but not more than two times as thick, it becomes necessary to resaw the board in two passes—one with each edge down. When the work-piece exceeds twice the saw's capacity, it is often possible to make two passes with the table saw and then finish the resawing job by hand or with a band saw.

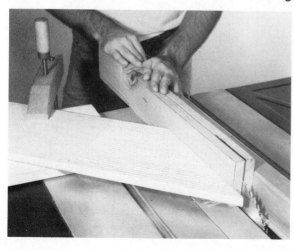

Figure 5-39: Resawing setup using a featherboard.

In either case, the cuts made on the table saw will help make the rest of the cut straight and reduce the amount of hand or band sawing necessary. It is not particularly easy to resaw a piece entirely on a band saw, because the blade has a tendency to weave in and out. The cuts made on the table saw help to assure the straightest line possible.

It is necessary to remove the blade guard when two passes are required to make the resawing cut. Be conscious of this increased hazard at all times and exercise extra care in keeping your hands away from the saw blade. Attach an auxiliary wood fence arrangement, like the one shown in Figure 5-40A, to the saw's regular metal fence. With this setup, two featherboards are used—one to apply pressure from the top and the other to hold the work tightly against the auxiliary wood fence. The blade height should be set so that the first cut is slightly more than half of the board thickness. When resawing hardwoods, the best procedure is to make a shallow cut first, then raise the blade so it extends above the work surface roughly 1/4" more than the stock width. Feed the material by holding it at the top and sides (Figure 5-40B). Never hold or push the piece from the end. When making the second cut, the first cut has a tendency to squeeze closed, so hold the saw kerf open with wedges. This two featherboard method is also very useful when cutting long, thin stock. When using this setup to simply rip stock, use a push stick to complete the cut.

A

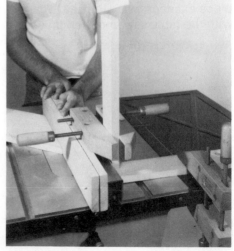

B

Figure 5-40: Another simple resawing setup.

Squaring Boards with Ripcuts. One of the prerequisites for using the rip fence as a guide is a straight even workpiece edge that can ride smoothly against the fence. Unfortunately, not all pieces of stock have such an even edge. This is particularly true of stock pieces which have been worked with the jig saw or band saw. Whatever the reason for the rough edge may be, it is apparent that some sort of squaring device is needed before the rip cut can be made. Fortunately, there are a number of squaring methods available, most of which employ the sliding table concept.

Method No. 1—This variation of the sliding table idea employs a squaring board with a guide fastened to its underside which fits into the miter gauge slot of the table. A stop or cleat which runs at a right angle to the saw blade is fastened to the forward edge of the sliding table and the work to be cut is butted firmly against this stop (Figure 5-41). The whole assembly is then fed past the saw blade. A similar variation of this cut-off board is also shown in Figure 5-42. In this case, the top board acts as the clamping jig.

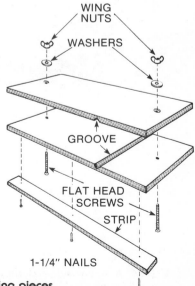

Figure 5-41: A sliding table squaring jig. The platform and the stop are made from 3/4" lumber or plywood. The hardwood slide should be slide-fit in the table slot.

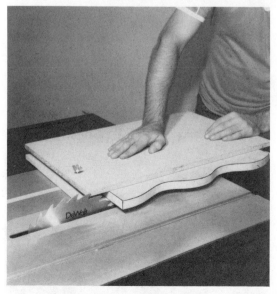

Figure 5-42: Another cut-off board jig used for squaring pieces.

Method No. 2—This method is a slight variation of the sliding table concept described in Method No. 1. In this case, no hold-downs are used. Instead, the table is fitted with a number of projecting pins or anchor points. The workpiece to be ripped is pressed down on this wood table and onto the anchor points which hold it in place for the cut (Figure 5-43).

Method No. 3—This method is extremely useful when it is necessary to clean up the raw edge on a large sheet of plywood. All that needs to be done is to clamp a straightedge to the underside of the work in the proper position. This straightedge will ride against the edge of the tabletop and guide the plywood into the blade (Figure 5-44). To use this method, the side of the table must be parallel with the saw blade. While this method will not work on all table saws, in the majority of cases the alignment between blade and table edge is sufficiently accurate for satisfactory results.

Method No. 4—A straightedge can also be nailed to the top surface of the work and the work guided in the same manner as was described for pattern sawing in Chapter 7. This particular method is extremely useful for plywood and for long taper cuts which cannot normally be handled with a tapering jig. The pattern sawing system of squaring workpieces works well on larger pieces because the guide acts as a hold-down to help keep the work in place.

Taper Ripping. Taper cuts, which are required in many woodworking projects, are made with the aid of a special jig. Taper jigs must have one straight side to ride against the rip fence and an angled side with which to set the amount of taper. As shown here, various types of tapered table legs can be cut for various furniture projects (Figure 5-45).

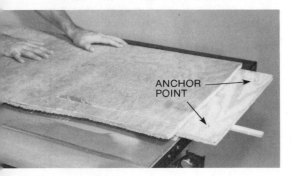

ANCHOR POINT

Figure 5-43: This squaring jig has anchor points to hold the work in place. Again, the sliding table idea is utilized.

Figure 5-44: A straightedge clamped to the workpiece rides against the edge of the table.

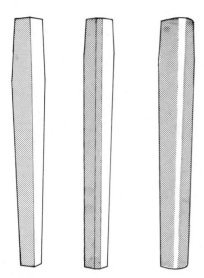

Figure 5-45: Examples of taper ripping.

Taper Cutting With A Template. One method of tapering square table legs is to use a template like the one shown in Figure 5-46. Template taper cuts are made in the following manner:

1. Position the rip fence at a distance from the blade that is equal to the combined width of the leg stock and the long template member. The leg should just clear the blade when the stock is placed against the template (Figure 5-47A).

2. With the stock positioned in the first notch of the template, cut a taper on two adjacent sides of the pieces.

3. Place the leg in the second notch of the template and make the two remaining cuts (Figure 5-47B).

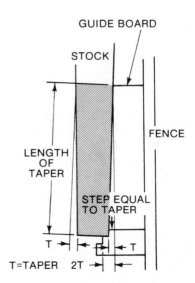

Figure 5-46: A template for cutting square table legs.

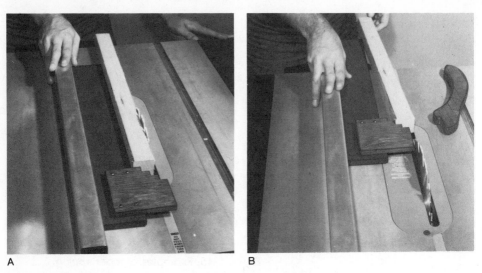

A   B

Figure 5-47: Making a taper cut with the taper template.

The position in which the stock is placed depends upon the length of the taper desired. For instance, when it is necessary to taper a 30″ leg for a distance of 24″, fasten the stock 24″ from the end. During all taper cuts, the blade should be set at a height which projects it about 1/8″ above the stock (as in ordinary ripping). The splitter guard should be used to prevent the stock from being caught on the back of the saw.

Another simple method when only one or two taper rips are needed is to lay out the required taper on your workpiece. Then, nail a parallel guide board on the workpiece with the guide board riding against the fence as shown in Figure 5-48.

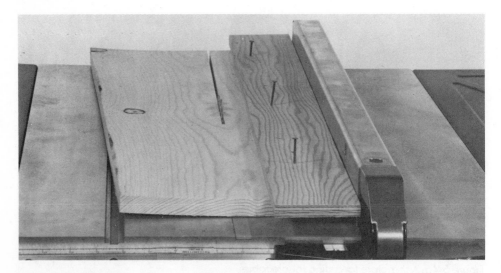

Figure 5-48: Simple method of cutting tapers.

Special Tapering Jigs. The tapering jig shown in Figure 5-49 is suitable for production work of all types. It may be purchased (see Chapter 2) or it can be made of wood in your shop. The jig is simply two straight pieces of wood, hinged at one end and connected at the other by a crosspiece. Keep the two pieces together as you attach the hinge. Either sheet metal or hardwood can be used to make the crosspiece.

After completing the jig, measure 12" in from the hinged end and mark a line across both pieces (Figure 5-50). The jig is set by measuring between these two marks to determine the taper per foot. For example, suppose you are building a footstool with legs that are 1' long, 3" wide at the top, and 2" wide at the bottom. This would require a 1" taper per foot. To set for this taper, open the jig 1" at the 1' mark.

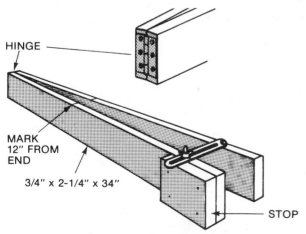

HINGE

MARK
12" FROM
END

3/4" x 2-1/4" x 34"

STOP

Figure 5-49: An adjustable taper jig suitable for production work.

This special taper jig can be used to cut a taper on each face of a square leg. Set the fence to equal the combined width of the jig and the workpiece. Make the first pass; then make the second pass on an adjacent face. Next, adjust the jig to twice its original setting and make the third and fourth passes on the next two adjacent faces. When the workpiece is square, the rip fence need not be readjusted.

This chapter, with the exception of the section on taper ripping, has dealt with straight crosscut and rip sawing. They are the backbone of all table saw operations. Miter, bevel, and compound angle cuts are the next steps in completely understanding the magic that a table saw can perform. These cuts are fully explained in Chapter 6.

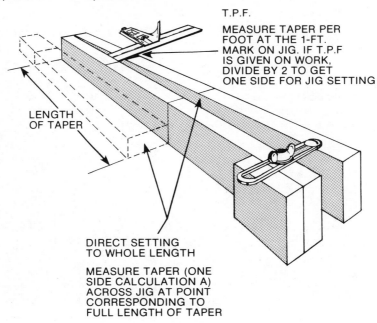

T.P.F.

MEASURE TAPER PER FOOT AT THE 1-FT. MARK ON JIG. IF T.P.F IS GIVEN ON WORK, DIVIDE BY 2 TO GET ONE SIDE FOR JIG SETTING

LENGTH OF TAPER

DIRECT SETTING TO WHOLE LENGTH

MEASURE TAPER (ONE SIDE CALCULATION A) ACROSS JIG AT POINT CORRESPONDING TO FULL LENGTH OF TAPER

Figure 5-50: Method of setting the adjustable taper jig.

Chapter 6
Miter, Bevel, and
Compound Angle Cutting

Besides cutting both straight rip cuts and crosscuts, the table saw performs a full range of miter and bevel operations (Figure 6-1). Bevel crosscuts and bevel rip cuts are made by tilting the saw arbor. This changes the angle of the saw blade in relation to the table surface. Miters require an adjustment to the miter gauge. Compound angle cuts result when both the saw blade and the miter gauge are set at an angle.

Accuracy in all types of angle sawing is vitally important. Otherwise, the cut pieces will not fit together properly. Fortunately, the table saw is a very precise cutting machine when correctly adjusted. But, no matter how accurate the table saw may be, it cannot eliminate human error. So, take the time to set blade and miter angles carefully. A test cut on a piece of scrap material is a good idea whenever possible. Remember, careless mistakes in angle sawing will cost you both time and money.

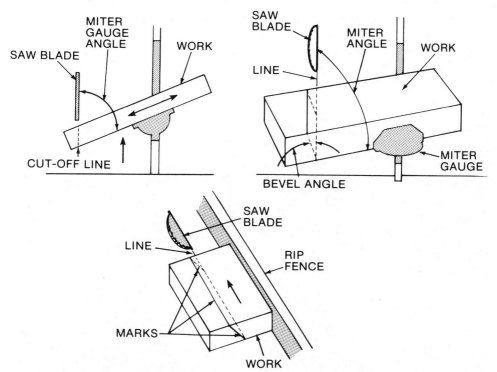

Figure 6-1: Three of the common angle cuts: (left to right) miter, bevel rip, and bevel miter.

85

MITERING. A miter cut is made in the same manner as a straight crosscut except that the miter gauge is set at an angle other than zero. The following are the most common miter joint angles:

Square	4 sides	45°
Hexagon	6 sides	30°
Octagon	8 sides	22-1/2°

Set the angle by sliding the angle control on the miter gauge to the desired setting and locking it in place by tightening the turndown screw. A second, alternate method of setting the angle is to draw the proper angle on the workpiece. The miter gauge is then adjusted until this cutoff line aligns with the saw blade, and the gauge is locked in place. **Note:** Remember to position the saw kerf on the waste side of the cutoff line.

Miter cuts can be made with the gauge set in either an open or closed position (Figure 6-2). The closed position offers advantages in a number of situations. It is the preferred position for cutting wide pieces because the open position often results in part of the miter gauge being located off the table at the beginning of the cut. The closed position is also preferred when working with very short pieces. The open position is usually preferred when cutting longer stock.

Cutting Miters. Before beginning any miter operation, it is best to understand what can go wrong when making a miter cut. Here are some of the most common causes of imperfect miters:

1. Improper alignment or adjustment of the table saw.
2. Workpiece warped or otherwise marred.
3. Dull saw blade or saw blade teeth incorrectly set.
4. Work pushed past the saw blade too quickly.
5. Work allowed to "creep" as the cut is being made.

A   B

Figure 6-2: (A) The open miter gauge position. (B) The closed cutting position.

Of these five points, the last is the most difficult to alleviate, for no matter how accurate the machine or how square and true the stock, the forward motion of the saw blade will pull the work, causing it to creep away from the miter gauge (Figure 6-3). This is true even when using the sharpest saw blades at the proper feed rate. Special attention must be given to the solid positioning of the stock against the miter gauge in order to prevent creeping.

The miter gauge hold-down device is one of the finest ways of counteracting workpiece creep during mitering operations (Figure 6-4). As with straight crosscuts, it holds the piece firmly on the table and against the miter gauge. Using the uppercut feature of the saw along with the hold-down device provides an extremely convenient setup for mitering. The stock is clamped into position and the miter gauge is locked in place on the table. Since there is no need to push the material through the blade when using the uppercut action, there is absolutely no chance of slippage or creep. The blade is simply raised up and through the piece, resulting in a true, accurate cut.

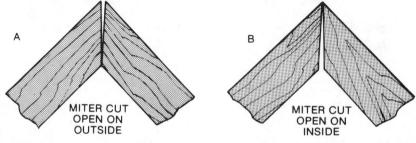

Figure 6-3: Results of creeping: (A) With the gauge in the closed position; (B) with the gauge in the open position.

Figure 6-4: Miter cutting using the hold-down clamp. The clamp helps to prevent creeping.

What's more, your hands never need be near the blade when the cut is being made with the uppercut feature. When two miter gauges are employed as shown in Figure 6-5, it is assured that all four cuts will be exact. The use of two miter gauges can be advantageous in a number of other situations as well. An obvious example is when frequent readjustment of a single gauge is necessary in order to make mating cuts. Another case is when the stock is shaped in such a way that it cannot be flipped over, as in the case of molding pieces which are not flat on both sides.

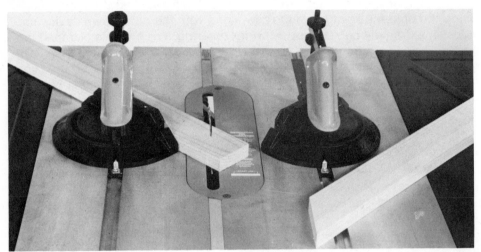

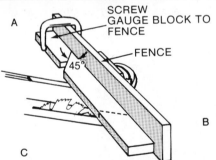

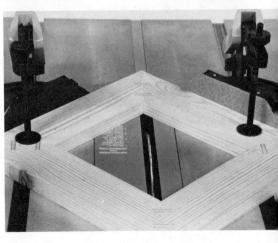

Figure 6-5: Using two miter gauges in miter operations (A). When doing this, you are assured all four cuts are going to be exact, giving you professional results (B). Another way of holding a miter cut (C).

Auxiliary miter gauge wood facing is another popular and practical anti-creep device. When the slight marking of the workpiece is not objectionable, an auxiliary wood face board with disappearing anchor points can serve as a suitable anticreep device (Figure 6-6). It can be used alone or as part of a clamp attachment system. The points of the screws are turned into the wood from the back side and are filed sharp to hold the workpiece in place. When the anchor points are neither wanted nor needed, they can be recessed into the wood face by simply turning out the screws the required number of revolutions.

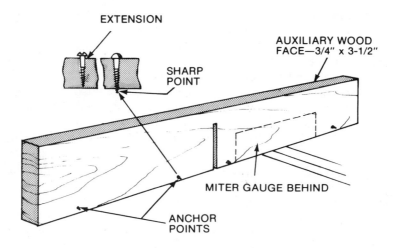

Figure 6-6: Mitering with auxiliary wood facing.

Joining Mitered and Tapered Pieces. The cutting of tapered pieces was discussed in Chapter 5. On occasion, such as when fastening a tapered leg to a table skirt board, it is necessary to join a tapered piece to a mitered one. If the taper angle is known, there is no problem. Simply set the miter gauge at this angle and make the cut. But if the angle of the taper is unknown, the miter cut angle can be determined (Figure 6-7) by using the following formula:

$$A = \frac{B - C}{2}.$$

Line Y is at 90° to the leg top starting at B, and Line X is parallel to Y starting at C. The distance A is used to draw the cut-line on the workpiece requiring the crosscut. It is highly recommended that a trial cut be made on a piece of scrap wood of the same dimensions before the actual cut is made.

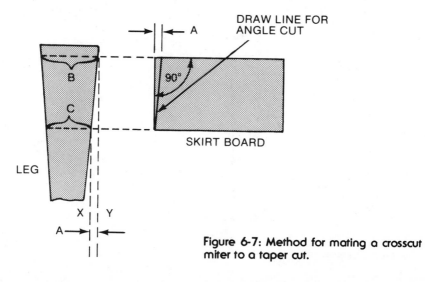

Figure 6-7: Method for mating a crosscut miter to a taper cut.

Mitering Jigs. Because the perfect miter cut is one of the most difficult in all of woodworking, it is often advisable to construct some type of mitering jig to help position and secure the work. This is particularly true when a large number of miter cuts must be made, as in construction or production work. A mitering jig is also a good idea if you are having trouble matching up left- and right-hand miters. This sometimes occurs when the miter gauge is swung from one side to the other or is moved from one table groove to the opposite one. Mitering jigs are also great time savers.

Any number of mitering jigs are capable of solving the problems mentioned above. A good style of jig for 10" table saws is shown in Figure 6-8. It consists of a 3/4" plywood table, roughly 16" by 24" in size. The top triangular piece of the jig is worked to an exact 90°. It is screwed in place. The metal clamps, which are available in most hardware stores, are also screwed into place. Cutouts on the base allow easy working of the clamp screws. Hardwood or metal bars which slide in the table slots guide the jig. Slight adjustments may be necessary to properly line up the miter jig; but once set up properly, the jig will cut a perfect miter every time.

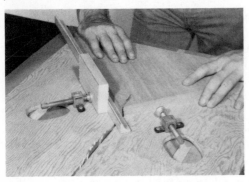

Figure 6-8: (A) Mitering jigs prevent creep and permit both right- and left-handed cutting. (B) Plans for the miter jig.

A

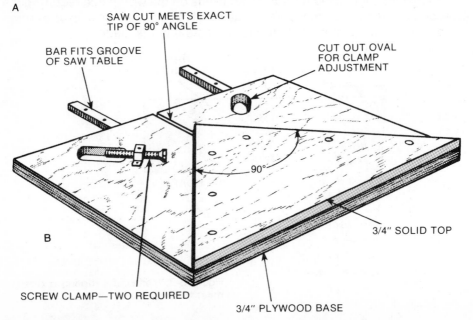

SAW CUT MEETS EXACT
TIP OF 90° ANGLE

BAR FITS GROOVE
OF SAW TABLE

CUT OUT OVAL
FOR CLAMP
ADJUSTMENT

90°

3/4" SOLID TOP

B

SCREW CLAMP—TWO REQUIRED

3/4" PLYWOOD BASE

A number of other simple mitering jigs are shown in Figure 6-9. While these do not offer the clamp feature discussed above, they all provide good support as well as consistent accuracy for both right- and left-handed cuts. These jigs need adjustment only once. All require that the work first be cut square to the net length desired. After this has been done, the miter is set by butting the square end of the work snug against the jig guide. Then, the cut is made. Any duplicate pieces cut on the jig will be accurate in both miter angle and length, provided the initial square cutoff length is accurate.

The jig shown in Figure 6-9A normally requires its own miter gauge and auxiliary fence. Moldings with narrow bases often must be supported upright to prevent wobbling when being cut. To eliminate this wobbling, use suitable pieces of scrapwood to hold the molding firmly upright.

Both miter jigs shown in Figures 6-9A and 6-9B can also be used in the following operations:

1. To cut across the diameter of a circular workpiece.
2. To cut a true diagonal across opposite corners of a square.
3. To cut diametrical slots across the end of a cylinder or turning square for mounting on the spur center in lathe work.

The sliding table jigs shown in Figures 6-8, 6-9B, C, D, and E are, quite naturally, limited to the miter cut determined by the angle of the guides. In this particular case, the angle is 45°. In production work, a job may call for the cutting of pieces at some different angle. In these cases, it often pays to construct a special miter jig set to this particular angle.

The jigs described above, and all jigs of this type for that matter, are permanent jigs which can be used over and over. When not in use, they should always be protected against dampness. To best provide for this protection, sand the jig carefully and apply several coats of shellac, beginning with a wash coat and ending with full strength applications. A resin-type sealer will also provide the protection necessary for a long useful life.

BEVEL OPERATIONS. Beveling operations call for tilting the saw arbor. The distinction between a cross bevel and a miter cut is very slight. When crosscut bevels are joined together, the result is often called a miter joint. Because of this, many people classify a cross bevel cut as a miter cut. In this book, however, only those cuts and joints which require a miter gauge setting will be called miter cuts. Those made with the blade at any angle other than 90° will be called bevels (Figure 6-10). Those made with adjustment to both the miter gauge and the saw arbor are called compound angle cuts, or bevel miter cuts.

Bevel Crosscutting. Bevel crosscutting is the same as straight crosscutting except that the workpiece is cut at an angle other than 90° (Figure 6-11). The miter gauge is used as the guiding device in bevel crosscutting. It should be set at 0°. Most operators prefer to work with the saw blade tilting away from the miter gauge. To make this angle adjustment, mark the angle of the cutoff line on the top and both sides of the workpiece; then set and lock the blade at this angle. Mark a pencil line on the kerf guide in front of the blade to help with alignment. The saw kerf should be located on the waste side of the cut. Hold the stock firmly against the miter gauge and feed the cut slowly, as you would any other crosscut.

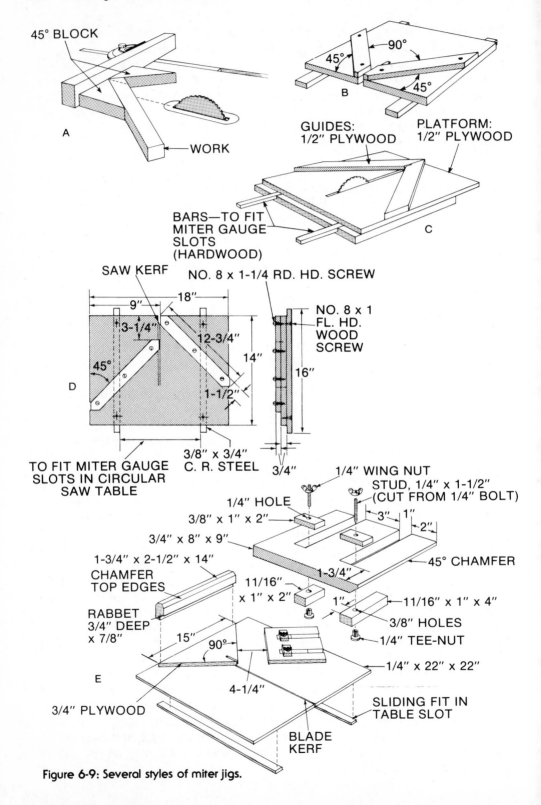

Figure 6-9: Several styles of miter jigs.

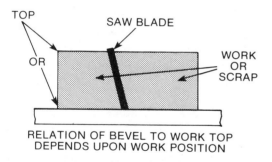

RELATION OF BEVEL TO WORK TOP
DEPENDS UPON WORK POSITION

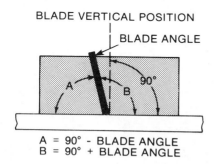

A = 90° - BLADE ANGLE
B = 90° + BLADE ANGLE

Figure 6-10: When bevel cutting, the placement of the resulting workpiece angle
depends upon on which side of the blade
your finished work (or the scrap) is located.

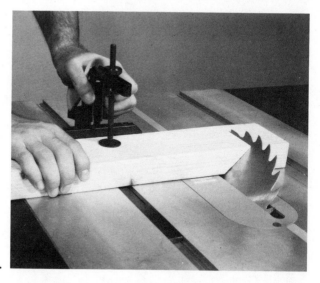

Figure 6-11: Bevel crosscutting.

The miter gauge hold-down clamp will help simplify the operation. As with
miter cuts, the hold-down and the uppercutting feature can be used to great
advantage on bevel crosscuts. Follow the instructions for straight uppercutting
given in Chapter 5 after making the tilt adjustment. Bevel crosscuts on
pieces with a width greater than 7-1/2" should not be made using the uppercut
feature. Use the procedure described in the previous paragraph for these cuts.

Bevel Ripping. To make a bevel rip cut, mark and align the workpiece in the manner already described under bevel crosscutting. Locate the guide fence so that the bottom of the cutoff line is aligned with the saw blade. Recheck the alignment position of bevel rip cuts by sighting from the back along the top cutoff line on the work to the blade. Take the saw kerf into consideration when doing this.

If the exact degree of the marked angle is not known, adjust the angle as you sight along this line (Figure 6-12). This alignment sighting is done before the rip fence is positioned and locked into place. Once all angle adjustments have been made and the fence properly set, adjust the blade height to about 1/8" to 1/4" above the work and make the cut as you would a regular rip cut (Figure 6-13). A high fence or auxiliary table fence are handy when bevel ripping (Figure 6-14).

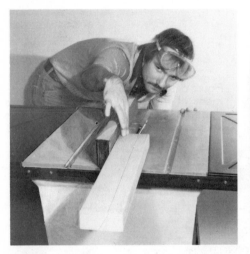 

Figure 6-12: Sighting the bevel rip cutoff line.   Figure 6-13: Making the bevel rip cut.

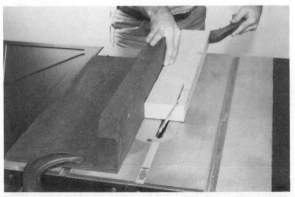

Figure 6-14: Using the auxiliary table fence. The cut can be started as shown, but must be finished by pushing against the supported stock between the table fence and blade.

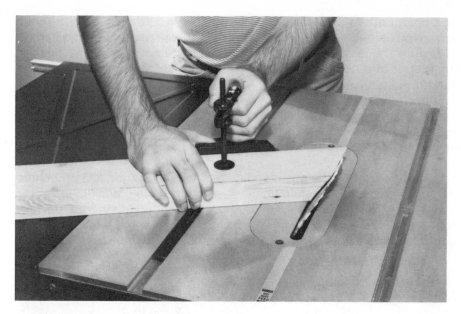

Figure 6-15: The compound angle cut.

COMPOUND ANGLE OR BEVEL MITER CUTS. Compound angle cuts, often called bevel miter cuts, are a combination miter cut and bevel (Figure 6-15). When making these cuts, position the miter gauge at the desired angle and lock it in place. Set up the workpiece as already described for bevel crosscutting and make the cut in the same manner. The combination of the saw blade set at an angle and the miter gauge set at an angle results in a compound angle cut. The table shown here lists the most commonly used compound angles.

TABLE OF COMPOUND ANGLES

Tilt of Work	Equivalent taper per inch	Four-Sided Butt		Four-Sided Miter		Six-Sided Miter		Eight-Sided Miter	
		Bevel Degrees	Miter Degrees	Bevel Degrees	Miter Degrees	Bevel Degrees	Miter Degrees	Bevel Degrees	Miter Degrees
5°	0.087	1/2	5	44-3/4	5	29-3/4	2-1/2	22-1/4	2
10°	0.176	1-1/2	9-3/4	44-1/4	9-3/4	29-1/2	5-1/2	22	4
15°	0.268	3-3/4	14-1/2	43-1/4	14-1/2	29	8-1/4	21-1/2	6
20°	0.364	6-1/4	18-3/4	41-3/4	18-3/4	28-1/4	11	21	8
25°	0.466	10	23	40	23	27-1/4	13-1/2	20-1/4	10
30°	0.577	14-1/2	26-1/2	37-3/4	26-1/2	26	16	19-1/2	11-3/4
35°	0.700	19-1/2	29-3/4	35-1/2	29-3/4	24-1/2	18-1/4	18-1/4	13-1/4
40°	0.839	24-1/2	32-3/4	32-1/2	32-3/4	22-3/4	20-1/4	17	15
45°	1.000	30	35-1/4	30	35-1/4	21	22-1/4	15-3/4	16-1/4
50°	1.19	36	37-1/2	27	37-1/2	19	23-3/4	14-1/2	17-1/2
55°	1.43	42	39-1/4	24	39-1/4	16-3/4	25-1/4	12-1/2	18-3/4
60°	1.73	48	41	21	41	14-1/2	26-1/2	11	19-3/4

Using Compound Angle Sawing. Compound angle cuts are used in the construction of boxes with tilted sides, peaked figures, pedestal stands, sawhorses, picture frames, and many other projects (Figure 6-16). The peaked roof of a doll or bird house requires such a cut. Also, tables having splayed legs with more than a 10° outward tilt require compound angle cuts for their construction.

The basic figure in which compound angle sawing is used is a box having four, six, or eight sides. In each case, the sides are always equally tilted. Figure 6-17 shows the method of calculating a four-sided miter box with sides tilted at 20°.

The compound angle table given earlier lists the saw setting at 5° intervals. Plan your work to match the specifications given for both blade tilt and miter gauge angle. The joints of a four-sided box can be butted or mitered; but six- and eight-sided figures should always have mitered joints, because a butt joint would be considered poor construction for such work.

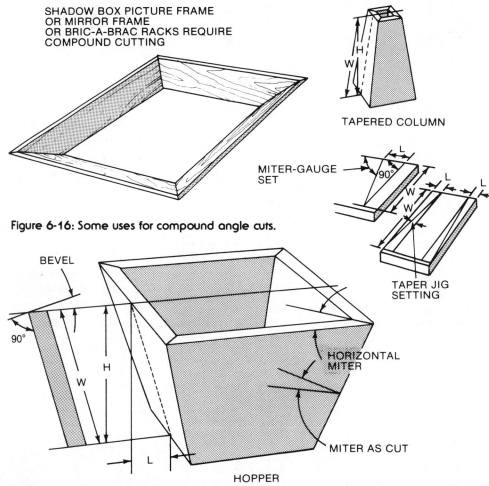

SHADOW BOX PICTURE FRAME
OR MIRROR FRAME
OR BRIC-A-BRAC RACKS REQUIRE
COMPOUND CUTTING

TAPERED COLUMN

MITER-GAUGE SET

TAPER JIG SETTING

Figure 6-16: Some uses for compound angle cuts.

BEVEL

90°

H

W

L

HORIZONTAL MITER

MITER AS CUT

HOPPER

Figure 6-17: A four-sided miter box employing compound angle cuts. The sides tilt outward 20°.

The actual sawing of a compound angle cut is as easy as making a common miter. Refer to the compound angle table and set the blade tilt and miter gauge to the amount given for the type of box and amount of slope required. Cut large work from individual boards, but if it is at all possible, cut all parts from one board. As shown in Figure 6-18, turn the stock over as you make alternate cuts. When the board has square edges, any miter gauge position can be used. Overall, however, the closed setting is best for work of this nature.

Forming Splayed Legs—As mentioned earlier in this chapter, compound angle cuts are used in the construction of tables and chairs with splayed legs. Compound cuts must be made at both the top and the bottom of the leg. Work of this type usually has less than 10° tilt. At these small angles, setting the blade to the necessary tilt will be sufficient to give a satisfactory joint. For a 10° tilt, as seen from both the front and end of the leg, the saw blade is tilted 10° and the miter gauge is swung 10°. When the tilt is 5° as seen from the front and 10° as seen from the end, tilt the saw to one of these angles and set the miter gauge to the other. Because the cut surfaces are parallel, both cuts are made at the same setting by simply sliding the work along the face of the miter gauge. The example shown in Figure 6-19 is a round leg. It should be aligned with a mark on the miter gauge facing to guard against twisting. Make certain that the work does not turn when you shift the piece from one end to the other. **Note:** Square table legs of more than 10° tilt must be backed off and treated the same as a corner block.

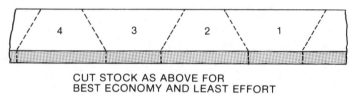

CUT STOCK AS ABOVE FOR
BEST ECONOMY AND LEAST EFFORT

Figure 6-18: Cut the stock as shown here for the best economy.

Figure 6-19: Cutting a compound angle on a table leg.

Corner Blocks—It is sometimes necessary to brace a four-sided figure with corner blocks (Figure 6-20). To make these blocks, first bevel rip the stock with the saw tilt set the same as for a four-sided butt joint (as shown in the compound angle table). This same block will also fit boxes assembled with miter joints, because the shape of these boxes will be the same. Level the tops and bottoms of corner blocks with compound cuts. When making these compound cuts, adjust the miter gauge to the setting given in the table. Tilt the saw blade to the same angle as the box sides. (This angle is not taken from the table.) If the sides of the box are removed, you will see why the angles used for corner blocks will work equally as well for splayed legs on tables, stools, and sawhorses.

The last two chapters have covered the basics—what every table saw owner must know. The following chapters will cover some of the specialty operations that truly give the table saw the ability to perform magic on a piece of wood.

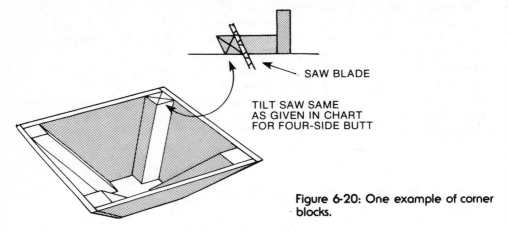

SAW BLADE

TILT SAW SAME
AS GIVEN IN CHART
FOR FOUR-SIDE BUTT

Figure 6-20: One example of corner blocks.

Chapter 7
Special Cutting
Techniques

The table saw is capable of performing a good number of special operations. These jobs include rabbeting, chamfer cutting, raised panel cutting, tenoning, pattern sawing, and a good deal more. Specialty jigs make wedge cutting, circular work, and the handling of unusually shaped pieces easy.

While most specialty cuts are made with a regular saw blade, a number require, or are easier to perform, with the dado cutterhead. All of the procedures described in this chapter are relatively easy and safe to do as long as the operator follows the proper procedures and precautions. Once you begin performing these operations, you will realize why it is so important to master the basic cutting techniques described in the two previous chapters. Although the end result and function of each of these special cuts differ greatly, there is little difference in the actual way the table saw is handled. The basic techniques always apply.

RABBET CUTTING. Rabbet cutting is cutting a groove or slot along the edge or end of a piece of stock. A rabbet cut can be made in several different ways: by making a series of successive saw cuts (Figure 7-1), by making two separate saw cuts at right angles to each other to remove a corner down the length of the stock, or by making a single pass along the edge or end with a dado cutter. This latter method is outlined in the next chapter. Rabbets can also be formed by using the molding cutterhead.

There are several ways of accomplishing the two saw cut method. The two most popular are given below. However, whatever the cutting method, the cut should always be pencil marked and the saw blade height and guide fence adjustments both made before any portion of the rabbet is cut (Figure 7-2A).

Method Number One—In this method, the cut which requires the workpiece to lie flat on the table surface should be made first (Figure 7-2B). When aligning for this cut, set the saw blade a little shy of the pencil mark. The second cut, made with the workpiece set on its edge, cleans out the corner and produces the rabbet (Figure 7-2C). Notice that this method results in a waste piece

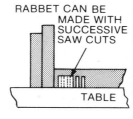

RABBET CAN BE MADE WITH SUCCESSIVE SAW CUTS

TABLE

Figure 7-1: Cutting a rabbet by making successive saw cuts.

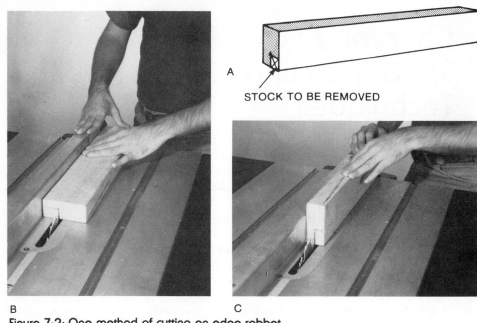

STOCK TO BE REMOVED

B   C

Figure 7-2: One method of cutting an edge rabbet.

that is not trapped between the blade and the guide fence. Had the cut been made in the reverse order, a trapped piece, known as an arrow, would have been left between the fence and the blade. This creates a potentially danger-ous situation—the scrap piece can be thrown back at the operator with con-siderable force after the cut has been completed. Always use a method which avoids trapped pieces. The following is another example.

Method Number Two—In this method, the first cut is made from the face of the wood piece (Figure 7-3A). The second cut is then made with the piece lying flat on the table surface as shown in Figure 7-3B. This second cut clears the rabbet with the scrap piece located on the outside. Again, align the first cut a little short of the required depth. Also, note that the second cut of this alternate method removes the supporting wood of the piece. So before using this method, make sure that there will be enough support wood left to properly hold up the piece. Otherwise it could drop down onto the turning saw blade, causing a hazardous situation. When it is necessary to use a push stick to move the piece past the blade, apply any pressure necessary to the supported por-tions of the wood, not to any part of the wood that is going to be cut away.

On end rabbets (Figure 7-4), make the rip cut first, so that there will be stock to bear against the fence. The work should be at least 4″ wide for safety, unless a tenoning jig (described later in this chapter) is used; and an auxiliary fence should be fastened to the rip fence for better support. End rabbets can also be made by crosscutting, instead of ripping.

As shown in Figure 7-5, it is frequently necessary to cut rabbets on both the edge and the end of the workpiece.

Bevel Rabbets. Except for one slight variation, the procedures described above are also used to produce bevel rabbets. The first cut is a bevel rip; the second cut is a straight rip.

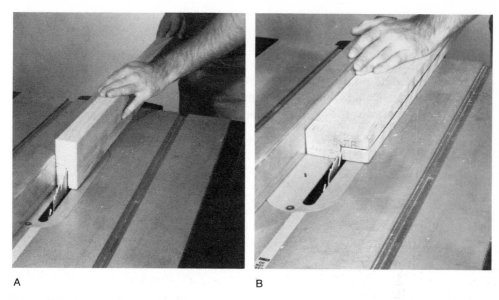

A   B

Figure 7-3: A second way of rabbet cutting.

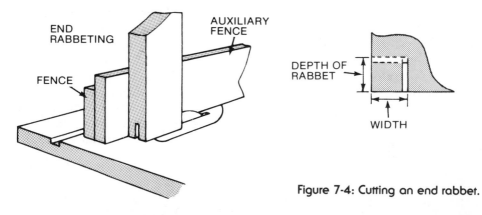

END RABBETING

AUXILIARY FENCE

FENCE

DEPTH OF RABBET

WIDTH

Figure 7-4: Cutting an end rabbet.

Figure 7-5: Rabbets can be cut all the way around a piece of stock.

CHAMFER CUTTING. A bevel cut along the top or bottom edge of a piece of stock is known as a chamfer cut (Figure 7-6). Chamfer cutting or chamfering can be done with the work set flat on the table or positioned on its edge or end. The correct positioning depends on the angle to which the blade is set.

When the angle between the top of the stock and the chamfer measures 45° or more, the cut is made with the workpiece lying flat on the tabletop. The basic bevel rip or crosscut procedure is used for this type of cut.

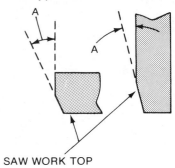

SAW WORK TOP

Figure 7-6: Various chamfering angles.

A = ANGLE OF THE BLADE

If the angle is less than 45°, the stock should be positioned on edge or end. During all edge cutting operations, a wide, wooden auxiliary fence should be attached to the metal rip fence. This will give extra support for the cut. The table insert must be in excellent condition so that there is no chance of a thin edge slipping into the insert opening. Use both hands to firmly hold the work against the auxiliary fence as the cut is being made. End cuts should be made with the aid of a tenoning jig. Adjust the blade to the proper height and angle, position the piece in the jig as shown in Figure 7-7, and make the cut. Chamfer cutting can be used to produce the octagonal shape necessary for spindle lathe woodworking.

Figure 7-7: Cutting a chamfer with a tenoning jig.

Raised Panel Cutting. Raised panel cutting is a simple way to add beauty to any door project. Basically, raised panel cutting is a combination of rabbeting and chamfering on all four sides of a piece of stock. This type of cutting calls for a wide auxiliary fence to be fastened to the saw's metal rip fence. This will provide additional support. Hold the piece firmly against the fence as the cut is being made (Figure 7-8). Several popular raised panel designs are shown in Figure 7-9. When the design requires a series of cuts, those along the edges and sides are made first. The flat or face cuts are made last. A number of raised panel cuts will end in a slight shoulder which adds a greater visual depth to the cut. Others do not have this shoulder. Although it is possible to make any one of these cuts using a saw blade, a dado cutterhead will reduce the number of individual setups required.

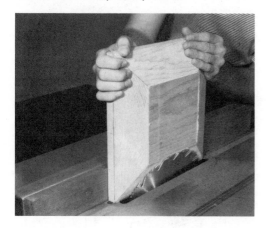

Figure 7-8: Cutting a raised panel.

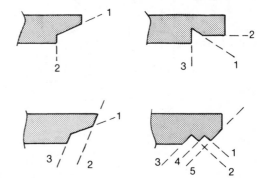

Figure 7-9: Several raised panel designs. Numbers represent the order of the cuts.

TENONING. Tenons are cut by rabbeting one or more of the edges (sides) of the stock. The four major types (one-sided, two-sided, three-sided, and four-sided) of tenons are shown in Figure 7-10. To center the tenons between the two workpiece faces, equalize the opposite rabbet cuts of the two-sided and three-sided tenons (each of these types has only one pair of opposing rabbet cuts), and equalize the two pairs of opposing rabbet cuts of the four-sided tenons. If the tenons are to be centered on the workpiece, opposite rabbets must be made with identical setups. If centering is not wanted (as frequently is desirable—see Chapter 10), the cuts will be made off center.

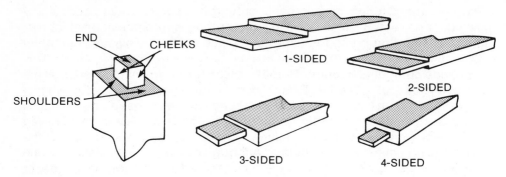

Figure 7-10: Parts of the tenon and the major types.

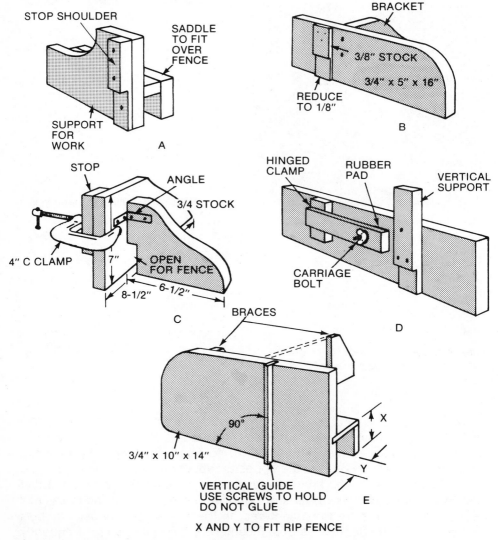

Figure 7-11: Simple tenoning jigs that you can make.

The usual procedure in making tenon cuts on the table saw is to make all into-the-end (cheek) cuts first. This requires you to hold the stock against the fence and down on the saw table. Then, push the workpiece through by hand. This works fairly well with wide stock, but "rocking" of narrower widths makes this method not only impractical but also unsafe.

Figure 7-11 illustrates five simple tenoning jigs that can be made from scrap stock. (Commercial tenoning or universal jigs that can be used with most table saws are available.) The shop-built tenoning jigs are useful for a wide variety of other cutting operations.

The tenoning jig shown in Figure 7-11C, for example, consists of two blocks of 3/4" hardwood, fitted together at right angles with screws and a pair of angle irons. One of the blocks is cut out to make a sliding fit over the saw fence. A 4" C-clamp provides a method of holding the work. The clamp is screw-fastened in place, as can be seen in the drawing, further support being provided by housing the clamp in a groove cut across the end of the main piece of wood. A narrow strip of wood provides a stop block for the work. The method of using the jig can be seen in the photo. The rear extension should be kept firmly in contact with the table while the work is being pushed into the saw. The cutout for the fence should be a snug sliding fit to eliminate side play.

The tenoning jig illustrated in Figure 7-11E, because of its high fence, is ideal for cutting tenons on long stock or for panel raising. But when making any of these jigs, remember that the main thing about the construction is simply "good construction." Make the jig solid and be sure that there is a good sliding fit if you want accurate results.

In putting work through with this jig, it is usually advisable (except in design D) to clamp the stock in place to eliminate any possible chance of slippage, as shown in Figure 7-12. This isn't always necessary. The depth and width of the stop shoulder and the cutout in the shoulder are determined by the jobs you habitually do.

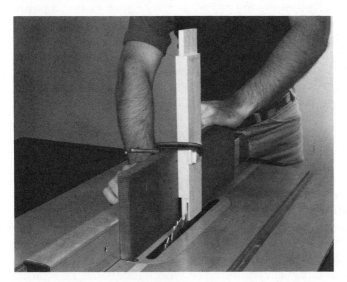

Figure 7-12: Simple tenoning jig in use.

If the stock isn't of exactly the same thickness, it is necessary to make both cheek cuts from the same side. In this case, make the outside cheek cut first on all the pieces and then reset the ripping fence to make the second cheek cut. It is possible to make both cheek cuts simultaneously if two saws of the same diameter and with a spacing block between them are put on the saw arbor (Figure 7-13). More details on multi-blade cutting are given later in this chapter.

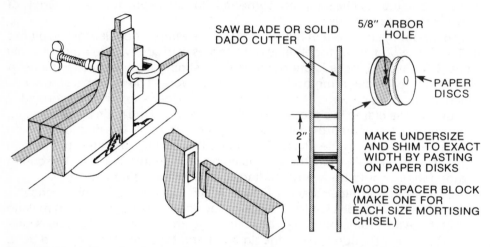

SAW BLADE OR SOLID DADO CUTTER

5/8" ARBOR HOLE

PAPER DISCS

2"

MAKE UNDERSIZE AND SHIM TO EXACT WIDTH BY PASTING ON PAPER DISKS

WOOD SPACER BLOCK (MAKE ONE FOR EACH SIZE MORTISING CHISEL)

Figure 7-13: Making cheek cuts with two saw blades and a spacing block.

COVE CUTTING. By clamping a straight guide fence to the saw table in a position that is out of line with the saw blade, it is possible to create cove molding for decorative and other purposes (Figure 7-14). The stock to be molded is run along this out-of-parallel fence and a number of light cuts are made until the desired depth is obtained. Determine the proper fence angle by using a parallel rule or four strips of wood nailed together to make a frame. For example, say a cove 1-1/2" wide by 3/4" deep is required (Figure 7-15). To begin, set the saw blade height to the desired 3/4" elevation, and then make the frame with the sides 1-1/2" apart for the setting of the parallels. Place this wood frame or the parallel rule over the saw blade so that it just touches the front and rear teeth of the exposed blade (Figure 7-16). When rotated by hand, the teeth of the saw blade should just nick the setting-out frame. This setting-out frame determines the proper angle for the fence. The fence itself is located by measuring to intersect the center line of the workpiece with the center line of the saw blade (Figure 7-17).

When cutting the cove shape, raise the saw blade to a height of no more than 1/8" above the table to make the first cut. The saw should then be raised another 1/8" and a second cut made. Repeat this operation until the required depth is reached, never raising the saw blade more than 1/8" at one time. For deep cuts, rough out the work with a number of straight saw or dado head cuts (Figure 7-18). The shape produced by the finishing cut will be an ellipse (Figure 7-19), so if a true circle is required, the woodpiece must be sanded with paper held over a true round guide.

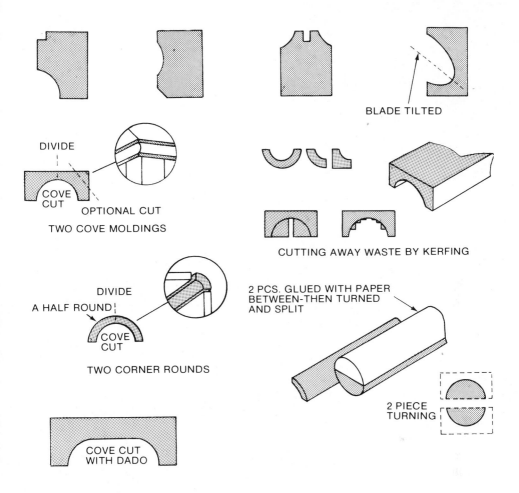

BLADE TILTED

DIVIDE

COVE CUT

OPTIONAL CUT

TWO COVE MOLDINGS

CUTTING AWAY WASTE BY KERFING

DIVIDE

A HALF ROUND

COVE CUT

TWO CORNER ROUNDS

2 PCS. GLUED WITH PAPER BETWEEN-THEN TURNED AND SPLIT

2 PIECE TURNING

COVE CUT WITH DADO

Figure 7-14: Different cove molding shapes and how to use them.

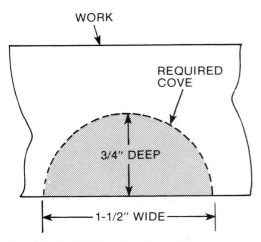

WORK

REQUIRED COVE

3/4" DEEP

1-1/2" WIDE

Figure 7-15: Details of a simple cove cut.

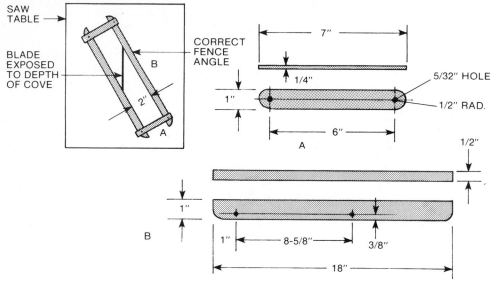

Figure 7-16: Plans for a parallel rule and how it is used to set up the guide board.

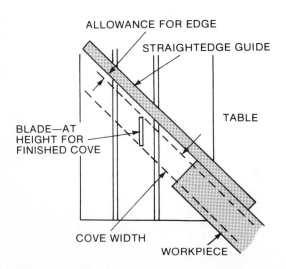

Figure 7-17: Setting up the cove cut.

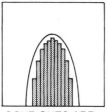

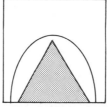

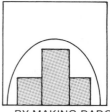

COVE CUTS ARE
SIMPLIFIED BY
FIRST ROUGHING
OUT WITH STRAIGHT
CUTS...OR

...BY ANGLE CUT-
TING INSIDE THE
CURVE AS MARKED
FROM THE PLAN...OR

...BY MAKING DADO
CUTS TO REMOVE
THE WASTE STOCK.

Figure 7-18: Cove cuts are simplified: (A) by first roughing out with straight cuts; (B) by angle cutting inside the curve as marked from the plan; (C) or by making dado cuts to remove the waste stock.

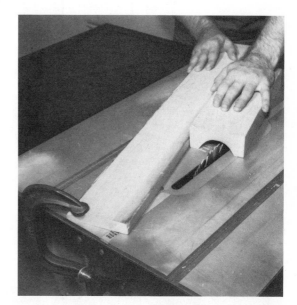

Figure 7-19: Making the cove cut.

By varying the angle at which the stock meets the blade (Figure 7-20), as well as the final elevation of the blade, a great variety of cove shapes and moldings can be formed. Twin coves can be formed by turning the stock end-for-end after each pass. Properly offset the auxiliary wood fence to account for the desired spacing between the two coves (Figure 7-21A). The coving method may also be used on edges (Figure 7-21B).

A combination blade or a ripping blade with a good amount of set are the two best blades for cove cutting operations. Carbide tipped blades are also very popular. In any case, the blade used must be sharp. A small saw produces the best circular shape. At times, a 6" dado saw can be used to finish the cut, but this saw should never be used to rough a cove cut.

As described in Chapter 9, cove cuts can also be made with a molding cutterhead. It is possible to make these cuts with one or two passes of the molding cutterhead—the most practical setup when a large number of shapes must be formed.

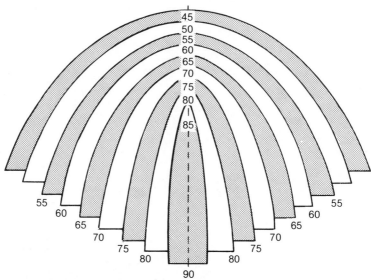

Figure 7-20: Full-size plan illustrates approximate shapes cut at various work angles.

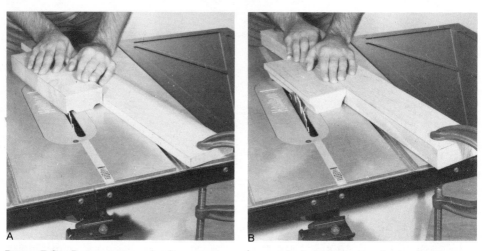

Figure 7-21: Twin coves and edge coves can be made by employing the basic setup.

KERFING. Many woodworking projects require the bending of wood pieces. In solving the problem of curved surfaces, the home craftsperson has a number of options at his or her disposal. The wood can be bent by steaming it, but this calls for special equipment. It is also possible to form the curve by sawing thick segments of wood. To thin-out the back section, cut a wide dado as shown in Figure 7-22. The thinned-out section must be reinforced with glue blocks. After the stock is thinned-out, soak it in hot water and bend it to the desired radius.

While the thinned-out method will produce a fairly small radius, the best method of bending wood pieces is to cut a series of saw kerfs to within 1/8" of the outside surface. This will make the material more flexible for bending. This method, known as kerfing, is easily accomplished with a table saw.

The stock's overall flexibility and the radius to which it can be curved are determined by the distance between the saw kerfs. The closer the kerfs, the more the wood can be bent. The first step in determining the proper kerf spacing is to decide on the radius of the curve or circle to be formed. After determining this radius, measure the same distance (as the radius) in from the end of the stock to be bent, and cut the first saw kerf at this point. The saw kerf can be made like any crosscut with the saw blade raised to within 1/8" of the top of the stock. Saw kerfs are best cut at right angles to the grain of the wood. This may make the wood a bit more difficult to bend, but there will be less chance of thinner pieces splitting. Cut the minimum amount of saw kerfs necessary for the desired flexibility. Making an excess number of saw kerfs weakens the wood and wastes time.

Figure 7-22: To thin-out stock for bending, cut a wide dado such as this.

After making the first saw kerf, clamp the stock to the table top with a C-clamp and raise the end of the stock until the kerf closes completely (Figure 7-23). The distance between the underside of the stock and the tabletop will be the same as the correct spacing distance for the saw kerfs.

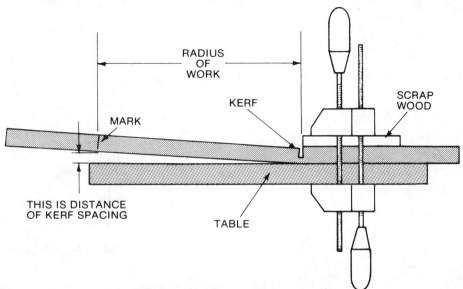

RADIUS
OF
WORK

KERF

SCRAP
WOOD

MARK

THIS IS DISTANCE
OF KERF SPACING

TABLE

Figure 7-23: Method of determining kerf spacing.

In most cases, bending operations require many saw kerfs. That is why it is a good idea to use a miter-gauge faceboard which serves as a spacing jig (Figure 7-24). To make this simple jig, run a saw slot through the faceboard and use a nail to serve as a guide. Space this nail away from the saw slot at a distance equal to the saw kerf spacing desired. Make the initial cut with the end of the workpiece butted snugly against the pin. Gauge each remaining cut by placing each new kerf over the guide pin (Figure 7-25). When kerfing must be done in an area some distance away from the end of the stock, make the first cut without the aid of the guide pin. A pencil mark on the kerf guide can also be used to space the cuts (Figure 7-26).

When all the saw kerfs have been cut into the wood, slowly bend the stock until the desired curve is formed (Figure 7-27). Wetting down the workpiece with warm water will increase bending ease. Tack a tie strip in place to hold the workpiece until it is attached to the assembly. It is even possible to form compound curves by kerfing both sides of the work. If the saw kerfs must be exposed, it is possible to glue veneers in place over the cuts.

Figure 7-24: Miter-gauge faceboard suitable for kerf spacing.

Figure 7-25: Using the guide pin spacing faceboard.

Figure 7-27: Bending the wood to the desired curve. Remember these three points when kerf cutting: (1) The closer the kerfs, the smoother the contour; (2) while the shorter tangents must be sanded, the closed kerfs are stronger; and (3) kerfs are best if they are together at the bend.

Figure 7-26: Spacing kerfs with a mark on the kerf guide.

PENCIL LINE

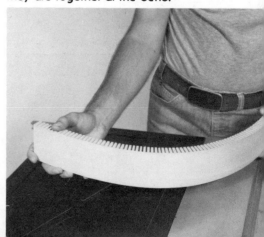

For exterior work, coat the kerfs with glue before making the bend. Plastic wood or putty can be used to fill the crevices after the bend has been made. When this filling is properly done, only close inspection will reveal the method used to make the bend.

A spiral curve can be formed if the kerfs are cut at a miter angle instead of straight across. The greater the miter angle, the greater the "looseness" of the spiral.

SAWCUT MOLDINGS. A number of attractive moldings can be formed by making cuts similar to those employed in kerfing operations. The shapes shown in Figure 7-28 are variations of "dentil molding." However, the term "dentil molding" is quite general and can be applied to many different shapes. The setup for cutting this type of molding closely resembles the one used for kerfing— auxiliary facing is fastened to the miter gauge and a nail is driven into this facing to act as a guide pin. Again, the amount of space between saw cuts is determined by the distance between guide pin and saw blade (Figure 7-29).

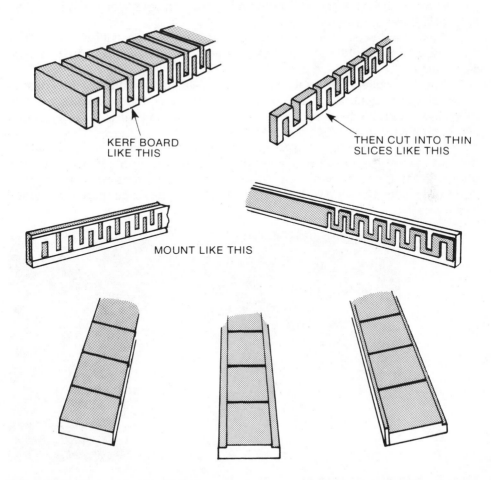

KERF BOARD
LIKE THIS

THEN CUT INTO THIN
SLICES LIKE THIS

MOUNT LIKE THIS

Figure 7-28: Typical sawcut moldings.

Figure 7-29: Making the dentil crosscuts.

After all the kerf-like crosscuts are made, the work is completed by setting the saw blade at a sufficiently high elevation and making a series of narrow rip cuts to form molding strips (Figure 7-30). Extremely narrow and exacting rip cuts of this nature require a special setup to assure the safest possible operation and the finest results. An auxiliary wood table fitted over the saw's tabletop will give the work the full support necessary to prevent the narrow strips from being pulled down into the table insert opening. The actual ripping procedure for sawcut molding is detailed below:

1. Cut the auxiliary wood table to the size necessary to fit the saw table.

2. With the saw blade lowered beneath the table surface, clamp the auxiliary table to the saw table.

3. Position the rip fence a distance away from the blade equal to the thickness of the molding strips desired.

4. Raise the saw blade so it will cut its own slot into the auxiliary wood table.

5. Position the molding firmly against the fence. Always use a push stick to safely move the workpiece past the saw blade.

This same auxiliary table setup can be used with many different thicknesses of molding. Always take care to position the fence so that the exact molding thickness is cut. When using the above ripping method with a hollow-ground blade, cuts as thin as 1/64" are possible.

The auxiliary table can also be used to make surface cuts on wide pieces that are then strip-cut to produce strips for assembly into decorative panels (Figure 7-31). Once the decorative strips are cut, they can be made into a panel by edge-to-edge bonding with contact adhesive, or the pieces can be enclosed in a frame.

Figure 7-30: Ripping thin moldings.

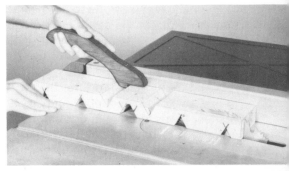

Figure 7-31: After the design has been cut into the wood, the blocks are strip-cut. The resulting strips are then joined edge-to-edge to form panels for such projects as room dividers, screens, and so on. While the design above was produced by making V and slot cuts, the types of decorative designs are almost infinite.

Another decorative panel cutting technique that can be done on your table saw is piercing. It is accomplished by making cuts on one side of the stock with the cutter blade projection slightly more than half the panel thickness. Then the panel is turned over and opposing cuts are made (Figure 7-32). Openings are created where these opposing cuts cross. While many shapes can be formed, precision setting of the blade-height is very important.

MULTI-BLADE CUTTING. Earlier in the chapter we discussed using two blades to cut tenons. The same setup can be used to double or triple (if using three blades) the output on repetitive sawing jobs that call for parallel cutting (Figure 7-33).

Figure 7-32: Making piercing cuts on a panel.

Figure 7-33: With a two-blade setup it is possible to produce a number of similar parts.

The major restrictions to multi-blade work are the length of the saw's arbor and the width of the saw slot of the table insert. For most multi-blade cutting, it is necessary to install a special insert as described in Chapter 1. Remember— **NEVER** operate the saw without a table insert. Washers determine the spacing of the blades.

When multi-blade cutting, the work is fed as for any rip cut. The rip fence is first set to the desired thickness and then the work is passed through the blades. If any drag is encountered, slow down the rate of feed.

Another application of multi-blade cutting is when making decorative woven panels (Figure 7-34). Using a flexible material such as hardboard, it is a simple task to interweave with thin wooden slats or a contrasting material like colorful plastic strips. The more saw cuts that are made and the closer they are spaced, the more flexible the panel material becomes. Clamps or stop blocks help control the start and completion of the cuts, assuring that uniformity is achieved.

Figure 7-34: Making a woven panel with a multi-blade setup.

INLAYS. To make wood inlays on a workpiece, cut a shallow kerf into the surface or edge of the stock using the repeat pass method with a hollow-ground blade (Figure 7-35). These kerfs are then filled with pieces of contrasting wood cut to fit them (Figure 7-36A). It is also possible to veneer the edges of the piece with thin strips that match or complement the inlay. A dado or molding cutterhead can also be used to make the kerf. As shown in Figure 7-36B, controlled kerfs can be cut into the wood face. (See the section on blind cutting in Chapter 8 for the methods to make these cuts.)

PATTERN SAWING. Sawing to a pattern, or "pattern sawing" as it is more often called, is one of the few production woodworking methods that is equally well adapted to the home workshop. Since it requires little more than a pattern and one of a few easily constructed types of jigs, this method is useful where several duplicate parts must be made. Not only does it eliminate much tedious layout work, but it enables scrap material to be quickly brought to shape. One of the advantages of the method is that even an inexperienced operator cannot possibly cut the material too small.

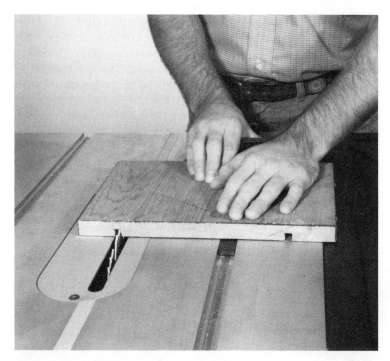

Figure 7-35: Making the cut for an inlay by the repeat pass method.

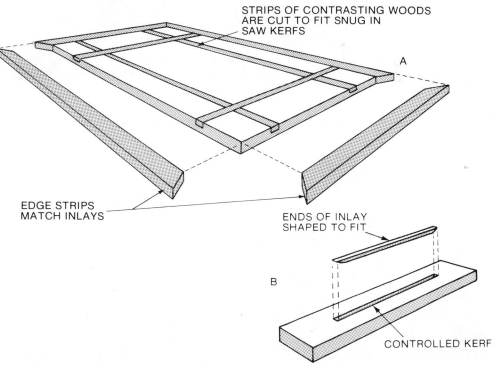

STRIPS OF CONTRASTING WOODS
ARE CUT TO FIT SNUG IN
SAW KERFS

A

EDGE STRIPS
MATCH INLAYS

ENDS OF INLAY
SHAPED TO FIT

B

CONTROLLED KERF

Figure 7-36: Simple inlay types.

There are several different jigs that may be used, depending upon the type of work. Odd-shaped pieces with straight sides may be cut to shape expeditiously with the table saw as shown in Figure 7-37. A wooden guide fence is clamped to the regular ripping fence, and this extra fence clears the saw table sufficiently to allow the material to slip below it. A small rabbet is cut on the lower side of the outer edge of this fence to permit the blade of the saw to be set so that the outer teeth are exactly flush with the edge of the wooden fence. A pattern cut to the shape of the article also is needed. This is fastened to the material with small nails. After the pattern is secured to the stock, it is guided along the wooden fence, and the work is thus trimmed to the exact shape of the pattern.

When it is undesirable to have the fine indentations of the nails in the surface of the work, a frame may be made as shown in Figure 7-38 to fit the workpiece snugly. This is used in the same manner as a regular pattern.

Figure 7-37: Cutting straight-sided odd shapes using pattern sawing and a template for cutting.

Figure 7-38: To avoid nails on the work, a box jig may be used when pattern sawing.

Another application of pattern sawing is shown in Figure 7-39. But, with this type of pattern sawing **no** pattern is necessary. The work itself is the pattern. Cut the cleats off flush with the edges of the work. Simply run each edge of the workpiece along the auxiliary fence. This same method can also be used to trim veneer edges flush with the main body of the wood to which it is applied.

OTHER SPECIALTY JIGS. As can be seen on the preceding pages, cutting jigs are essential to many specialty operations. The following easily constructed jigs will further expand the capabilities of your table saw.

Notched Jigs. Very small pieces or those which are extremely odd shaped often pose unique problems. Many times these pieces cannot be cut safely or accurately with the use of the rip fence or miter gauge alone. In these cases, a notched jig often provides the solution as shown in Figure 7-40.

The jig is basically a piece of wood with parallel sides. The notch cut into this piece can either be in the shape of the part you wish to keep or the shape of the part that is to be discarded. In most cases, the jig will ride along the rip fence and act as both carrier and gauge. As shown in Figure 7-41, jobs such as tenon cheek-cuts can be made with the use of notched jigs. This jig allows for the exact positioning of even the most unusually shaped workpieces.

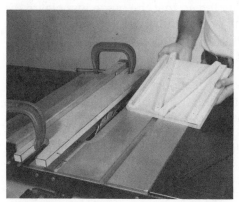
Figure 7-39: Another pattern sawing setup.

Figure 7-40: Simple notched jig.

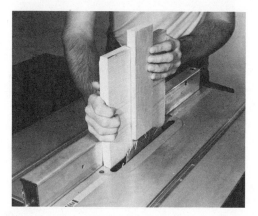
Figure 7-41: Making tenon cheek-cuts with a notched jig.

The function of a notched jig is in most cases quite specific, so making generalizations concerning the use of notched jigs is not easy. However, there are a number of general situations where a notched jig can be quite helpful. Whenever the workpiece is so small or oddly shaped that it cannot be safely hand-held, or when other safety precautions call for it, use a notched jig. If use of the ordinary guiding devices, the rip fence and the miter gauge, are impossible or pose a safety threat, the use of a notched jig is in order. Often, when a large number of identical parts must be formed, the answer is the construction of a special notched jig. In any case, the jigs must be made very accurately, so you can see their impracticality when only one or two pieces need be formed. At such times when accuracy is all important, but the work really does not justify the construction of a special notched jig, it is probably best to lay out the piece, cut just outside the guide lines, and finish the job with a belt or disk sander.

Wedge Cutting Jigs. Wedge cutting typifies the special function of notched jigs. To cut wedges or triangular pieces, it is necessary to make a wood jig. For example, one should be used for cutting glue or corner blocks (Figure 7-42). Several sizes and shapes should be available for cutting other common items (Figure 7-43). Regardless of design, the jig is notched to produce the desired taper, and the saw fence is adjusted so that the blade just clears the jig as it passes along the fence. After the stock is crosscut from wide material, all other cuts are made with the grain of the material. As each wedge is cut, the stock is flopped in the notch. The jig is first pushed forward, then withdrawn with the wedge in the notch.

For best results, select stock free of knots. It should also have the straightest grain possible. There will be no need to sand the wedges if a hollow-ground combination blade is used to make the cuts. In order to assure chisel points on the wedges, the width of the stock from which the wedges are cut must equal the length of the notch. When blunt points are desired, make the notch in the jig deeper.

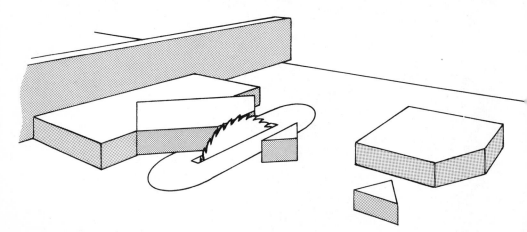

Figure 7-42: Wedge jig suitable for cutting glue or corner blocks.

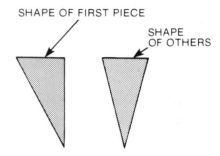

SHAPE OF FIRST PIECE

SHAPE OF OTHERS

Figure 7-43: Two wedge cutting jigs.

Adjustable Wedge Cutting Jigs—When a good number of wedges have to be formed, designing an individual template for each one is neither practical nor economical. An adjustable wedge cutting jig (Figure 7-44) is the answer. A bolt, located at the front of the jig, is turned in or out as required to set the taper. The head of the bolt rides against the rip fence and therefore should be ground and polished to prevent any marring of the fence. It is also quite possible to make a wedge cutting jig from solid lumber. To visualize this jig, imagine the wedge formed by the bolt to be of solid wood contacting the fence. Whenever cutting wedges, always use some type of jig. Never under any circumstances should you attempt to cut wedges freehand.

Figure 7-44: Adjustable wedge cutting jig.

CIRCLE CUTTING. Circular cuts can be easily made on the table saw with the aid of a pivot setup. The pivot is no more than a nail that is driven through the center of the workpiece into a plywood platform. The platform is attached to bars that fit into the miter gauge slots of the table. This assembly is clamped down fast to prevent the work from shifting. This is very important, for if the work moves, a perfect circle will be ruined.

To make this pivot cut, first remove most of the waste stock by making tangent cuts along the perimeter of the desired circle (Figure 7-45). After removing this waste stock, clamp the platform in a position so that the work center line is near the front of the saw blade. Cut thick stock by making repeat passes. Raise the blade 1/16" after each complete rotation. Start the saw and rotate the work into the blade in the direction indicated by the arrow in Figure 7-46.

A beveled edge is possible by simply tilting the saw arbor (Figure 7-47). Make the bevel cut after you have formed the circle with the blade in the vertical position. The bevel will be flat when the final pass is made with the work center line on the blade center line.

Figure 7-45: Cutting away the scrap to make circular cuts easier.

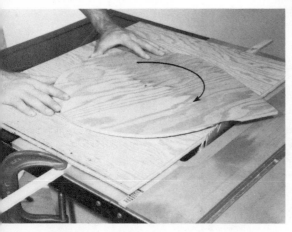

Figure 7-46: Making a simple circular cut. Note the direction of rotation.

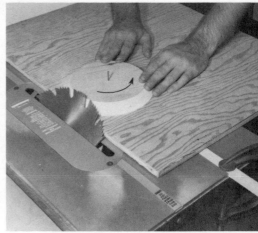

Figure 7-47: Circular bevel cuts.

Coving circular edges can be done if the work is cut with the blade tilted and the wood positioned almost in front of the blade (Figure 7-48). Repeat passes are required for this cut. Raise the blade 1/16" for each rotation. Changing the work position or the tilt angle will alter the final result. Experiment on scrap stock to find the most interesting effects.

Working with dado cutterheads is discussed in the next chapter. However, pivot cutting with the dado head is best covered here. Pivot cutting with the dado will result in the type of shape shown in Figure 7-49 if the cut is not completely through the work. Notice that the waste side of the stock is beveled while the good side is square. This cut also requires repeat cuts.

A rabbet can be cut on circular pieces using the pivot technique and the dado cutterhead (Figure 7-50). Circular work can also be rabbeted using vertical support. Clamp or screw the support piece to the rip fence. The pivot nail is driven through the center of the material as shown in Figure 7-51. Start by slowly raising the cutter as you hold the work. Use the fine elevation control to do this. Turn the work very slowly and grip it firmly to the support piece to complete the rabbet cut.

Molding cutterhead attachments can also be used to cut these edges and surface cuts. The resulting shape cut with a pivot setup will differ from that cut in a straight line, so experiment on scrap pieces to determine the desired shape.

Figure 7-48: Circular cove work.

Figure 7-49: One example of circular dado cutting.

Figure 7-50: Cutting a rabbet on a circular piece using a dado.

Figure 7-51: Vertical setup for cutting circular rabbets.

Cutting Spirals. Spirals on a table saw can be cut with either a saw blade or dado cutter. Using a miter gauge with an auxiliary fence, firmly hold the round stock down on the saw table and slowly turn it toward the blade or cutters. The angle at which the miter gauge is set determines the lead of the spiral, while the depth-of-cut is controlled by the height of the blade or cutters above the table. It is best to keep the projection to a minimum. If you feed slowly, the cutting action will automatically hold the pitch. There is no limit to the length or diameter of work which may be handled this way. Even a dowel may be spiraled (Figure 7-52).

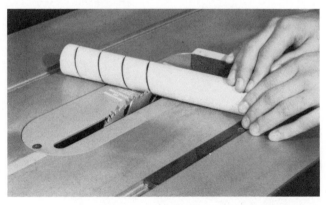

Figure 7-52: Use a regular blade to cut a spiral in a dowel.

Chapter 8
Using a
Dado Head

A dado head is perhaps the most versatile of all table saw accessories. Dado heads are used primarily for the cutting of grooves, dadoes, and rabbets in widths from 1/8″ to 13/16″, but are capable of much more, especially in the areas of joint design and decorative cutting. While it is true that a regular saw blade can accomplish many of these cuts using the repeat pass method, dado heads can make the same cuts in only one or two passes. Increased accuracy and decreased cutting time make the dado head well worth the initial investment.

The three basic cuts in dado work are the groove, the dado, and the rabbet (Figure 8-1). A groove is a cut made into the woodpiece in such a way that the direction of the cut runs parallel with the grain of the wood. A dado is a cut made at a right angle to the grain of the wood. Groove cutting uses the rip fence for support; dado cutting employs the miter gauge. When either a groove or a dado is made along the edge or end of a board, it is known as a rabbet cut.

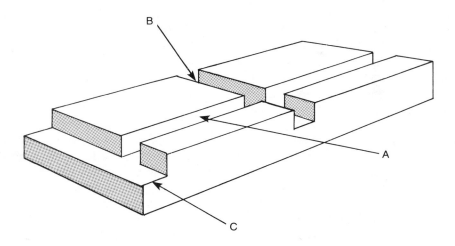

Figure 8-1: The three basic dado cuts: (A) a groove; (B) a dado; (C) a rabbet.

Basic descriptions of the various types of dado head types are given in Chapter 2. Always refer to the instructions supplied with the specific accessory whenever mounting the dado or adjusting its cutting width. When using any dado head, the table saw's regular insert must be removed and replaced with a special wider variety (Figure 8-2). Care must be taken to insure that the dado

125

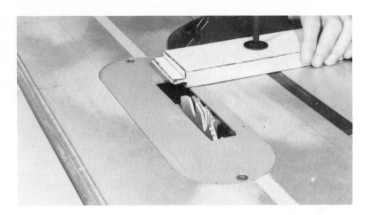

Figure 8-2: A wider table insert, suitable for dadoing operations.

head does not strike the table insert. This is especially true if you plan to cut a bevel with the dado head. In fact, a number of table saw manufacturers recommend that the dado head never be moved from the vertical position and that no type of bevel sawing should be attempted with this accessory.

Using a dado of the correct size is very important. The greater the diameter of the outside saw blade, the greater the speed (feet per minute of travel) of the blade's cutting edge. This greater speed means a greater load on the table saw motor. The wide kerfs which dadoes cut also increase the motor load. A dado that is too large and is set at a wide cutting width can overload the saw's motor. To prevent this, any dado you use should be of a smaller diameter than the saw blades normally used on the saw. The dado should be at least 2″ less than the blade capacity of the table saw. The dado illustrated throughout this book is 4″ less (a 6″ diameter as opposed to a saw capacity of 10″). **Note:** Never use an adjustable wobbler type dado head on badly twisted or warped wood.

Using the Standard Type Dado Head. There are a number of operational points which pertain to the use of any standard type dado head. Some of these were discussed in Chapter 2, but they are best repeated here. Standard dado heads consist of two outside saws, each 1/8″ thick, whose teeth have no set. Although these saws do not make a finished cut, they are adequately smooth for nearly all types of work. Any tool markings can be quickly sanded away. The inside cutters or chippers of the dado assembly vary in thickness. There is usually a number of 1/8″ and 1/16″ chippers. They are used in combination to make dado assemblies of various thicknesses. In all cases, the cutters should be heavily swaged and arranged so that this heavy portion falls in the gullets of the outside saw (Figure 8-3A). The saw and chipper must overlap (Figure 8-3B), with "a" being the outside saw, "b" the inside cutter, and "c" a paper washer or washers. These paper washers are not needed unless you must very precisely control the exact cutting width. For example, a 1/4″ dado or groove is made by using the two outside saws arranged as shown in Figure 8-3C. Notice that the cutter teeth of one saw are positioned so that they line up with the raker teeth on the other saw. Dado heads should never be used for any through cutting operation. Their job is to cut partway through or into a piece of stock. Also, never use the inside chippers without the two outer saws.

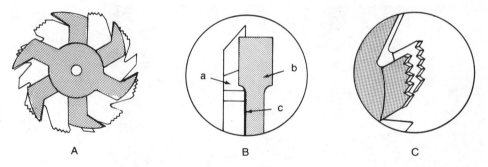

Figure 8-3: The parts of a standard dado head assembly and their proper adjustment.

Mounting the Dado Head—All types of dado heads, both standard and adjustable, are fitted and secured to the saw arbor in the same manner as an ordinary saw blade (Figure 8-4). Always use the special dado table insert having a slot wide enough to accommodate a full-width dado head. All heads should be fully assembled and/or adjusted before they are mounted. Be sure that the saw arbor is free of dirt and sawdust. This is important because a dado head is quite a bit of metal revolving at a fairly high speed. If the head is not running true on the arbor, it will set up a terrific vibration. Also, the blade guard, splitter, and antikickback fingers cannot be used during dado operations and must be removed from the saw or lifted and swung out of the way.

Figure 8-4: Mounting the dado head.

Aligning the Dado Cutterhead—Several factors make aligning the dado head with the workpiece quite different from aligning ordinary saw blades. The major reason is that all grooving and dado cuts are made on the underside of the workpiece. Another reason is that dado cuts can vary greatly in width from one cut to the next.

Using a ruler is one way of positioning the dado head for grooving operations. One important fact to keep in mind when using this method is that the measurement must always be taken from the tooth closest to the fence (Figure 8-5). Disconnect the power source and rotate the arbor by hand to find the closest tooth. When using an adjustable dado, rotate the blade by hand to find the nearest approach of blade teeth to the fence, and take the measurement from that point.

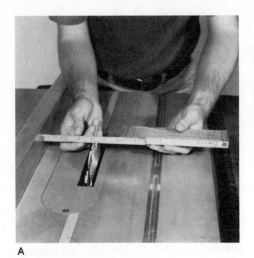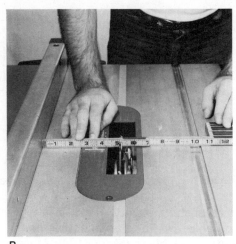

A   B

Figure 8-5: Positioning the dado head. (A) The standard type dado. (B) The adjustable unit.

Another method of aligning the dado head is to mark "groove lines" on the top surface of the workpiece. Sight along these lines to the extreme tooth sides of either the standard or adjustable dado heads (Figure 8-6). It is a good idea to make a test cut on a piece of scrap material to check your setting.

Figure 8-6: Positioning the dado head by sighting along "groove lines."

Perhaps the easiest way of correctly positioning the stock against the miter gauge is to draw dado guide lines on the top and leading edges of the work-piece and make the proper alignment by eye. For increased accuracy, make a cut in a piece of scrapwood clamped to the miter gauge. After this sample cut has been made, return the miter gauge back to the front of the table, turn the table saw off, and mark the cut edges on the table surface or kerf guide (Figure 8-7). Use these lines to help position the real workpiece.

The Basic Groove Cut. As mentioned at the beginning of this chapter, grooving (or ploughing as it is sometimes called) is making a cut that runs with the grain of the woodpiece. In other words, it is the same as ripping a piece, but it is not a through cutting operation. The rip fence is used as the guide for all grooving operations.

Figure 8-7: Marking the kerf guide to help align a groove.

To make a simple groove cut (Figure 8-8), first raise the dado head to the depth of the groove required and slide the rip fence to the correct position. When raising the dado to the desired depth-of-cut, keep in mind that the maximum depth-of-cut is produced by the tooth tips as they pass by the vertical center line of the cutter. This depth can be measured with a ruler (Figure 8-9).

Figure 8-8: A simple groove cut.

Figure 8-9: Measuring to set the depth-of-cut.

The workpiece must be held firmly in place at all times during the cut. To assure this, it is often necessary to clamp a featherboard to the fence directly above the work, as shown in Figure 8-10. Because the dado head takes a bigger bite out of the wood than an ordinary saw blade, the possibility of kickback is increased. As a precaution against kickback, the depth-of-cut should be limited as outlined on the following page.

Softwood (in inches)		Hardwood (in inches)	
Wide	Deep	Wide	Deep
1/8	1-1/4	1/8	5/8
1/4	1	1/4	1/2
3/8	7/8	3/8	7/16
1/2	3/4	1/2	3/8
5/8	5/8	5/8	5/16
3/4	1/2	3/4	1/4
13/16	3/8	13/16	3/16

Figure 8-10: This featherboard arrangement is useful for holding narrow pieces in place for grooving.

If the depth-of-cut is greater than these limitations, it will be necessary to make several passes, increasing the dado elevation with each pass (as indicated in the table) until the desired depth is reached. During each pass, slowly feed the work into the dado head, applying sufficient side pressure to hold the work in against the rip fence to keep it on line. When it is necessary to cut a groove wider than that which the dado head can provide, make the cut in several passes. If it is not more than twice the maximum width, set the dado head to slightly greater than half the required width and make two cuts. Each cut must overlap at the center to make up the required width. When the total width is over twice the capacity of the cutter, set the dado head up for a cut slightly greater than one-third the width, and make three cuts. For best results, make the two outside cuts first, aligning each carefully with its respective side of the groove, as shown in Figure 8-11. Once you make the two end cuts, the center cut or cuts can be made without paying too much attention to alignment. Just be sure that each of these center cuts overlaps the adjacent ones by at least 1/16".

The Dado Cut. Dado cuts are made across the grain of the stock. Dado cutting is closely related to crosscutting except, as in grooving, it is not a through cutting operation. The basic dado cut is made in the same way as the straight crosscut (Figure 8-12). The miter gauge is used as the guiding device. An auxiliary face board can be used to provide added support for longer pieces. Clamping a yardstick or rule to the miter gauge face board is a great aid when a series

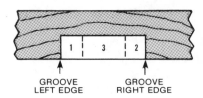

Figure 8-11: The order for making a repeat pass groove.

Figure 8-12: Cutting a dado.

of evenly spaced cuts must be made in the same board (Figure 8-13). Angle dadoes can also be made by adjusting the miter gauge to the desired setting (Figure 8-14). This type of angled cut has many applications in cabinet and general construction work. Dado cuts can be utilized to make many types of decorative pieces. To cut a corner dado, place the wood piece into a V-block held snugly against the miter gauge as shown in Figure 8-15.

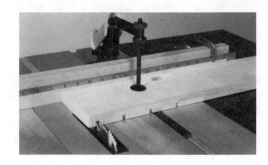

Figure 8-13: Measuring regularly spaced dadoes.

Figure 8-14: Cutting angle dadoes.

Figure 8-15: Cutting a corner dado using a V-block.

When aligning a dado cut, follow the principles outlined in the previous section on groove cutting. Adhere to the width and depth limitations given in the chart found in that section. The procedures concerning cuts which exceed the capacity of the dado head also apply to dado operations.

Methods of Making Repeat Dado Cuts—It is often necessary to cut a series of regularly spaced, repeating dadoes. This is especially true when constructing cabinets, chests, shelves, and other such items. As mentioned previously, clamping a yardstick or rule to the auxiliary face board of the miter gauge is the simplest way of making this operation easier.

A better, more accurate way of making regular repeat cuts is to use the miter gauge in combination with a stop rod. To position the next dado cut, simply fit the stop rod into the last dado made (Figure 8-16). Also, the rip fence, when fitted with a stop block to control the location of the dadoes, is another way of cutting repeat dadoes (Figure 8-17). Still another method is the use of a notched block, as shown in Figure 8-18. When the desired distance between dadoes is equal, the steps of the notched block should be equal. When uneven spacing is required, cut the steps into the notched block accordingly.

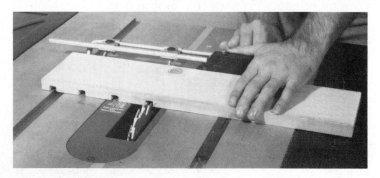

Figure 8-16: Making repeat cuts using the stop rod.

Figure 8-17: Using the rip fence with stop blocks to locate the dado cut.

Figure 8-18: The notched block setup for locating dadoes.

Cutting Blind Grooves or Dadoes. Any groove or dado cut which stops short of one or both ends of the workpiece is known as a blind groove or blind dado. Blind cuts are commonly used in the construction of spline joints. The many uses of splined joints are covered in Chapters 6 and 10.

When making a blind groove, use clamps to locate the beginning and end of the cut (Figure 8-19). Determine the position of these clamps by holding the workpiece alongside the saw in the required position. For blind cutting in longer pieces of wood, clamp an auxiliary wood fence to the regular rip fence. Then, attach stop blocks to this auxiliary fence.

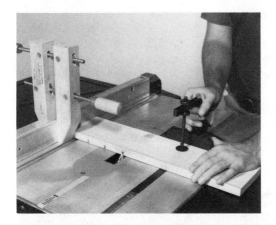

Figure 8-19: Using clamps to position a blind cut.

The first step in making this type of cut is to set the saw blade to the depth-of-cut required. This necessitates an adjustment of the fine adjustment elevation knob of the saw. Turn the knob all the way to the right (lower the blade). Then, using the slide control, lock the dado assembly in place just below the surface of the table. Next, raise the dado to the cutting height desired by turning the fine adjustment knob to the left. Blind cuts to a maximum depth of 1-1/4" are possible. Count the number of turns required to raise the blade to this height. Count both full turns and partial turns. After this count has been taken, lower the blade so it is once again flush with the table. (Use the fine adjustment knob to lower the blade.) Place the workpiece in the proper position. Secure it in place by clamping a block over the workpiece and onto the fence. For safe cutting, it is very important that the piece be firmly held to the table surface.

Turn on the saw, and while it is running, raise the blade to the predetermined height by turning the fine elevation knob the required number of turns and partial turns. When the dado reaches its correct height, feed the stock to the back stop to complete the cut. When the cut is complete, turn off the saw and wait until the dado stops turning. It is now safe to remove the workpiece. At no time, in any manner whatsoever, should the workpiece be lowered down onto a rotating cutter to make a dado or groove cut, blind or otherwise.

As shown in Figure 8-20, a stop block clamped to the table, fence, or auxiliary saw table can be used when making either blind or stop cuts. The stop block functions to determine the length of the cut. In any case, the blind corner of the groove or dado will have to be squared with a chisel.

Figure 8-20: Stop blocks used to position blind cuts.

Rabbeting Using the Dado Cutterhead. The procedure for the cutting of rabbets using the normal saw blade and the two-cut method is given in the preceding chapter. Rabbets can also be cut in a single pass using the dado cutter. Assemble or adjust the dado to a width that is more than wide enough to remove the required amount of wood. When cutting a rabbet along the end of a piece of stock, use the miter gauge as the guiding device (Figure 8-21). To cut a rabbet along the edge of a piece of stock, use an auxiliary wood fence with a cutout section. The cutout section provides for cutter clearance and allows for more flexibility in the positioning of the work (Figure 8-22).

Figure 8-21: Cutting a rabbet along the end of a piece of stock.

Figure 8-22: Auxiliary rip fence facing with a cutout section suitable for edge rabbet cutting.

Constructing this type of wood fence is a simple job. Secure a facing board to the regular metal rip fence with wood screws. It should be at least 3/4" thick. Lower the dado assembly beneath the table surface and position the rip fence over the insert so that the dado will cut away part of the wood facing when it is raised above the table. After rechecking the fence alignment and clamping it down in place, use the uppercut feature of the saw to make the cut. With part of the wood fence cut away, the rabbet can be easily formed.

As in end rabbeting, assemble the dado to a width wider than is required. Next, move the rip fence to correctly align the dado head with the workpiece. The rabbet can then be made by positioning the stock against the auxiliary wood fence and running it past the dado cutter (Figure 8-23).

Figure 8-23: Cutting a rabbet along an edge.

Cutting Edge Grooves. The setup described in Chapter 5 for the resawing of stock can also be used for cutting grooves in the edges of long workpieces. Raise the dado head to the required depth-of-cut and position the rip fence and the auxiliary wood table so that the workpiece rests in the proper location (Figure 8-24). It is also possible to use a featherboard in place of the auxiliary wood table. Whatever setup you use, make the edge grooving cut as you would a regular resawing cut. In addition to edge grooving and resawing, this setup is also suitable for molding cutting.

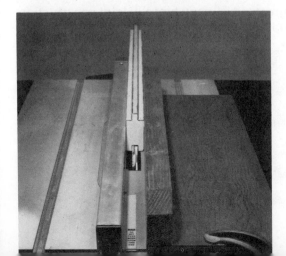

Figure 8-24: Cutting edge grooves with the auxiliary wood table setup.

Figure 8-25: One type of decorative cut made with the dado cutterhead.

Other Uses for the Dado Head. The dado cutterhead can be used to make many types of decorative cuts. Follow safe cutting procedures and allow your imagination to be your guide. The piece illustrated in Figure 8-25 was formed by cutting a series of mitered dadoes. The dado projection was set on half the stock thickness. After all cuts on one side of the piece are made, the stock is flipped over and the procedure is repeated.

Repeat passes are also useful for making extra wide grooves and hollowing out pieces (Figure 8-26).

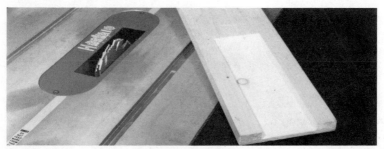

Figure 8-26: A hollowing job done with repeat passes of the dado cutter.

By using two distinct dado height settings, it is possible to cut the special two step groove shown in Figure 8-27. The deepest cut is made first. The rip fence is then adjusted and the second, shallower groove is cut. It is very important when doing this type of cut that the workpiece bears on the table on both sides of the dado assembly. Use a featherboard for support as you push the work past the blades. With narrower pieces, employ a push stick to do this job safely.

The dado cutterhead is also a great aid in many types of joint construction. These uses are discussed in Chapters 10, 11, and 12.

Figure 8-27: Forming the special two step groove.

Chapter 9
Using the
Molding Cutter

A molding cutterhead complete with an assortment of shaping knives makes a fine addition to any workshop. When mounted on the table saw arbor, the molding cutterhead enables you to shape many standard and original molding designs on the edges or faces of workpieces. The different and unique knife shapes, plus the fact that both partial and combination cuts can be made, greatly increase the shaping capabilities of the molding cutter. Corner molds, picture frames, cabinet door lips, table edges, edge joints, and many other jobs which would normally require the use of a shaper can be worked on a table saw with this accessory.

When done properly, cutting moldings with a cutterhead and knives is fast, clean, and safe. Immediately after their use, the cutter knives should be thoroughly cleaned of all dirt and resins and coated with a light oil. This will prevent the formation of rust on the cutting edges. Always store the knives so that the cutting edges will be protected. Never leave a set of knives locked in the cutterhead during storage.

Setting Up for Molding Cuts—The molding head unit consists of a cutterhead containing three grooves. Sets of steel knives are mounted into these cutterhead grooves and securely held fast with screws (Figure 9-1). The grooves into which the shaping knives are fitted should be kept free of sawdust or other debris which could prevent the knives from seating properly.

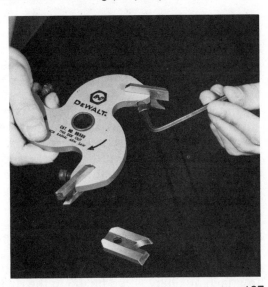

Figure 9-1: Mounting the knives on the cutterhead.

Assemble the molding cutter on the saw arbor in the same manner as an ordinary saw blade (Figure 9-2). Follow all specific instructions given by the manufacturer of the cutterhead. During all molding operations, the blade guard, splitter, and antikickback finger assembly cannot be used and must be removed from the table saw. Because of this, extra care must be exercised when making molding cuts. The standard saw blade insert must also be replaced by a molding insert, which has a wide enough slot to accommodate the cutters. (With most table saws, the dado head insert will work nicely.) In some special cases, it may be necessary to make a special insert of plywood or hardboard, shaped to duplicate the standard insert. This is especially true of molding cuts which require only a small portion of the knives to project above the table. An insert which fits close to the cutting knives provides the safest way of doing such a job. Another common use for this thinner wooden insert is when molding thin work on edge. The thin insert prevents the work-piece from slipping into the opening around the cutterhead.

Figure 9-2: The molding cutterhead assembly on the saw arbor.

After cutting the insert to shape with a band or saber saw, drill and countersink the two holes for the table-insert hold-down screws. Then, mount the desired type of knives on the cutterhead and lower it completely beneath the table surface. Screw the wooden table insert firmly into place. Next, start the saw and raise the molding cutterhead up and through the wooden insert. Use the fine adjustment knob to raise the cutter in gradual increments. With this method, the knives will cut their own custom-made insert. Be sure to wear eye protection or goggles. Always elevate the cutterhead slightly higher than is actually required to assure cutter clearance. Never attempt this cut without first screwing or clamping the insert firmly in place. After the insert cut is made, the cutterhead can be readjusted to the level required for the actual work cut.

Before using the molding cutters, turn the head manually to see that it is running true and that the head assembly clears all of the table saw parts. Also, be absolutely sure that the assembly is properly mounted and its knives securely fitted into their grooves. When making these checks, **disconnect the machine from its power source.**

Auxiliary Molding Fence—When using the molding cutterhead, it is necessary to attach auxiliary wood facing to the rip fence of the table saw (Figure 9-3).

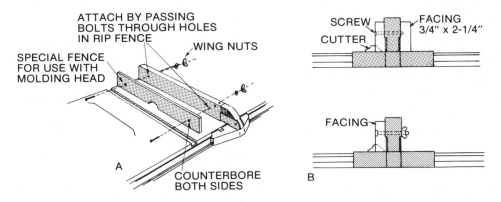

Figure 9-3: Auxiliary wood facing for molding operations.

Facings made of straight-grained hardwood are best. One-inch stock is ideal, but 3/4" stock is quite acceptable. Clamp the facing to the fence on top of a 1" thick scrap board. Then, use a set of planer and jointer knives in the cutterhead to cut a semicircular notch in the bottom edge of the facing. Use the uppercutting feature of the saw to make the cutout (about 1" deep) after the fence is correctly positioned over the insert. Make certain that there is no possibility of the molding cutter striking the metal rip fence as the uppercut is being made. Attach the wood facing with countersunk nuts and bolts run through the holes provided in the rip fence (Figure 9-4). If the holes for the bolts are counterbored on both sides of the wood facing, it may be used on either side of the rip fence, putting it to either left or right of the molding head.

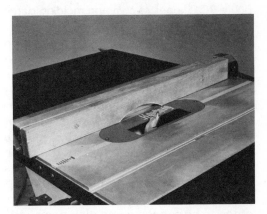

Figure 9-4: The cutaway portion of the auxiliary facing.

Types of Shaping Knives. The molding cutterhead is one table saw attachment which works extremely well with the imagination of the operator. With the wide assortment of cutters available it is possible to make an almost unlimited number of edge or end molding designs. The knives can also be used to cut surface decorations (like grooving operations with the dado head). Because most table saw molding cutters are identical with standard shaper cutters, any molds formed with a cutter on the shaper can be duplicated on the table saw using the same shape cutter.

Figure 9-5: Shapes of common molding cutterhead blades.

Shaping knives designed for the cutting of cabinet door lips, bead molding, wedge tongue, glue joints, and others, are designed to accomplish a specific job and are usually set to the full profile. The most popular full profile shapes are shown in Figure 9-5. In addition to cutting full profiles, these knives can be used to make partial profiles. Partial cuts can be mixed in combination to form almost any type of original molding design (Figure 9-6). Some knife designs, such as the 1/4" and 1/2" quarter-round, are known as combination cutters and are most often set to cut only a partial profile. This portion may be used to form an entire molding in itself, or it may be just part of an edge which is then completed by making repeated passes with different cutters.

Cuts made with individual knives can be planned to slightly meet one another, to be spaced some distance apart, or to overlap. To help in the planning of combination cuts, it is a good idea to make a record of each cutter profile. To do this, make ink outlines of your cutters on 4" squares of vellum or tracing paper. Two or more of these papers can then be stacked together and moved about to create the desired design—after which you can trace the result onto another paper on which you can also note the cutters, angles, etc., to be used for the cutting operations.

General Cutting Techniques. Many of the operational techniques described in Chapter 8 for dado cutter use also pertain to the molding cutterhead. For

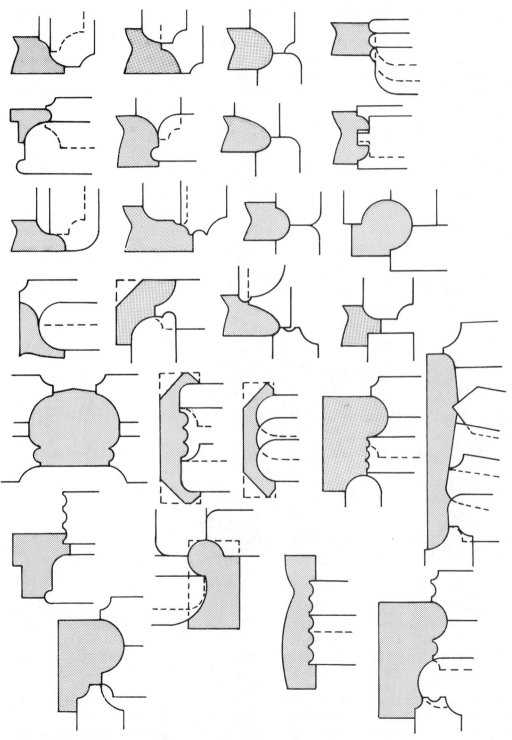

Figure 9-6: Combination moldings made with two or more cuts.

example, like a dado head, the molding cutterhead removes a considerable amount of stock. It follows that molding cuts should not be made too deeply or too quickly, especially when working with hardwoods. Deep cuts can be made, but they must be cut in stages. Simply adjust the tool projection after each pass. If the molding cutterhead slows up or the work begins to clatter, you are cutting too fast or too deeply. When either of these occurs, stop feeding and move the workpiece back from the knives, allow the cutterhead to attain its full speed, and then resume cutting at a slower feed rate. It may also be necessary to reduce the depth-of-cut. Follow this general rule: Limit your cuts in softwoods to depths of no more than 1/4" to 3/8"; hardwoods should be limited to depths ranging from 1/8" to 1/4".

The easiest and smoothest molding cuts are those made with the grain of the woodpiece. Cuts made across the grain are normally slightly rougher, so be sure to hold the work firmly in place. Cuts made with the grain, whether they are at the edge or somewhere along the width of the work, are made following the principles applied to basic rip cuts. The workpiece rides against the auxiliary molding fence. Cross-grain moldings are normally cut with the workpiece positioned firmly against the miter gauge if the stock is relatively narrow in width (Figure 9-7). When it is 6" or wider, end or cross-grained cuts can be made in the same way as those made with the grain, using the auxiliary fence to guide the workpiece.

Figure 9-7: Molding end grain with the miter gauge.

A molding cutterhead can be used with the saw arbor tilted to make a bevel cut. It can't be used, however, through the full range of bevel positions unless a special table insert is made as described earlier in this chapter. At too great an angle, the cutting assembly or knives will strike the standard molding table insert. This maximum angle will vary depending on the type of cutting knives being used. Never tilt the molding assembly while the table saw is running. Disconnect the tool from its power supply, elevate and tilt the assembly to the bevel desired, and test for clearance by rotating the cutter assembly by hand. Be absolutely sure the molding cutter sufficiently clears the assembly before turning the power on.

Edge Molding. While there are many operations which can be done with the molding cutterhead on the table saw, the shaping of edges is its primary purpose. While edge work is best done in a flat position (Figure 9-8A), it can also be done on edge (Figure 9-8B). A high auxiliary fence is sometimes handy when cutting large workpieces on the edge.

A

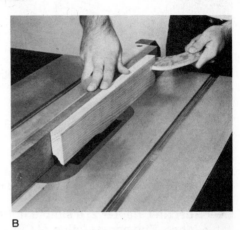
B

Figure 9-8: (A) Cutting a molding with the grain flat on the table and with the workpiece riding against the auxiliary molding fence. (B) Cutting a molding on edge.

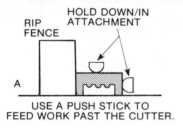

RIP FENCE

HOLD DOWN/IN ATTACHMENT

A

USE A PUSH STICK TO FEED WORK PAST THE CUTTER.

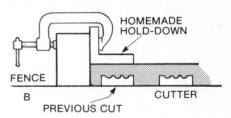

HOMEMADE HOLD-DOWN

FENCE

B

PREVIOUS CUT

CUTTER

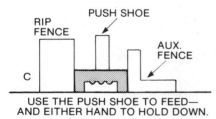

RIP FENCE

PUSH SHOE

AUX. FENCE

C

USE THE PUSH SHOE TO FEED— AND EITHER HAND TO HOLD DOWN.

Figure 9-9: Several methods of holding down edge moldings.

There is no special technique involved when edge cutting beyond setting the cutterhead to proper height while the auxiliary fence is located to provide the proper width, and watching the grain of the wood. Do **not** try to mold the edge opposite from the fence because any deviation from a true, straight feed can result in widening of the cut. If molding is done against the fence, a deviation results only in narrowing the cut, which can be corrected by a second pass.

When cutting edge moldings, it is a good idea to use some type of hold-down. As shown in Figure 9-9, this may be commercial hold-down fingers, such as

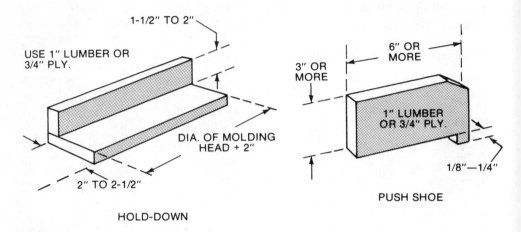

Figure 9-10: Construction of a simple hold-down and a push shoe.

described in Chapter 2, a simple hold-down, or a push shoe and an auxiliary table fence. The construction of the auxiliary table fence is given in Chapter 5, while the simple wood hold-down and push shoe are given here in Figure 9-10. The auxiliary table fence can also be employed when molding on edge (Figure 9-11). A tenoning jig (see Chapter 7) is also valuable when cutting edge moldings, especially for cuts across the edge of narrow stock (Figure 9-12).

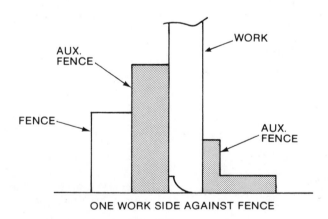

ONE WORK SIDE AGAINST FENCE

Figure 9-11: Edge molding with an auxiliary table fence.

Edge work on tabletops and other large surfaces should be done, whenever possible, in a flat position. Shaping should start across one end and should proceed right around so that each succeeding cut will remove any possible splinters from the end of the preceding one. On cuts parallel with the grain of the wood, observe that the cut is **with** the grain and not against it (edges 2 and 4, Figure 9-13). That is, cutting from D to A is with the grain and correct; cutting

Figure 9-12: The tenoning jig is essential for safe, accurate cuts across the edge of narrow stock.

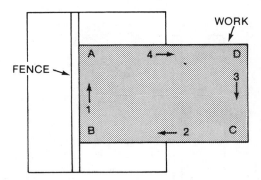

Figure 9-13: Method of shaping all four edges.

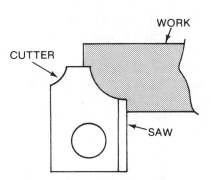

Figure 9-14: Nicking the end grain with a saw blade helps to position the molding cut.

from A to D is against the grain and may cause splintering. End-grain cuts, particularly on circular or elliptical work, can often be improved by first nicking lightly with the table saw, as shown in Figure 9-14.

Perfect circles are best worked against a V-block fence as shown in Figure 9-15. The jig should be centered with the center of the molding cutterhead. Figure 9-16 shows the method used in shaping oval work. A mark must be placed on the fence to indicate the center of the cutter, and the work must be kept in contact with this mark. Always clamp an auxiliary wood strip to the molding fence if the work is so thin that it slips under the cutout in the fence.

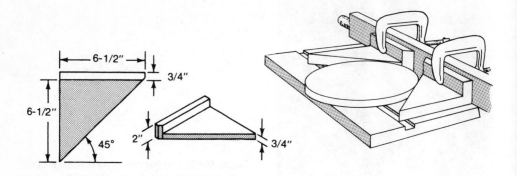

Figure 9-15: V-blocks used for molding the edges of circular pieces.

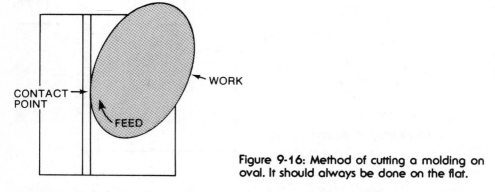

Figure 9-16: Method of cutting a molding on oval. It should always be done on the flat.

To the same end, ovals should not be shaped on edge unless a special wood table insert is made up to prevent the work from falling below the level of the table.

Strip Molding. The simplest way to make strip molding is to place the stock against the molding fence and push it through. Each side of a wide board is thus shaped, after which the mold is ripped off with the table saw. Cutting can be either on the edge, as in Figure 9-17, or the work can be pushed through flat.

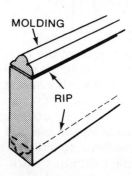

Figure 9-17: Rip method of cutting strip moldings.

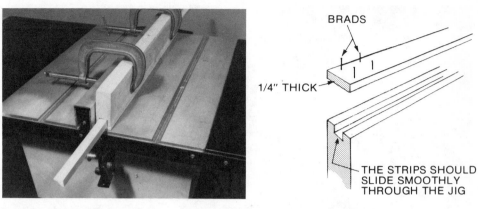

BRADS

1/4" THICK

THE STRIPS SHOULD
SLIDE SMOOTHLY
THROUGH THE JIG

Figure 9-18: Strip jig setup for cutting large quantities of moldings.

The jig shown in Figure 9-18 provides another means of cutting strip moldings. Follow the specifications given in the drawing when constructing your
jig. The channel opening must be of sufficient width and height to accommodate the workpiece. The piece bradded to the main body of the jig is cut
away at the center to allow for clear passage of the cutting knives. To cut a
strip molding using this jig, simply clamp the jig firmly against the saw fence
and run the strip through the jig. When the correct knife is used, many moldings
can be cut in a single pass through the jig. Those moldings which require combination cuts are made by running the piece through the jig as often as is necessary to produce the desired result.

Ornamental Moldings. The molding cutterhead attachment can be used
to cut a wide variety of decorative moldings with the appearance of hand carved
work. Some of the more popular examples of surface cuts are shown in Figure
9-19, but only the imagination of the operator limits the number of distinct
molding designs. There is nothing complex in cutting these moldings. In fact,
there are several ways in which they can be cut.

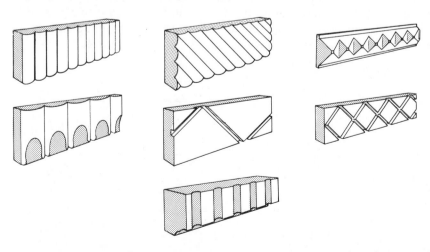

Figure 9-19: Types of ornamental molding.

A   B

Figure 9-20: (A) Setup for cutting bead molding. (B) The guide pin in the miter gauge face board.

Cutting Method No. 1—This method is simply a repetition of the desired molding cut. A guide pin or guide board is used to space the cuts. The guide board is the finer setup of the two, because many shapes cannot be spaced accurately with a pin set to the work itself. The operation shown in Figure 9-20A is bead molding being cut with a bead molding cutter. The guide board is a separate saw cut strip nailed to the edge of the work. Details for its construction are outlined in Chapter 7. For this bead cut, the saw kerfs should be spaced a strong 5/8" apart (Figure 9-21). The guide pin is a nail driven into the miter-gauge faceboard (Figure 9-20B). This pin can be located in any position because the spacing is determined by the guide board and not the work itself. The projection of the cutter should be high enough to assure a full round is cut. The cuts are made following the standard precautions for molding cutter work. Simply continue cutting and spacing until the full length of work is machined. After cutting this wide molding, the work can be ripped into strips of the desired thicknesses. It's also possible to further ornament these strips by running molding cuts lengthwise on the strip in the ordinary manner.

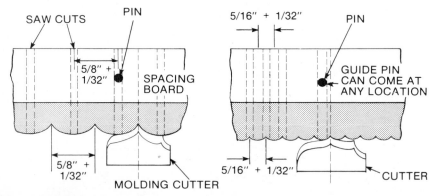

Figure 9-21: Cutting diagram for bead molding.

Cutting Method No. 2—An alternate method of using the guide board is to locate it on top of the work (Figure 9-22). Fasten the board to the workpiece. The guide board on top setup is particularly useful in production work, since the board itself is not touched by the cutter. Also, each edge on the guide board can have a different spacing of saw cuts suitable for specific moldings. Since this type of work involves cross-grain cutting, the molding cutters must be sharp. As in other cuts of this nature, the end of the cut will have a tendency to splinter out. This is particularly true of the guide-on-top method described above, since this method does not offer a fresh backing for each cut.

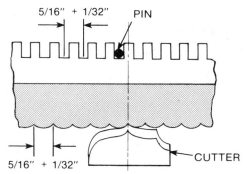

Figure 9-22: Guide board on top of the workpiece.

Cutting Method No. 3—A waste board is one method of spacing which is most useful when only occasional cuts of this type are made (Figure 9-23). After each molding is cut, the waste board is run over the jointer to slice off 1/4" or whatever spacing is needed for the work.

Figure 9-23: Using a waste board to space molding cuts.

In addition to making moldings, all the methods described in this section can be used to work up imitation carved panel effects. The only difference will be in the size of the work. When these cuts are combined with ornamental cuts made on a drill press and shaper, the possibilities are almost endless.

Forming Dowels. By making surface cuts with a molding cutterhead and the proper knives, it is possible to cut dowels of various diameters on a table saw. A number of standard molding cutters can be used to obtain the desired results.

To make dowels, surface cut one side of the piece. Then, turn the stock over and make a second and final surface cut on the opposite side (Figure 9-24). A thin strip of wood may be left connecting the dowel with the main body of the work. This can be easily broken with the fingers to free the dowels. The connecting piece can then be sanded smooth.

Figure 9-24: Cutting dowels with a molding cutterhead.

Rabbeting. Rabbeting operations are done quickly and easily with a straight knife set mounted to the molding cutterhead (Figure 9-25). This method has obvious advantages over the two saw out procedure used with ordinary saw blades. The method closely resembles that used with the dado head and is extremely useful when making shallow cuts. Remember to follow the depth-of-cut limitations given earlier in this chapter. Make several light passes if necessary.

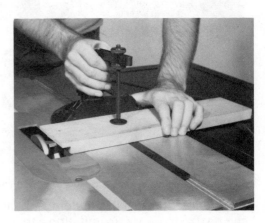

Figure 9-25: Cutting a rabbet with a straight molding knife.

Tenon Cutting. A molding cutterhead equipped with straight knives provides a fast, clean method of cutting tenons. Tenons measuring up to 1" wide can be cut in a single pass of the cutting knives (Figure 9-26). Longer cuts are formed by simply walking the workpiece across the cutters until the desired width is achieved. When more than one cut is necessary, the first cut should be made on the inside to form the shoulder.

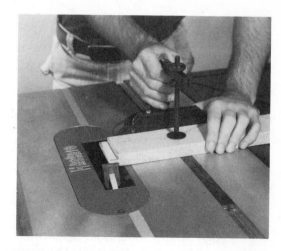

Figure 9-26: Shaping a tenon.

Panel Raising. By simply tilting the saw arbor slightly and using the same application of straight knives as in tenon cutting, it is possible to do raised panel cutting to any width desired.

Cove Cutting. Large cove moldings of exceptional smoothness can be cut with molding knives. To make a cove cut, the work must be fed obliquely into the cutterhead (Figure 9-27). This setup is described in detail in Chapter 7.

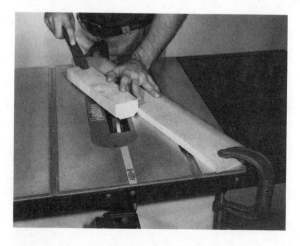

Figure 9-27: Cutting a cove.

The maximum depth-of-cut possible is about 11/16″. The angle of the feed controls the width of the cut. For example, the smallest cove (Figure 9-28A) was cut with a 1/2″ knife in the usual position, that is, straight into the cutter. The mold is 1″ wide—the entire width of the cutter being used. Sample cove B was cut with a 30° feed. The depth is the same as A, but the width of the cut is increased to about 1-1/2″. With a 60° feed (Figure 9-28C), the width of the cove is increased to about 1-5/8″, the maximum width possible for any cut. It is possible to make these cuts in a single pass, although two passes are preferred when working with dense woods, such as those used in cabinet construction. After cove cutting, the molded portion can be ripped to any width desired.

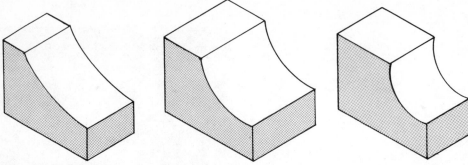

Figure 9-28: Three different cove sizes.

Jointing and Planing. When a jointer isn't available, a molding cutterhead with straight knives can be used to do a good job for both jointing and planing. To join an edge, first clamp the work to a guide board which is known to have a true edge. The work should be entirely inside the straight edge of the guide board as shown in Figure 9-29. The work is advanced to the cutters as shown in Figure 9-30. In this setup, the straight edge serves as a guide and guarantees an accurate edge will be cut on the work. Set the cutterhead so that a small rabbet is cut in the guide board at the same time the edge is being formed on the work.

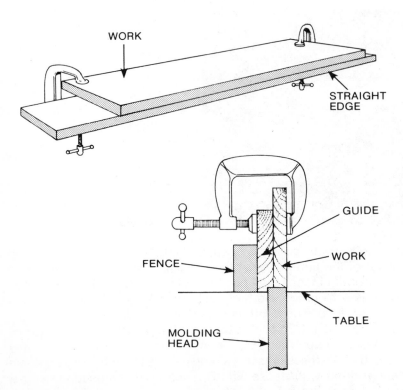

Figure 9-29: The guide board arrangement for jointing an edge.

Figure 9-30: Jointing an edge.

   The first step in the planing operation is to nail a runner to each edge of the work (Figure 9-31). As was the case in the jointing operation, the entire surface of the work must lie within the projection of the runners, as indicated by the straight edge across the work (Figure 9-32). Also shown in Figure 9-32 is a guide board arrangement for planing. The numbers represent the order of cuts. The first cut is made at the center of the work. Successive cuts are taken on either side by setting the fence more than 1" for each new cut. If the surface being planed is true and smooth, the runners are not necessary, because a narrow strip of uncut wood at either side will serve the same purpose. When the board is evenly warped, it is possible to work it without using runners. But if there is a twist in the work or unequal warping, the runners must be nailed in place before the work can be planed.

Figure 9-31: Planing a board. Use straight molding knives.

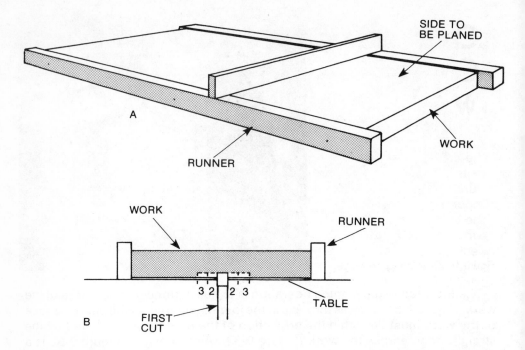

Figure 9-32: (A) Guide board arrangement for planing. (B) The order of cuts for the planing operation.

Chapter 10
Common
Wood Joints

The satisfaction obtained from any woodworking project comes not only from its initial appeal, but also from its continued attractiveness with use. Both its durability and its pristine appearance are important. The integrity of joints is important to both of these aspects.

The term "joint" generally means the close securing or fastening together of two or more smooth, even surfaces. The construction quality of any wood project depends primarily on the quality of the joints. They must be neat, strong, and rigid to give the finished piece its necessary instant appeal and long-lasting durability. Keep in mind that destructive forces may be (1) applied from the exterior of a joint or (2) induced by internal forces. External forces may be those applied by sitting on a chair or racking caused by pushing a case across a rough floor. Internal forces may be from shrinking of wood parts or the steady pull of poorly mated parts forced together by clamping pressure. Proper joint selection will alleviate the first type while correction for the second type may be concerned with good manufacturing practice, such as selection of wood species, uniformity of moisture content, and joint accuracy.

There is considerable latitude possible in joint design between a plain butt joint and a joint designed for maximum strength and durability. Some of these may even cause little or no change in external appearance. In other instances, considerable breadth in joint selection is possible if it does not show in the finished item. As a general rule, it is best to select the simplest joints that will do the job satisfactorily.

BUTT JOINTS. The butt joint is the simplest of all woodworking joints (Figure 10-1). But, it's also the weakest of the wood joints and is often shunned because the end grain is left exposed.

Although this joint is extremely easy to make, great care must be taken to see that the edges to be joined are absolutely square. The best way to assure this squareness is to perform the necessary crosscutting operations extremely carefully. Plain butt end grain to end grain or end grain to side grain joints have little strength unless they are further reinforced by either dowels or wood glue blocks.

Doweling Butt Joint. Dowels are round sticks of wood made of birch or maple. They are either smooth or grooved. The standard sizes measure from 1/4" to 1-1/2" in diameter, and 36", 42", or 48" in length. They also may be obtained in usual working lengths, pointed, grooved, and ready for use. The purpose of the grooved surface is to allow the glue to flow more freely into the joint. Grooves can be cut into dowels with a spiral cut on the table saw. The diameter

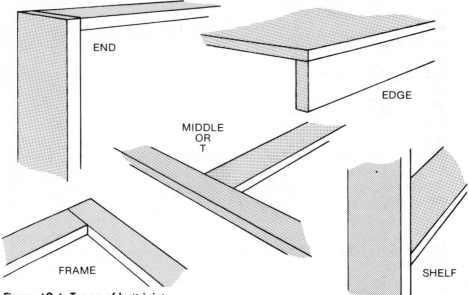

Figure 10-1: Types of butt joints.

of the dowel used to hold together the joint should be no more than half the overall thickness of the board it secures. The depth of the hole, of course, will vary with the type of joint, the strength desired, and the type of wood used.

There are two basic doweling methods (Figure 10-2), the open method and the blind method. In the open dowel method, a hole is drilled completely through one piece of wood and deeply into or sometimes completely through the piece to be joined. The dowel is then coated with glue and pushed through the holes to join the pieces. Saw off the dowel flush to the outer surface. Measure the dowel a bit long for open doweling. This will make cutting it off flush to the outer surface an easier job.

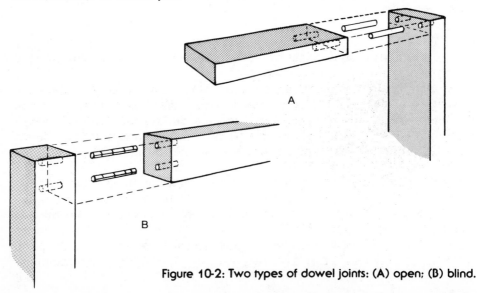

Figure 10-2: Two types of dowel joints: (A) open; (B) blind.

With the blind doweling method, neither piece is drilled completely through. Instead, holes are drilled partway into each piece from the joined faces. The depth of these holes should be roughly four times the diameter of the dowel used. The dowel is then glue coated and inserted into one of the holes. The second piece is then pressed onto the protruding dowel. The length of the dowel rod should always be cut about 1/8" to 1/4" shorter than the total of the two holes. Chamfer the dowel at each end to aid in location during assembly. The fit of the dowel should not be so tight that the glue is all pushed to the bottom of the hole. Optimum size is a snug fit, such that the dowel, spline, or tenon can be pushed in with a finger but not loose enough to wobble in the hole. A 1/64" clearance is a good fit to obtain.

Consistency of dowel and hole diameter is difficult to obtain. Holes and dowels should be checked frequently for uniformity of diameter. Gluing should be done soon after machining to prevent change of size by change of moisture content.

The layout of dowel holes must be accurate (Figure 10-3), especially when blind doweling. Once the holes are gauged, the most popular method of aligning the holes is to use dowel centers or "pops," as shown in Figure 10-4A. Here, after drilling the holes for the dowels in one piece of wood, you insert dowel centers in these holes. Then, you align the two pieces of wood as they will be joined. When you press them together, the points on the dowel centers mark the second piece of wood. It is now possible to drill holes at these center marks. When the pieces are connected with dowels, the blind dowel joint is perfectly aligned. Dowel centers come in assorted sizes to fit holes from 1/8" to 1" in diameter.

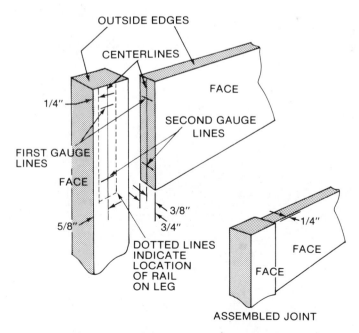

Figure 10-3: Gauging for the dowel holes in a typical leg and rail butt joint.

When locating dowel holes in a series of boards that will be joined edge-to-edge, position the board edges and butt them surface to surface. Using a combination square (Figure 10-4B), mark the hole location on one edge and carry the line across all the pieces. Identify the board faces which will be at the top after assembly. Drill dowel holes in the edges at the cross lines, using a dowel jig or drill guide such as the one shown in Figure 10-4C, that will gauge holes automatically.

When doweling joints other than those at edges, it is a good idea to make a template of stiff cardboard, thin plywood, hardboard, or even sheet metal if the long-term use justifies it. Drill 1/16" or smaller dowel center holes at the desired locations. Locate the template accurately first on one piece, then the other, to mark dowel centers with a center punch or awl (Figure 10-4D).

Since most of the strength of an assembly joint comes from side or face grain, a complete spread of glue on the sides of the dowel hole is desirable. If the glue is to be spread either on the dowel or in the hole, spreading glue in the hole is usually more desirable. Spreading glue on both the dowel and the hole is better than spreading on only one.

Glue or Corner Blocks. Glue blocks are small, square or triangular pieces of wood used to strengthen and support the two adjoining surfaces of a butt joint (Figure 10-5). Remember that while this joint reinforcement features a strong face-to-face gluing surface, varying moisture contents will cause a differential wood movement, since the grain direction of the block and the substrate are at right angles to each other. This will highly stress the joint. Because of this, a number of short blocks are preferable to one long one.

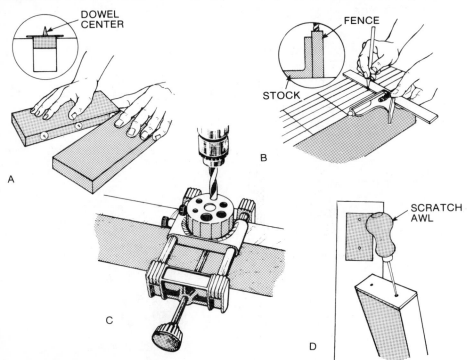

Figure 10-4: Methods of aligning dowel holes.

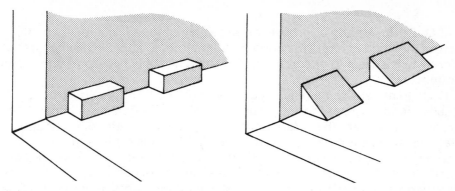

Figure 10-5: Square and triangular glue blocks.

GROOVED JOINTS. Grooved joints are a group of joints which have the following characteristics in common: They all have a groove or recess cut into one member, either with the grain or across the grain, into which the edge or end, in whole or in part, of another member is fitted. The two most common grooved joints are the rabbet and the dado. The cuts for these joints can be made with a saw blade (using the repeated cut technique), dado cutters, or a molding cutterhead.

Rabbet Joints. As has already been mentioned, a rabbet is a groove cut into the edge or end of a piece of wood (Figure 10-6A). The width of the cut usually equals the thickness of the insert, while the depth of the rabbet ranges from one-half to two-thirds the thickness of the part in which it is made (Figure 10-6B). When using plywood, it is sometimes desirable to cut the rabbet so deep that only the surface veneer remains on the part (Figure 10-6C). While this conceals unattractive plywood edges, it makes a rather weak joint. Of course, rabbet joints can be reinforced with glue blocks (Figure 10-6D).

When planning rabbet joints, make cuts in relation to how the project will be seen. That is, it is most acceptable to cut the L-shape in the side members so the partial end grain that remains won't be overly visible (Figure 10-6E). The methods of making rabbet cuts are fully covered in Chapter 7.

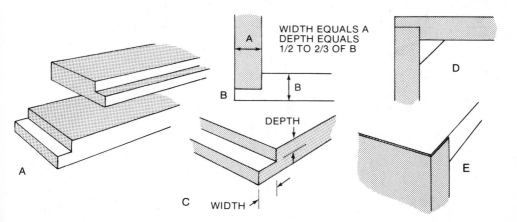

Figure 10-6: Rabbet cuts and how they are used for joints.

DADO JOINTS. A dado or groove, as already mentioned, is a recess or slot cut across the grain or along the grain. It differs from a rabbet in having three surfaces—two sides and one bottom; the rabbet has only two—one side and one bottom.

Dado joints are commonly used in cabinet and furniture construction. Basically, dado joints are formed when one piece of wood is set into a dado or groove cut into another. Variations of the standard dado joint abound. The standard or housed dado joint (Figure 10-7A) consists of a groove cut into one piece of wood which is exactly the same thickness as the second piece joined to it. The easiest and most reliable method of cutting grooves for standard dado joints is with a dado head set to the exact width required (see Chapter 8). It is also possible to form the groove by making several passing cuts with a standard saw blade and knocking out the waste with a chisel. These dado cuts can be cut at any angle to the edge of the workpiece.

Dadoes can also stop short of one or both sides of the workpiece (Figure 10-7B). It is necessary to clamp one or two stop blocks to the saw's rip fence during this operation. Follow the instructions for blind grooving given in Chapter 8 when making this type of cut. Other variations of dado joints are described below.

Dado-and-Rabbet. This joint is often used in the construction of drawers. As shown in Figure 10-7C, it is also an extremely fine joint to use when making shelves. Don't make either cut more than one-half of the way through the board thickness.

Full-Dovetail Dado. This joint locks the shelf against pulling free (Figure 10-7D). As shown in Figure 10-8, a single dovetail joint can be easily cut on the table saw. Set the saw blade to an angle of 5° to 7° to cut both the tongue and the dovetail slot. The stock between the two angle cuts of the groove is cleared away with a series of cuts with the blade set in a vertical position. Cutting accuracy and precision depth-of-cut setting are the two most important factors in completing a successful dovetail dado joint.

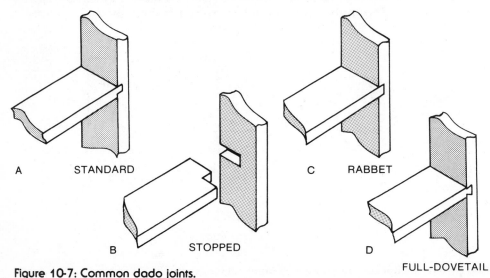

A   STANDARD   C   RABBET

B   STOPPED   D

FULL-DOVETAIL

Figure 10-7: Common dado joints.

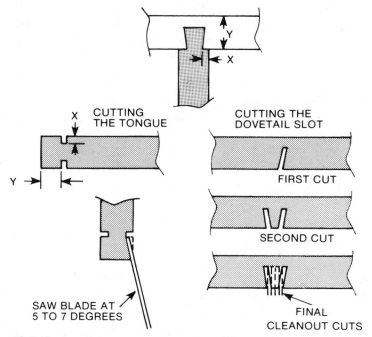

Figure 10-8: Cutting a dovetail for the dovetail dado.

Half-Dovetail Dado. This joint will support more weight than the full-dovetail style. It is, however, formed the same way as the full-dovetail except that angle cuts are made only on the top side of the cut.

Tongue-and-Groove. The tongue-and-groove joint (Figure 10-9), used most often for edge-to-edge gluing, can be cut with a dado head. The groove is cut in a single pass with a head of the correct thickness. To cut the tongue, place a spacer collar the same thickness as the groove between the blades of the dado head. Locate a chipper on the outside of each blade to remove the waste stock.

There are many different methods of securing grooved joints. Adhesives, alone or in combination with dowels, are the most widely used.

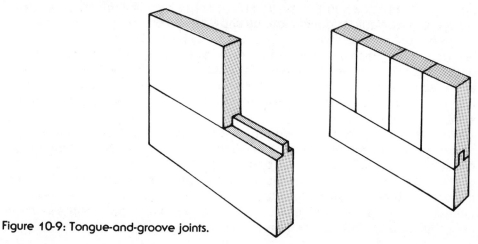

Figure 10-9: Tongue-and-groove joints.

LAP JOINTS. In lap or halving joints, half the thickness of each member is cut away so that when jointed together, their upper and lower surfaces will be flush. The three most common forms of the lap joint are the end, tee, and middle, as shown in Figure 10-10. The ordinary joint comprises two pieces of equal width. Start by ripping the stock to the required width and then cut the various pieces to length. Mark roughly with pencil the areas to be cut away. You are then ready to make the joint. Set the saw to cut exactly half the depth of the wood thickness. Check the setting by cutting from both sides of a scrap piece. The second cut should meet the first exactly, completely severing the test block.

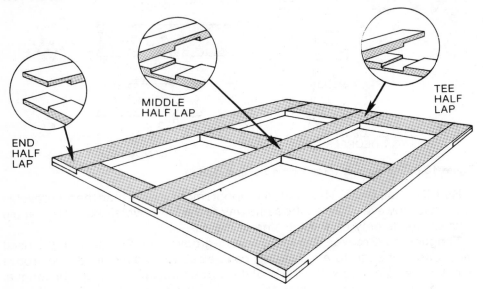

Figure 10-10: Three common lap joints.

If the joint is an end or corner lap, place one end of the work against the saw blade and move the fence, or any other form of stop, until it contacts the opposite end, as shown in Figure 10-11A. A scrap piece of the stock will then set the exact shoulder dimension, as shown in Figure 10-11B. Make the cut. Clean out the surplus stock by making successive cuts. If the joint is a middle lap, rip a scrap piece of the stock in two, as in Figure 10-11C. To cut the middle or cross lap, make one of the shoulder cuts, setting the saw to a pencil mark and erecting a stop at the end of the work, as can be seen in Figure 10-11D. Use the renailed spacer block to set the second cut. Clean out the surplus with successive cuts.

When the joint is being cut with the dado head, the end lap joint is cut just as described. The middle lap also follows the same general practice, the spacer block being ripped in two by the dado setup being used. In all cases, the use of a spacer block is advantageous. It is surprisingly accurate, and, of course, the only method to use in a production setup where many similar pieces are being run. The use of a spacer block for other less-used forms of the joint follows the same general procedure.

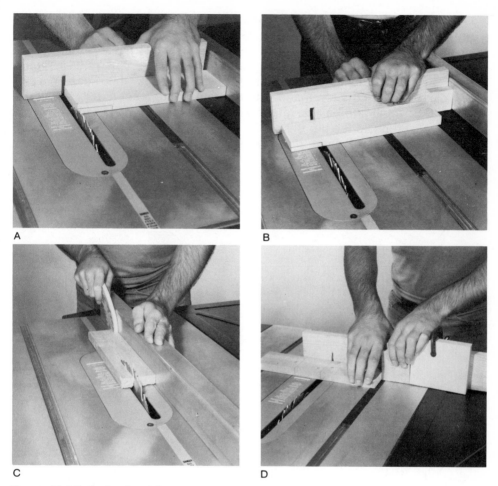

Figure 10-11: Cutting lap joints.

Occasionally, the tee and the end lap cuts are beveled as shown in Figure 10-12. The mating bevel provides a degree of interlock action which tends to make the joint stronger. An end-to-end half-lap is frequently used to extend the length of a piece of stock. The longer the lap, the stronger the joint.

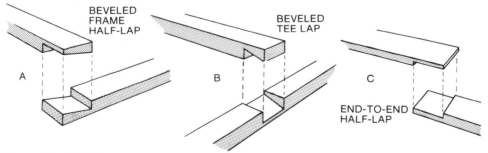

Figure 10-12: (A) Beveled end half-lap; (B) beveled tee half-lap; and (C) end-to-end half-lap.

   Oblique or angled half-laps are used when the pieces that join don't form a right angle with each other. When using such a joint, it is wise to provide a small shoulder, as shown in Figure 10-13, to make the joint stronger. A variation of the angled half-lap is the so-called "three-way lap" illustrated in Figure 10-14. This joint is employed to join three pieces of stock while keeping a single thickness. The cuts are made with the miter gauge set at 60°.
   The full-dovetail and half-dovetail laps shown in Figure 10-15 are elaborate versions of the basic tee lap described earlier. The mortise and tenon of the dovetail are cut in the same manner as the dovetail dadoes detailed earlier in this chapter.

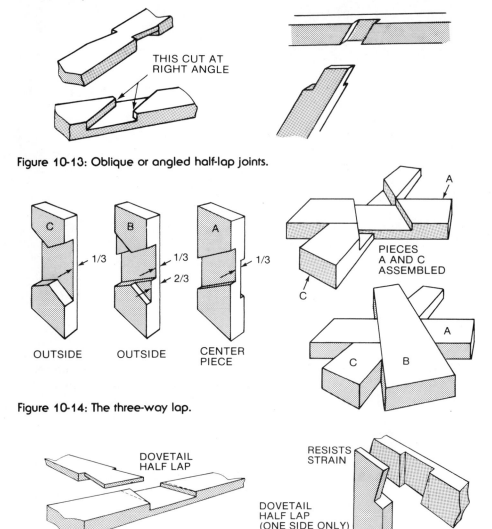

Figure 10-13: Oblique or angled half-lap joints.

Figure 10-14: The three-way lap.

Figure 10-15: Full-dovetail and half-dovetail lap joints.

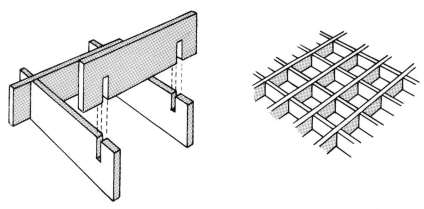

Figure 10-16: Edge half-laps can be used to form egg crate patterns or to form interlock joints.

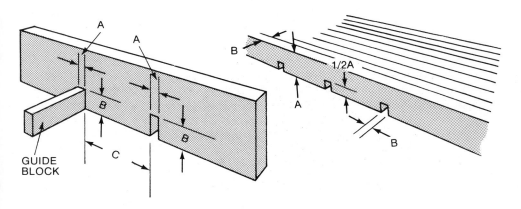

Figure 10-17: The jig for cutting egg crate patterns and how it is laid out: A = material thickness; B = 1/2 material width; C = spacing of partitions.

Edge half-laps, which are used to form egg crate patterns and to interlock sides of projects (Figure 10-16), are made in the same manner as middle laps, except that the grooves are cut into the edge of the stock instead of the surface. The formula for sizing the cuts is basically that the width of the groove matches the thickness of the stock, the depth of the cut equals one-half the width. While edge half-laps for egg crate or grid patterns can be cut freehand, the pieces can be ganged together, or a jig such as shown in Figure 10-17 can be used. With the jig secured to the miter gauge, make the first cut by butting the edge of the stock against the side of the guide block. Other cuts are made by locating the last notch cut over the guide block. Incidentally, this jig can be used to automatically position workpieces when cutting equally-spaced dadoes.

MITER JOINTS. When an attractive appearance is of primary importance, a miter joint often solves the problem. For instance, a miter joint provides the means of forming an uninterrupted wood grain around the edges or corners of cabinets, picture frames, or furniture pieces. Miter joints are also used in the construction of moldings around doors, windows, and panels. The joining ends or edges are usually cut at a 45° angle, although cuts of slightly less than 45° are often needed when fitting new molding to older, settled casings. This slight angle discrepancy does not normally create a problem and is hardly noticeable once the pieces are placed in position and painted or stained. In fact, one of the greatest advantages of miter joints is their definite "finished" appearance whether left natural, painted, or stained. Miter joints have one slight disadvantage: they are relatively weak unless reinforced in some way. This is due to the fact that the miter joint's surfaces only butt against one another and in most cases contain about 50% end wood. As shown in Figure 10-18, corrugated nails, dowels, splines, and keys are all used to help reinforce miter joints.

Miter joints, as described in Chapter 6, can be formed with the workpiece placed flat or on edge. The standard setting for the miter gauge or the saw blade is 45° (Figure 10-19). These angles should always be checked for accuracy by making a test cut into a piece of scrap.

Stops are frequently used when cutting miters. An adjustable stop like the one shown in Figure 10-20 is a valuable convenience. This stop will eliminate hunting for a block and clamp every time you undertake a new job. The adjustable stop shown is simply a sliding block that works in a groove cut in the auxiliary miter gauge facing. As an added feature, you may wish to house a yardstick in the lower face of the auxiliary miter face. This will make it possible

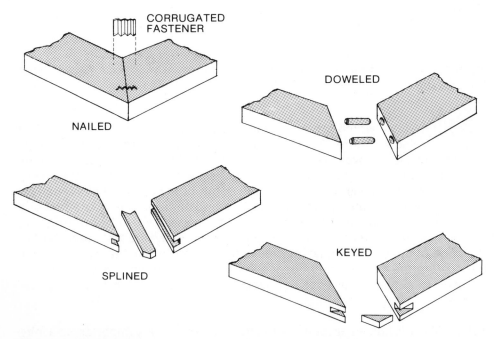

Figure 10-18: Methods of fastening miter joints.

Figure 10-19: Cutting a miter joint against the miter gauge.

Figure 10-20: Using an adjustable stop block to cut identical miter pieces.

to set the stop block without measuring and pencil marking the work. A miter gauge stop rod can also be used as a stop when making a number of identical pieces (Figure 10-21).

To find the length of a molding for a picture frame, first cut the rabbet and then add two widths of the molding, measured from the rabbet to the back, to the length of the picture (Figure 10-22).

Figure 10-21: Using the miter gauge stop rod on miter cuts when making a number of identical pieces.

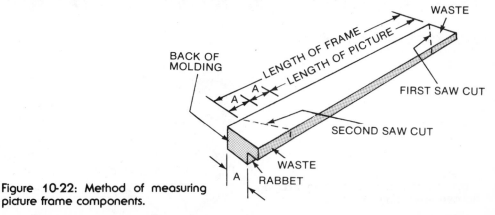

Figure 10-22: Method of measuring picture frame components.

Splined Miter Joints. The splined miter is no more than a basic miter joint employing a spline for added support. Since the strength of this joint depends on its grain running at an opposed angle to the joint, the grain must run across the narrow width of a spline, not along its length. Making the splines themselves isn't a difficult job. In fact, if the same blade is always used to cut the grooves for the splined miter joints, the splines may be made in advance for use whenever needed.

The splines can be fashioned out of hardwood, hardboard, or plywood. Many woodworkers prefer 1/8" plywood, not only because its thickness is guaranteed, but also because its equal strength in each direction offers a great advantage. In most cases, the standard combination saw blade cuts a 1/8" saw kerf, so cutting a groove to match these splines poses no problem.

Figure 10-23 shows how hardwood splines are cut. The spacing of the kerfs determines the thickness of the splines. Use of a hollow-ground blade will help prevent the thin stock from splitting. The width of the spline depends on the depth of the spline groove; usually 1" wide is sufficient for most miters. Actually, splines for edge miters should be about three-quarters the thickness of the stock. Sand the splines smooth before using them.

Cutting Splined Miter Joints—There are several jigs that can be used to assure a well cut spline. One of the simplest is the spline stop block shown in Figure 10-24. The slotted jig illustrated in Figure 10-25 also gives desirable results. Remember that the spline groove must be perpendicular to the miter bevel.

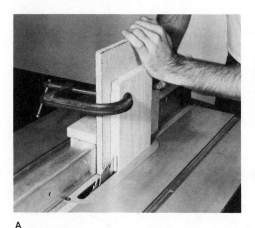
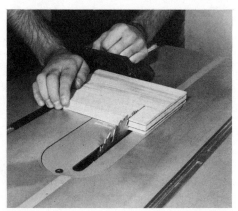

A   B

Figure 10-23: Method of cutting hardwood splines.

Figure 10-24: Stop block method of cutting splined miter joints.

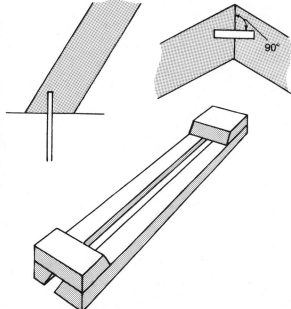

Figure 10-25: The slotted jig, cut to match the bevel angle, automatically holds the work at the proper slant. The spline grooves must be perpendicular to the bevel.

When cutting a spline groove for a frame miter, the first pass is made with the stock forming a closed angle with the table at the front of the saw blade (Figure 10-26A). The second cut is made with the same side of the workpiece against the fence; however, the angle is now open (Figure 10-26B). Use a tenoning jig or some type of hold-down when making these cuts.

When all of the pieces have been grooved, the splines are glued in place. Reinforced in this manner, the miter joints are very strong. As shown in Figure 10-27, splines can be used to reinforce pieces of wood that are edge glued.

Feathered or Keyed Miter Joints. This joint is very similar to the splined miter, except that the splines are placed in the outside edge of the corner. The feathered or keyed miter joints are generally used when making objects which are wide and flat. To form the joint, cut the two miters in the conventional manner, and clamp the pieces together in a tenoning jig or one such as that shown in Figure 10-28. One or more slots are then cut across the joint and the slip-feathers or keys (triangular splines made of plywood or hardboard) are secured into the slots. Sand the work smooth. The result is a strong, reinforced miter joint.

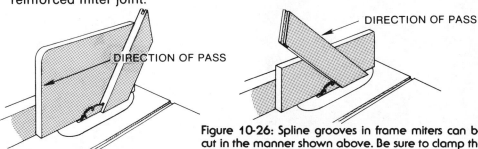

Figure 10-26: Spline grooves in frame miters can be cut in the manner shown above. Be sure to clamp the workpiece in a tenoning jig.

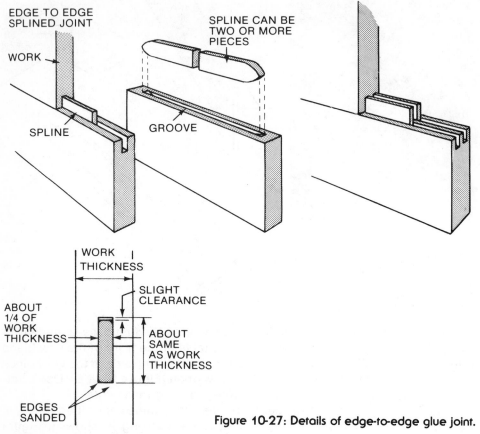

Figure 10-27: Details of edge-to-edge glue joint.

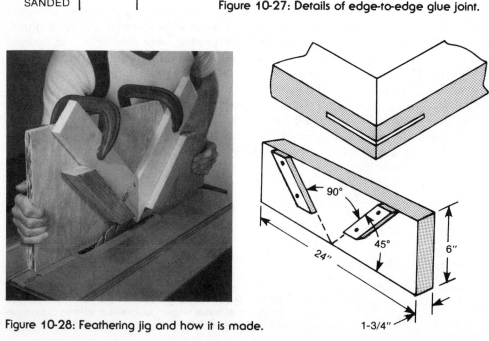

Figure 10-28: Feathering jig and how it is made.

Lap Miter Joints. At times, it's desirable to show the miter from only one side of the joint. In such cases, and where strength is important, use a lap miter joint (Figure 10-29). This joint has the appearance of a conventional miter joint from one side, but it is considerably stronger due to an increase in glue surface area.

Polygon Miter Joints. A polygon is a figure of any number of equal sides. To make such a figure (other than a square or rectangular surface), miters of some angle other than 45° are needed. To find this angle for a flat polygon (Figure 10-30), divide the number of sides into 180°.

$$\text{pentagon} = \frac{180}{5} = 36°;$$

$$\text{hexagon} = \frac{180}{6} = 30°;$$

$$\text{octagon} = \frac{180}{8} = 22\text{-}1/2°.$$

To cut a polygon, set the miter gauge per your calculations and make the cut as described in Chapter 6. Then, the second cut of a segment can be made by flipping it end-for-end.

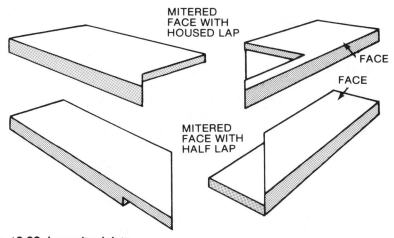

MITERED FACE WITH HOUSED LAP

FACE

FACE

MITERED FACE WITH HALF LAP

Figure 10-29: Lap miter joints.

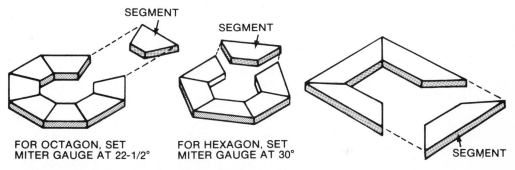

SEGMENT

SEGMENT

FOR OCTAGON, SET MITER GAUGE AT 22-1/2°

FOR HEXAGON, SET MITER GAUGE AT 30°

SEGMENT

Figure 10-30: Setting for flat polygon miter joints.

When constructing an on-edge polygon (Figure 10-31), cut the beveled segments by tilting the saw blade to the required angle given in the table below:

FIGURE	SIDES	ANGLE
Triangle	3	60°*
Square	4	45°
Pentagon	5	36°
Hexagon	6	30°
Heptagon	7	25-3/4°
Octagon	8	22-1/2°
Nonagon	9	20°
Decagon	10	18°
Undecagon	11	16-1/2°
Dodecagon	12	15°

*Note: Cannot be cut on the table saw except by devising a jig to hold the work.

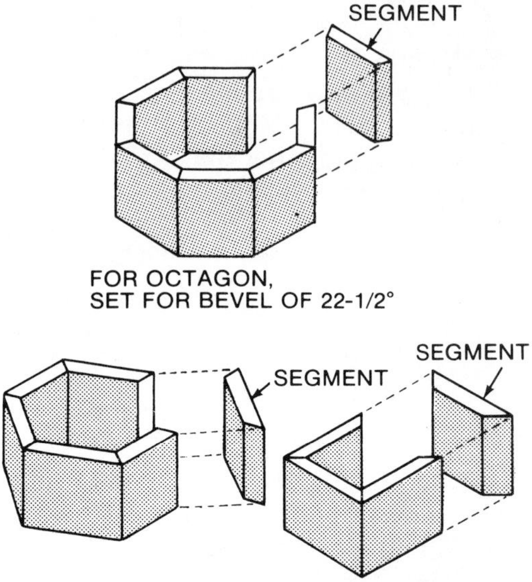

FOR OCTAGON,
SET FOR BEVEL OF 22-1/2°

FOR HEXAGON,
SET FOR BEVEL OF 30°

FOR SQUARE, SET
FOR BEVEL OF 45°

SEGMENT

Figure 10-31: Setting for on-edge polygon miter joints.

Compound Angle Joints. As explained earlier in Chapter 6, a compound angle is a miter and bevel cut made in one pass through the saw blade. That is, a compound angle requires both the miter and bevel settings; for example, when making a shadow box picture frame (Figure 10-32).

To form a closed, equal-sided figure, the correct compound angles for the desired number of sides and the desired tilt of the sides (Figure 10-33) must be chosen. Use the following settings for the most common compound angle cuts:

	4 SIDES		6 SIDES		8 SIDES	
Tilt	Bevel	Miter	Bevel	Miter	Bevel	Miter
5°	44-3/4°	5°	29-3/4°	2-1/2°	22-1/4°	2°
10°	44-1/4°	9-3/4°	29-1/2°	5-1/2°	22°	4°
15°	43-1/4°	14-1/2°	29°	8-1/4°	21-1/2°	6°
20°	42°	19°	28-1/4°	11°	21°	8°
25°	40°	23°	27-1/4°	13-1/2°	20-1/4°	10°
30°	37-3/4°	26-1/2°	26°	16°	19-1/4°	11-3/4°
35°	35-1/4°	29-3/4°	24-1/2°	18-1/4°	18-1/4°	13-1/4°
40°	32-3/4°	32-3/4°	22-3/4°	20-1/4°	17°	15°
45°	30°	35-1/4°	21°	22-1/4°	15-3/4°	16-1/4°
50°	27°	37-1/2°	19°	23-3/4°	14-1/4°	17-1/2°
55°	24°	39-1/4°	16-3/4°	25-1/4°	12-3/4°	18-1/2°
60°	21°	41°	14-1/2°	26-1/2°	11°	19-3/4°

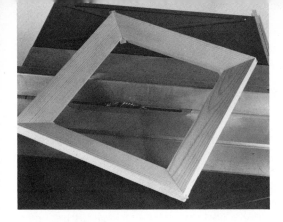

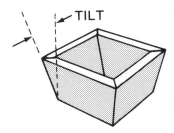

Common Wood Joints 173

Figure 10-32: Typical shadow box picture frame.

Figure 10-33: Shape of compound angle box.

A compound angle cut can be easily assembled by using a spline. The groove for the spline can be cut without changing the bevel setting. Caution must be exercised in this operation because the blade guard must be swung out of its normal position for these cuts. Set the fence so the spline groove will be in the approximate center of the material. Lightly pencil mark an X on the back side of all four pieces of the frame. Then, set the blade depth-of-cut for approximately 3/8″. Hold the pencil marked side away from the fence and make the cut as illustrated in Figure 10-34. Be certain to return the saw blade guard back to its normal position over the blade when these cuts are completed.

Figure 10-35 shows the use of splines in assembled and partially assembled compound joints, as well as polygon miter joints.

Figure 10-34: Cutting a compound angle spline.

Figure 10-35: Various splined miter joint frames.

MORTISE-AND-TENON JOINTS. The mortise-and-tenon joint is without exception the most important and most used joint in high-quality furniture construction. It is also one of the strongest of all wood joints.

The enclosed mortise (those with material on four sides) may be cut by hand or with power equipment such as a router or a drill press equipped with a mortising attachment. Open type mortises can be cut on the table saw.

The cutting of the standard tenon is described in Chapter 7. If you plan to cut quite a few tenons, it's a good idea to use a base stop and a backing block. Both the stop and block are easy to make and can be saved for future use.

When using the stop and block method, make the shoulder cuts of the tenon first (Figure 10-36A). Now, using a backing block equal to the thickness of the tenon and the saw blade, make the first cheek cut (Figure 10-36B). After this first cut is made, remove the backing block, snug the face of the work against the jig, and make the second cheek cut. The base stop shown in Figure 10-36C is approximately 1/4" in thickness. This cutting system eliminates any errors due to variations in the thickness of the work. This method is highly useful in production work. However, when only one or two joints are to be made, it is much easier to pencil-in guide lines and simply turn the work over when making the two cheek cuts. This eliminates the need for base and backing blocks.

A

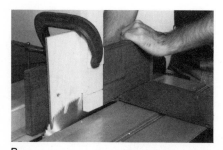

B

C

Figure 10-36: Cutting a tenon with a saw blade.

The dado cutter can be used to cut standard tenons. Set the arbor height at an elevation equal to the thickness of the stock to be removed on one side of the tenon. Position the work firmly against the miter gauge. Use a stop block or stop rod set to the length of the tenon to help secure the work. Cut this half of the tenon in one or two passes depending on the amount of wood that it is necessary to remove. Feed the work slowly to counteract the natural tendency of the work to creep away from the miter gauge. Remember, precision is of the utmost importance in joint construction. Now, reverse the work and cut the other side (Figure 10-37). When the tenon is longer than the width of the dado head, make the inside cut first. The work can then be stepped over to make the necessary extra cuts. In doing production work, a notched stop block can help you cut grooves and tenons as quickly as possible. It is especially helpful with wide tenons. Each step on the notch block advances the workpiece 11/16", the maximum width of cut attainable. With the aid of the notched block, you cover the required area in the least number of cuts.

Tenons can also be cut with a molding cutterhead. Details for the use of a molding cutterhead are given in Chapter 9.

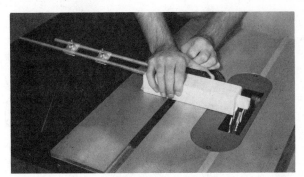

Figure 10-37: Cutting a tenon with a dado head. The stop rods keep the cut accurate.

In addition to the standard or blind mortise-and-tenon joint (Figure 10-38A), some of the more common ones and their uses are described below. When assembling any of these joints, apply plenty of glue, clamp the joint securely, and give the adhesive sufficient time to set before applying any pressure to the joint.

Round Tenon-and-Mortise (Figure 10-38B). The so-called "round" tenon is a standard tenon except that the corners are round rather than square. The mortise slot for this joint can be made with a router or a drill bit.

Through Mortise-and-Tenon (Figure 10-38C). This joint, useful in some types of furniture, is made like the blind type, except that the end of the tenon is exposed. Where extra strength and resistance to pulling apart are required, wedges can be used. The two ends of the mortise are sloped outward to provide room for the wedges, which are about half the tenon in length.

Barefaced Mortise-and-Tenon Joint (Figure 10-38D). When the rails and legs of tables and stools are made flush, very little wood is left between the mortise and the face of the leg if a regular tenon is used. To strengthen the joint in such cases, the tenon is made on the inside part of the rail and therefore has only one shoulder. Note that barefaced mortise-and-tenon joints can be used only when the mortise member is thicker than the tenon member.

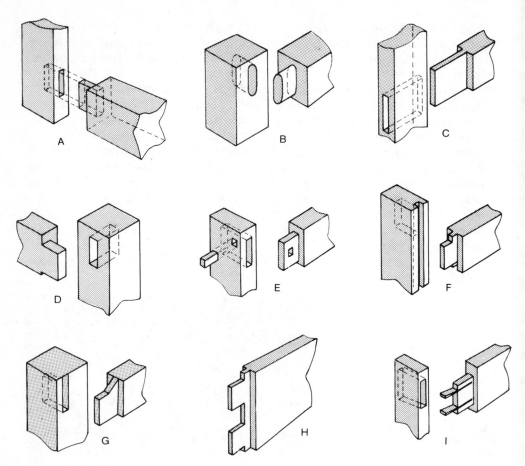

Figure 10-38: Various types of mortise-and-tenon joints.

Pinned Mortise-and-Tenon Joint (Figure 10-38E). A blind mortise-and-tenon joint is sometimes strengthened by driving a pin through it. On reproductions of Elizabethan or Jacobean tables, benches, or stools, such pins are a feature of the design and are usually made square or triangular. When the appearance is unimportant, ordinary dowels are used.

Haunched Mortise-and-Tenon Joint (Figure 10-38F). This joint is frequently used in frame-and-panel construction because it contributes strength to the joint. While the regular haunched joint has the tenon partially exposed at the top of the joint, the **concealed haunched tenon** (Figure 10-38G) offers the strength of the haunched tenon, without any exposure. The **double haunched tenon** (Figure 10-38H) is frequently used for rails in bed construction. It is a very strong joint.

Fox-Wedged Tenon (Figure 10-38I). As well as adding strength to the joint, the fox- or through-wedged tenon also resists pulling apart. The reason for this is that the two ends of the mortise slope outward to provide room for the wedges as shown. This wedge should be approximately one half the length of the tenon. The **blind-wedged mortise-and-tenon** (Figure 10-38J) utilizes

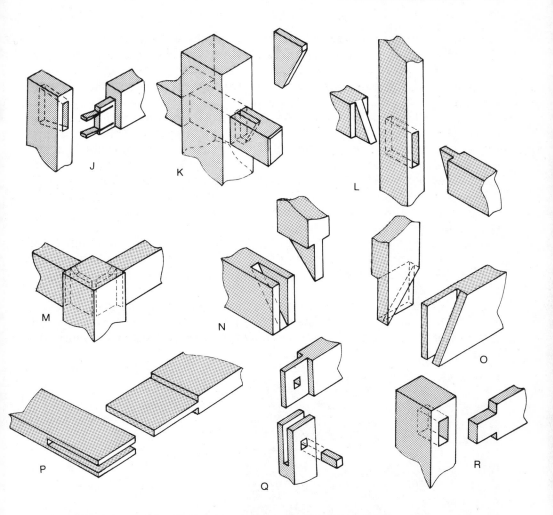

all the principles of the through-wedge tenon, but is used in cases where the fox-wedged is neither possible nor desirable.

Tusk Mortise-and-Tenon (Figure 10-38K). The tusk tenon that goes right through and is locked with a key, peg, or wedge goes back to medieval days. They were more common in some middle European countries than in Great Britain, but they may be found in some Colonial furniture. The use of a wedged or keyed tenon would improve an ordinary tenon, where the fit is not good.

Rail Mortise-and-Tenon (Figure 10-38L). This popular rail joint is actually a through mortise in which two tenons are mitered so that they meet inside.

Miter Mortise-and-Tenon #1 (Figure 10-38M). There are three basic types of mitered tenons. The first kind are often used to attach aprons or rails to legs. In some cases, especially when the apron or rail is flush with the leg, a standard tenon won't be sufficiently long enough to give the joint strength. The joint can be designed to employ either a closed or open mortise.

Miter Mortise-and-Tenon #2 (Figure 10-38N). This mitered mortise-tenon joint is good for frame construction where strength and good appearance are important. The tenon is made so that the angled shoulder cuts are done first and the cheek cuts remove the triangular-shaped waste pieces.

Miter Mortise-and-Tenon #3 (Figure 10-38O). This is a variation of the miter lap joint, except that it includes a tenon. One side has the appearance of a frame half-lap; the other, the more attractive side, looks like a miter. The design provides a good amount of glue area.

Open Mortise-and-Tenon (Figure 10-38P). An open mortise is a slot cut in one piece to receive the tenon that is on the mating part. This joint (sometimes called the slip joint) is commonly employed in simple frame construction where an exposed tenon end isn't objectionable. Where resistance to pulling apart is needed, a key can be used to hold the tenon in place (Figure 10-38Q).

Stub Tenon (Figure 10-38R). This simple joint is one of the weakest of all the mortise-and-tenon joints. However, it is easy and quick to make, and it is used in some frame construction jobs.

Figure 10-39 shows how to cut a tenon on round stock. The miter gauge must be held **very** firmly. A clamp may be used to hold the stock in position and it's a good idea to employ the rip fence as a stop. Turn the work very slowly— **keep hands clear.**

In this chapter, we have covered the most common joints used in woodworking. In Chapter 11, we'll take a look at some of the "special" woodworking joints; while in Chapter 12, we'll see how they can be put to use in furniture construction.

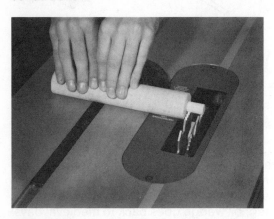

Figure 10-39: Cutting a tenon on round stock.

Chapter 11
Special
Wood Joints

In addition to the joints described in the previous chapter, there are many others used in cabinet and furniture construction. In fact, as stated at the beginning of Chapter 10, there are hundreds of distinct wood joints and variations of each. Most woodworkers will use only a small fraction of these in their projects. Yet, having the widest possible knowledge of the types of joints available will assure that the right joint is being used for the right job. Described below are a number of highly practical and neat joint designs.

BOX OR FINGER-LAP JOINTS. The so-called "box" or "finger-lap" joint, which is seen on many varieties of small boxes (Figure 11-1), is very handy for much work that falls within the scope of the home workshop, as it forms a strong joint which presents a good amount of gluing surface, besides being neat in appearance. With the aid of a simple jig, these joints may be cut rapidly and accurately on a table saw fitted with a dado head.

Figure 11-1: Typical box joint assembled.

When making box joints, the width of the fingers should never equal more than the thickness of the stock (Figure 11-2A). Even on a shallow project made of 3/4" or thicker stock, it is better to have thinner fingers; heavy fingers appear incongruous. A good width for stock ranging in thickness from 3/8" to 1" is 3/8" (Figure 11-2B). A 1/4" finger is effective for stock in the 1/4" to 1/2" range. For stock less than 1/4", match the finger width to the thickness of the material or slightly less. When two different stock thicknesses are employed, use the thinner one for the fingers and grooves (Figure 11-2C).

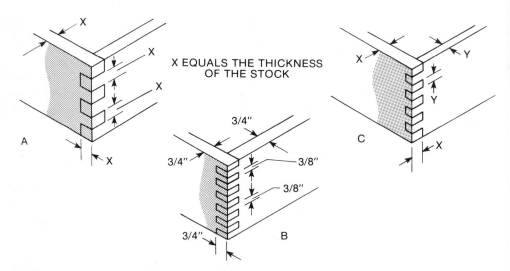

Figure 11-2: Methods for determining the dimensions for the fingers and grooves of a box joint.

While there are several jigs that can be used to simplify box joint making, the one shown in Figure 11-3 gives the most accurate results. To make this jig, cut a piece of 3/4" thick stock to the approximate width of the saw table. The width of the fence should be about 3-1/2". The fence can be fastened to the miter gauge as described in Chapter 5. If the design of your miter gauge doesn't permit the fastening of a fence to it, a separate finger-joint jig can be made as shown in Figure 11-4. The hardwood or steel bar runners must be sized and spaced to fit the miter gauge grooves in the table. These runners must be square with the face of the fence and are fastened to the fence with screws.

With either fence jig in place on the saw table, a dado cutter of the thickness selected for the joint is placed on the arbor, and the fence is then run across the cutter, producing the groove shown at D in Figure 11-3. The fence is then removed, a distance equal in width to the groove is marked to the left of the groove as shown, and another groove (C) is cut through the fence, as indicated. In the last groove, a square lug, 1-1/2" long, is fitted to a sliding fit; it should be a little loose so that it may be wedged to one side or the other in order that you may make your joints tight or loose as desired (Figure 11-5). A line (A) is then squared across the fence in the center of a groove (D) and another line (B) in the center of the space between C and D. Accuracy is extremely important in spacing the second cut (D).

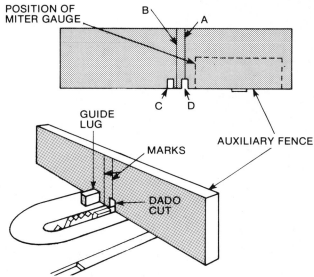

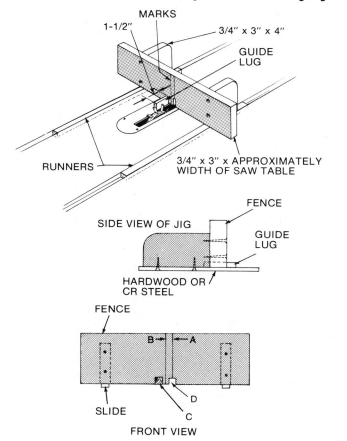

POSITION OF
MITER GAUGE

B

A

C   D

GUIDE
LUG

MARKS

AUXILIARY FENCE

DADO
CUT

Figure 11-3: Auxiliary fence arrangement for a miter gauge.

MARKS

1-1/2"

3/4" x 3" x 4"

GUIDE
LUG

RUNNERS

3/4" x 3" x APPROXIMATELY
WIDTH OF SAW TABLE

FENCE

SIDE VIEW OF JIG

GUIDE
LUG

HARDWOOD OR
CR STEEL

FENCE

B →   ← A

SLIDE

D

C

FRONT VIEW

Figure 11-4: Separate auxiliary fence jig for box joint making.

Figure 11-5: The guide lug controls the position of the workpieces as subsequent cuts are made.

To use the jig for making the joint, set the two pieces of stock to be joined against the auxiliary miter gauge facing. Position the edge of one piece even with line A, and the edge of the other piece even with line B. With the pieces in this position, make the first cut by pushing the work across the dado cutter. After making this cut, shift the work so that the groove just cut sets over the guide lug. Now make the second cut. Position the second groove over the guide lug and make the third cut (Figure 11-6A). Proceed in this manner until the entire width of the piece is cut (Figure 11-6B). At all times the position of the two pieces of stock being cut should never change in relation to one another. This is why it is important to have a guide lug of sufficient length to catch both pieces. The two pieces can also be clamped or even lightly nailed together to insure against shifting. In any case, adjustments can be made by moving the auxiliary facing slightly to the left or right.

A   B

Figure 11-6: In using the box-joint jig, line up the guide lug and dado cutters, and cut the groove like this.

182

A jig of the type just described will work only if the same thickness of stock is to be cut continuously. The auxiliary facing can be varied by holding it to the miter gauge with two bolts inserted through a long slot (Figure 11-7). A small guide pin is substituted for the guide lug. When using this variable jig, set the dado cutters to the width desired and set the fence so that the distance between the side of the cutter and the side of the guide pin is the same as the width of the cutter. The small guide pin works for all sizes of cuts, each groove being set tightly against the side of the pin nearest the cutter. This jig setup, however, requires more care, since the fence must be correctly set for each job and the cuts gauged by holding their inside faces firmly against the guide pin.

While precision is good in making a box joint, don't make the fit between the fingers and grooves so tight that it must be mated with a mallet. A slip is much better. If the joint is too loose, it can be tightened by drilling a hole through the assembled joint and inserting a dowel (Figure 11-8).

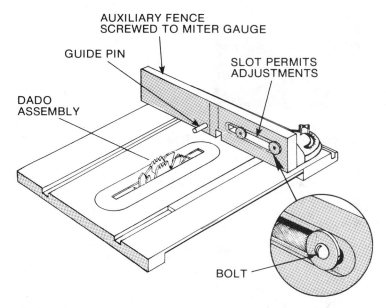

Figure 11-7: An adjustable box-joint jig suitable for stock of varied thicknesses.

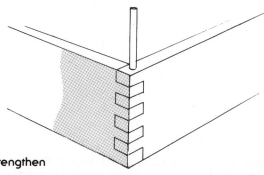

Figure 11-8: Dowels can be used to strengthen box joints.

To minimize the effect of the exposed end grain, many workers cut the grooves slightly deeper than is necessary in order to allow the fingers to project a bit (Figure 11-9). Before finishing, the projections are sanded flush. This treatment is generally more attractive than the texture that remains after a saw cut.

As shown in Figure 11-10, the box or finger-lap joint can be used as a pivot joint. To accomplish this, first drill a hole for a dowel, and then shorten the fingers slightly. Round or dress the corners of the fingers so the parts can move freely after the dowel is inserted. Of course, one of the major uses of the pivot or swivel joint is as the support for gate-leg tables. Figure 11-11 shows the layout of the joint and how it is assembled.

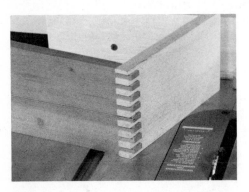

Figure 11-9: Frequently it is wise to let the fingers project, then sand them flush.

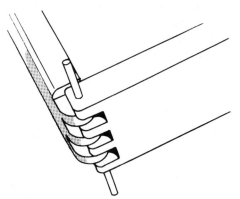

Figure 11-10: Typical pivot joint.

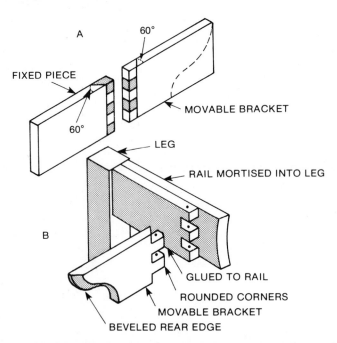

A

60°

FIXED PIECE

MOVABLE BRACKET

60°

LEG

RAIL MORTISED INTO LEG

B

GLUED TO RAIL

ROUNDED CORNERS

MOVABLE BRACKET

BEVELED REAR EDGE

Figure 11-11: Using the finger-lap joint as the support bracket for a gate-leg table: (A) The layout of the joint; (B) the joint ready for assembly.

RABBET-AND-GROOVE JOINTS. The rabbet-and-groove joint—sometimes called rabbeted dado—is both stronger and neater than the basic rabbeted joint. A typical rabbet-and-groove along with its formula is shown in Figure 11-12A. It is most commonly used in drawer construction (Figure 11-12B). In case of construction where the end grain of the rabbet-and-groove joint may be objectionable, you can frequently cover it with a corner guard (Figure 11-12C).

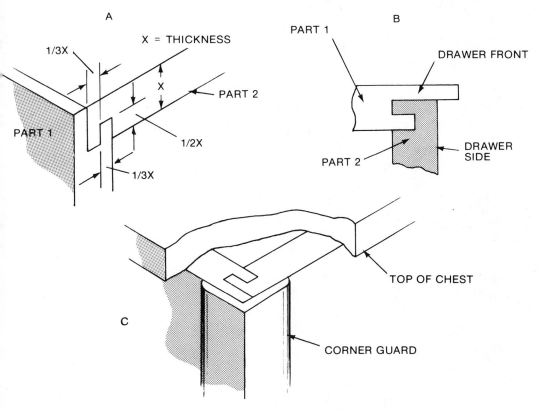

Figure 11-12: Formula for rabbet-and-groove joint.

To make the cuts necessary for the rabbet-and-groove joint, proceed as follows:

1. Mount a proper width dado arrangement on the saw arbor. Set the depth-of-cut to one-half the thickness of Part 1. Then, using the rip fence as a stop, cut the groove in Part 1 (Figure 11-13A).

2. As shown in Figure 11-13B, the set cut in Part 1 can be made with the dado, or you can change to a standard saw blade to remove the waste after the dado cut in Part 2 is made.

3. Reset the depth-of-cut of the dado set to the same depth as the thickness of Part 1. Then, mount Part 2 against a tenoning jig and cut the groove in Part 2 (Figure 11-13C).

4. Assemble the joint as shown in Figure 11-13D.

When making a drawer with a lip, such as the one illustrated in Figure 11-12B, the groove cut in Step 1 must be deeper to provide for the lip.

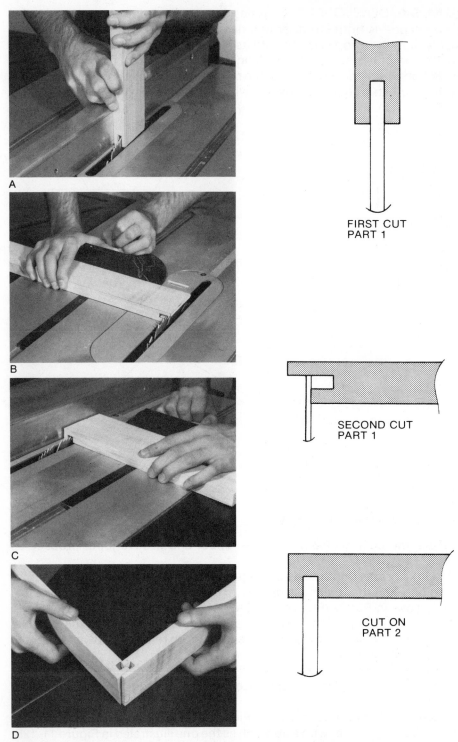

FIRST CUT
PART 1

SECOND CUT
PART 1

CUT ON
PART 2

Figure 11-13: The cuts and assembly of the rabbet-and-groove joint.

COMBINATION MITER JOINTS. The miter joints described in Chapter 10 are sufficient for most woodworking tasks. However, where strength, appearance, and durability are very important, then consider the use of one of the following combination miters.

Tongue-and-Groove Miter Joints. The tongue-and-groove miter is a standard miter joint that incorporates a tongue-and-groove interlock to prevent the parts from sliding or creeping apart. However, accuracy is very critical when making this joint.

To make this joint, first cut the mating edges at a 45° angle in the normal mitering technique discussed in Chapter 10. Then, assemble the dado cutters on the arbor to obtain the width of groove you desire. Tilt the dado cutters to 45° and set the projection of them above the saw table to the depth of the groove. Make the groove cut on the miter center line of Part A.

A cut is made in Part B with the cutters at the same angle, but with their projection adjusted as shown in Figure 11-14. A second projection adjustment is necessary to remove stock from the other side of the tongue. After the tongue has been formed, the remaining stock can be removed with the dado or a standard saw blade. As with all joint cutting operations, it's a good idea to make trial pieces before cutting good stock.

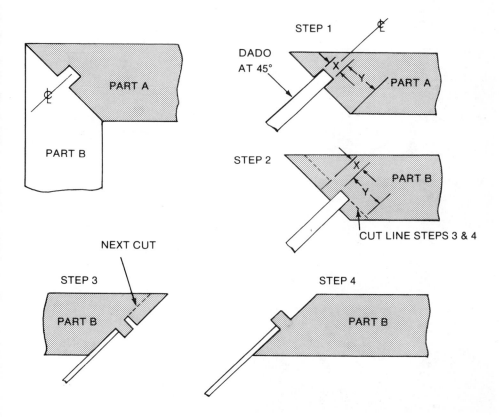

Figure 11-14: Steps in making a tongue-and-groove miter joint.

Housed Miter Joints. This joint is generally used for joining pieces that are of different thicknesses. It offers good glue area and appearance. Follow these steps in making a housed miter:

1. Start by marking the 45° miter angle on the thicker piece. Set the saw blade projection at a height equal to the thickness of this piece (Part 1) minus the thickness of the thinner piece (Part 2). The distance from the fence to the outer surface of the saw blade should equal the thickness of the thinner stock. Make the cut to the miter line (Figure 11-15A).

2. Make the miter cut on Part 1 so that it begins precisely at the corner and meets the bottom inside corner of the shoulder cut (Figure 11-15B). The proper blade projection is critical in this step.

3. On the thinner piece (Part 2), make a simple miter cut (Figure 11-15C). If the pieces are cut accurately, a good joint will be formed (Figure 11-15D).

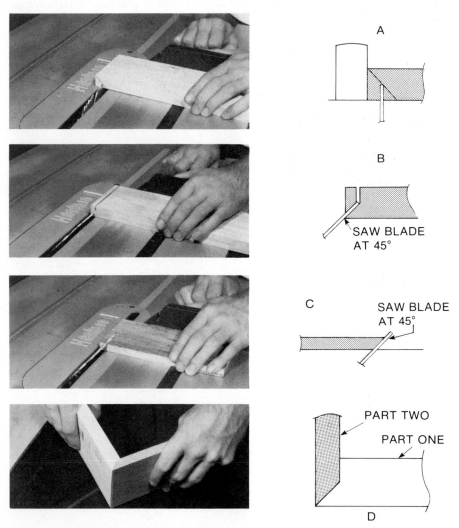

Figure 11-15: Steps in making a housed miter joint.

The housed miter can also be made with stock of even thickness. The procedure for making this joint is the same as for stock of uneven thickness, except that the blade is tilted at 35°.

Rabbeted Miter Joints. This joint, as the name implies, is part miter and part rabbet (Figure 11-16A). The rabbeted miter can be used to good advantage in the construction of cabinet bases and sides. Although slightly more complicated to make than the basic rabbet joint and miter joint, the mitered rabbet has excellent holding qualities. The square-cut section of this joint simplifies nailing and gluing procedures. When used as a cabinet base joint, Part 1, as shown in Figure 11-16B, should be the end or side piece. Also, any nails used to secure the joint should be driven in through this piece. If dowels are used to secure heavier pieces, fit them through the square step of Part 1 in the same positions as the nails (Figure 11-16C). Before beginning the cut, be absolutely sure the dimensional relationships given here for the rabbeted miter joint are understood and followed.

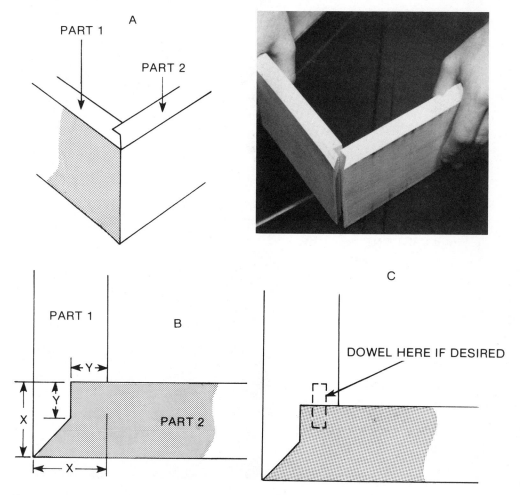

Figure 11-16: The rabbeted miter joint and its formulas.

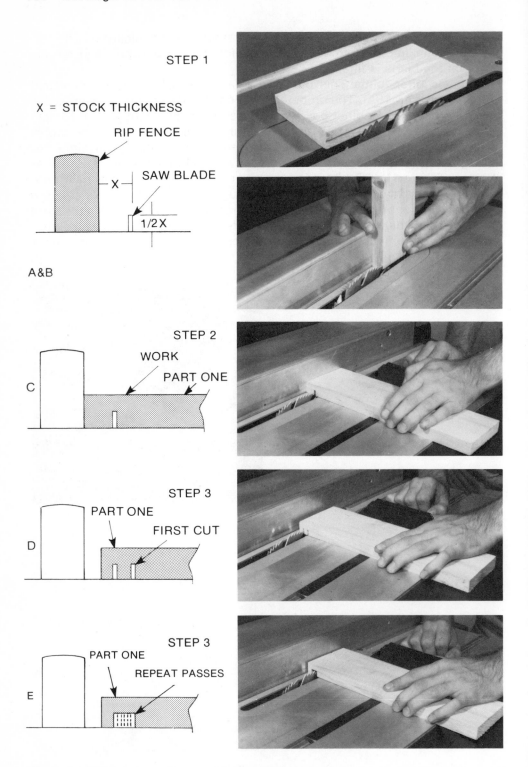

STEP 1

X = STOCK THICKNESS

RIP FENCE

SAW BLADE

X

1/2 X

A&B

STEP 2

WORK

PART ONE

C

STEP 3

PART ONE

FIRST CUT

D

STEP 3

PART ONE

REPEAT PASSES

E

Figure 11-17: Steps in making a rabbeted miter joint.

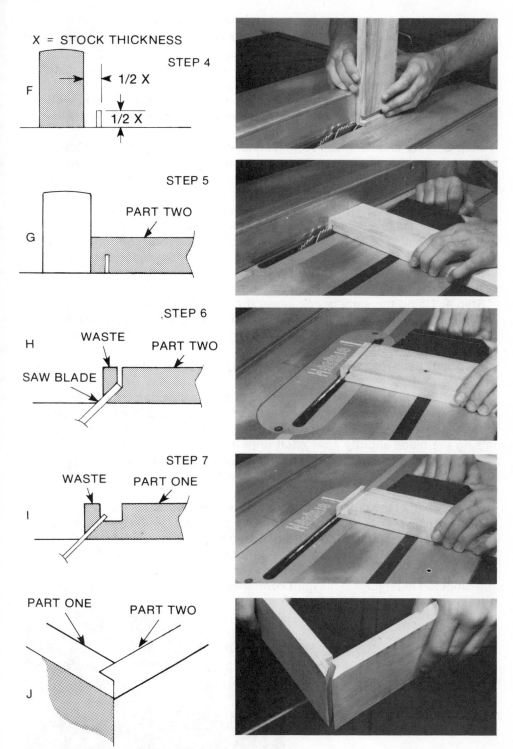

X = STOCK THICKNESS

STEP 4

1/2 X

1/2 X

F

STEP 5

PART TWO

G

,STEP 6

WASTE

PART TWO

H

SAW BLADE

STEP 7

WASTE   PART ONE

I

PART ONE   PART TWO

J

Figure 11-17: Steps in making a rabbeted miter joint.

The cutting procedure (Figure 11-17) is as follows:

Step 1. Raise the saw blade to a projection equal to one-half the thickness of the work. Check this setting on a piece of scrap stock (Figure 11-17A). Using a scrap piece of stock, or one of the workpieces, set the rip fence at a distance equal to the thickness of the stock, as measured from the free (outer) side of the blade (Figure 11-17B). The saw blade must be positioned flush with the face of the work. Before proceeding, recheck the saw height and fence settings for exactness.

Step 2. After checking the settings, make the first cut in Part 1 (Figure 11-17C). Pencil guide lines are not necessary for the cut, but marking the workpieces for easy identification is a good idea. When several joints are being formed, all similar pieces should be cut before advancing to the next step.

Step 3. With the saw blade set at the same depth-of-cut and the rip fence moved away, make a second cut slightly more than halfway to the end of the workpiece (Figure 11-17D). It's important to go beyond the halfway point. Then, make repeat passes to remove the material between the two kerfs (Figure 11-17E). If there are several pieces to cut, it may be wise to switch to a dado cutter for the cleaning operation.

Step 4. Using the same piece, leave the saw blade projection unchanged, and reset the rip fence so that the distance from it to the free (outside) face of the saw blade equals half the stock thickness (Figure 11-17F). This cut will be made on Part 2.

Step 5. Butt the end of Part 2 against the rip fence and make the cut as shown in Figure 11-17G.

Step 6. Set the saw blade at a 45° bevel and make the miter cut on Part 2 (Figure 11-17H). The miter cut and the inside bottom corner of the kerf should just meet. Since blade projection is so important, it is best to make several passes, raising the blade slightly after each until the projection is correct.

Step 7. The same miter cut is made on Part 1 with the contact point at the very corner of the work (Figure 11-17I). Saw blade projection in this step isn't as critical.

Step 8. If all of the cuts are made accurately, Parts 1 and 2 should mate perfectly (Figure 11-17J). While glue is usually sufficient to hold this joint, dowels and nails can be employed as described earlier in this chapter.

Lock Miter Joints. The lock miter joint shown in Figure 11-18 again is an improvement over the tongue-and-groove miter, the housed miter joint, and the rabbeted miter joint. This joint combines the neat appearance of a mitered corner with the strength of a dado corner.

Figure 11-18: Lock miter joint.

In becoming familiar with the lock miter joint, it is advisable to first draw the markings on a piece of paper. Figure 11-19A shows the first operation, which consists of marking the true miter line, and setting off three dimensions. These three dimensions are in proportion to the width of the stock, taking as a basis the dado combination which most closely approximates one-quarter the width of the stock. Thus, for 1" stock, you would use a 1/4" dado combination, etc. Figure 11-19B illustrates the necessary lines ruled in, and Figure 11-19C shows the joint shaded to picture how it will make up in wood.

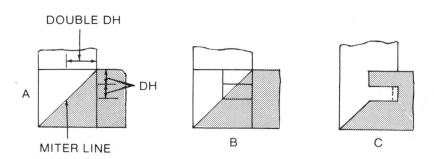

Figure 11-19: Laying out a lock miter joint.

The sequence of steps for cutting a lock miter are given in Figure 11-20. The mitered portion shouldn't surpass half the joint, as shown—or preferably less. Make cuts 1 and 2 with the dado head. (The grooves can also be done by making repeated passes with a regular saw blade.) Use a regular blade to make cuts 3 through 6; the latter two are made at a 45° bevel angle, with the workpieces flat. A few sample joints will quickly point out the exact method of procedure. You will find that the width and depth of the dado cuts can be varied considerably while still maintaining the general features of the joint. Thus, in working 3/4" stock, you would still use a 1/4" dado combination, with a resulting shorter portion of true miter. Again, the projecting ears of the joint can be made shorter than the specified "double dado head combination," as shown by the dotted lines in Figure 11-19C.

One important feature in the construction of lock miters will become apparent from a study of Figure 11-21. You'll notice that each side of any single board has the same kind of cut. That is, any one board should be cut the same—two ears or two rabbets. Working in this manner, the joint becomes a true locking type and need only be clamped in one direction when gluing-up, as shown in the drawing.

Lock Corner Joint. This is another strong corner joint which must be made accurately if it's going to hold the glue. To successfully make this joint in 3/4" stock, follow the steps shown in Figure 11-22. To make Part A, cut a dado 5/8" from the edge; then make a 1/8" by 1/8" rabbet on the same edge and a 1/8" by 1/2" rabbet at the other corner. In Part B, make a groove 3/4" deep and 3/8" wide; then make one pass with a regular blade. With thicker stock, the dimensions can be varied just as long as the general features of the joint remain.

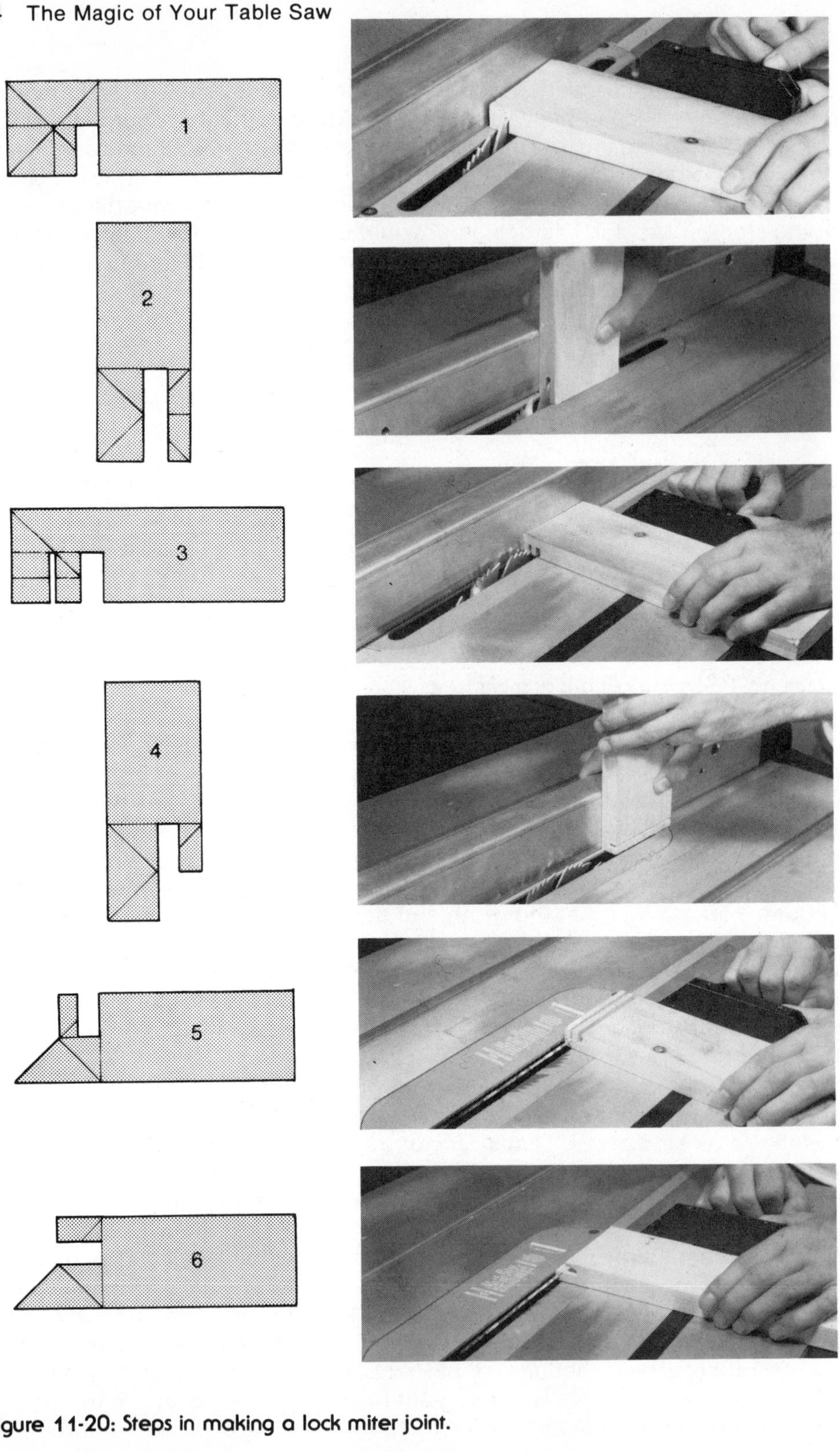

Figure 11-20: Steps in making a lock miter joint.

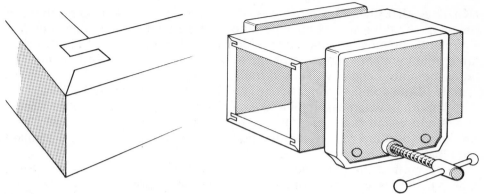

Figure 11-21: Gluing up a lock miter joint.

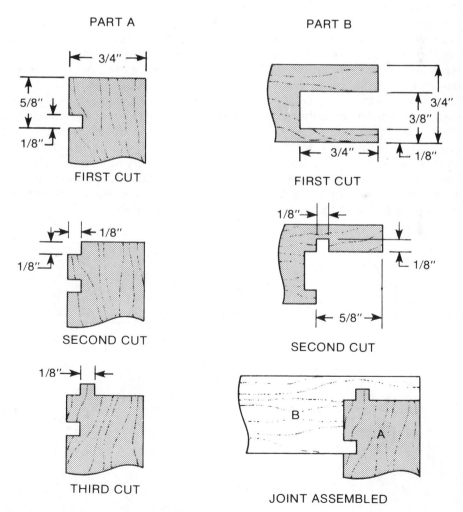

PART A

3/4"

5/8"

1/8"

FIRST CUT

1/8"

1/8"

SECOND CUT

1/8"

THIRD CUT

PART B

3/4"

3/8"

1/8"

3/4"

FIRST CUT

1/8"

1/8"

5/8"

SECOND CUT

B

A

JOINT ASSEMBLED

Figure 11-22: Steps in making a lock corner joint.

MOLDING CUTTER JOINTS. There are several good cabinetmaking joints that can be cut on the table saw using a molding head cutter. Of the cutters shown in Chapter 9, the most popular cutters for this task are the glue or milled drawer knife, rule joint knife, cove and bead knife, ogee knife, and ovolo knife. The latter three are generally used on frame-panel constructions.

Milled Glue Joints. As mentioned in Chapter 10, the edge-to-edge joint is very important when assembling solid lumber slabs for table and desk tops, chairs and bench seats, and other similar furniture construction items. And one of the best methods of jointing boards edge-to-edge is to use the milled glue joint.

The design of the glue joint cutter (Figure 11-23A) is such that one knife makes both cuts necessary for the job. That is, the shaped edges of the tongue-and-groove will fit perfectly when the second piece of stock is flipped for the mating cut (Figure 11-23B), thus providing an interlock action so pieces won't move during assembly. It also gives an extra glue area.

A good fit of the milled glue joint can only be achieved if the mating edges of the stock are dressed for a tight fit before they are shaped and if the molding fence of the table saw is accurately set up. When setting up the molding guide fence, make certain that the center line of the work is exactly in line with the center line of the knives (Figure 11-23C). It is also necessary to adjust the cutterhead so that the lowest cutting part of the knives will just lightly contact the stock. After making these two adjustments, take two pieces of scrap stock which are of the same thickness, and run each over the knives (Figure 11-23D). Flip one piece over and test fit the two together. The fit should be perfect. If one side projects more than the other, make the necessary adjustments to center the joint. Never make a glue joint of this type without first checking the fit on scrap stock. If the adjustments are not exactly precise, one piece will be offset from the other, and the joint will have to be resurfaced.

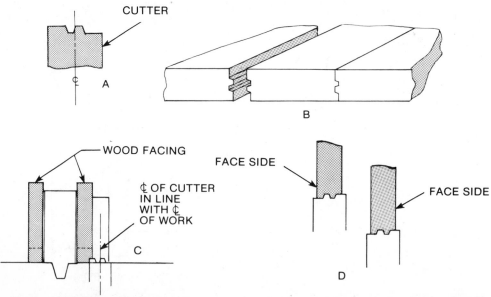

Figure 11-23: The milled glue joint.

Milled Drawer Joint. The milled drawer joint is also made with the glue joint cutter. Although several joints are suitable for drawer construction (see Chapter 12), few of these can surpass the overall quality of the milled drawer joint. The drawer front can be flush with the sides or it can have a lip (Figure 11-24).

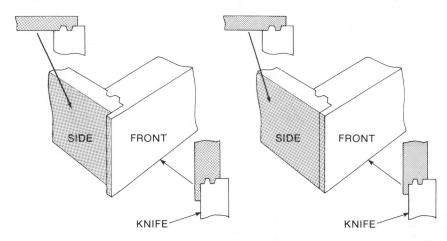

Figure 11-24: Two styles of drawer fronts—with or without a lip.

To cut the front of the drawer, mount the workpiece to a tenoning jig (Figure 11-25). When planning to use a lip, it is usually necessary to set the cutterhead with paper or cardboard washers so that the knives will cut the approximate 1/8" lip when the stock is mounted next to the jig (Figure 11-26). Use a backing block behind the work, making certain that the cutting depth is set to the approximate thickness of the side stock. The shaping operation of the joint can be made easier if you first form a conventional rabbet to remove the bulk of the waste stock.

When cutting the side pieces, set the workpiece against the stop so that the mark on the knife (Figure 11-27) is precisely in line with the end of the work. Again, use a backing block to prevent tearing. Keep in mind that the miter gauge must be set at exactly 90° when making the cut (Figure 11-28).

Figure 11-25: Holding the work in a homemade tenoning jig.

Figure 11-26: Installing paper or cardboard washers to space-out the drawer lip.

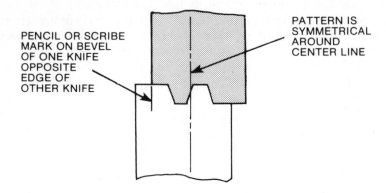

PENCIL OR SCRIBE
MARK ON BEVEL
OF ONE KNIFE
OPPOSITE
EDGE OF
OTHER KNIFE

PATTERN IS
SYMMETRICAL
AROUND
CENTER LINE

Figure 11-27: Match the knives as shown; then mark the knife.

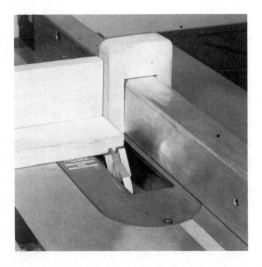

Figure 11-28: Cutting the side member of the drawer.

Rule Joint. The rule joint—better known as the drop-leaf table joint—is used on a tabletop whose size is extended by means of drop-leaves hinged to it. A table of this style usually has one fixed part and two leaves. The rule joint, because of its neater appearance, is used instead of the butt joint by the experienced craftsperson.

Before cutting the rule joint, make certain that you square the workpieces to dimensions, being particularly careful to see that the two edges are square and true. Then, set a marking gauge to half the thickness of the knuckle of a drop-leaf hinge; next, gauge the lines on the end grain of the board on both ends, holding the block of the gauge against the underside of the boards (Figure 11-29). The drop-leaf hinge itself is like a butt hinge, except that one leaf is longer than the other. The screw holes are countersunk on the rear side of the hinge, so that the knuckle can be set into the wood and flush with the underside of the top.

The rule joint can either be made with a set of cutters made especially for this joint (Figure 11-30A), or you can make the cuts with quarter-round and cove knives (Figure 11-30B). When using the latter, the fixed top is cut with the quarter-round knife, while the leaf is cut with a cove knife. The radius of the cutter knives must match perfectly, and the setup must be made so the parts have equal shoulders.

To complete the joint, the hinges are recessed and fastened to the underside of the tabletop and leaf. Screw the hinges in place on the tabletop. With the tabletop and leaf upside down, flat, and using paper matches as spacers between the tabletop and the leaf, screw the hinges into place on the leaf.

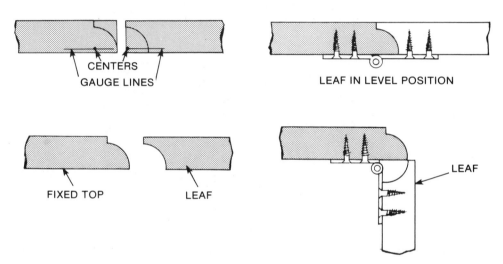

Figure 11-29: The rule joint.

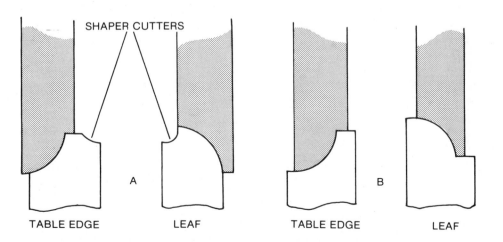

Figure 11-30: Cutting the rule joint.

Door Panel Sticking. Sticking is the term used to describe the shape of the inside edge of the frame that is employed in panel-frame joint construction. The sticking may be square or molded (Figure 11-31). Some of the more popular molded stickings can be cut with ovolo, ogee, and bead and cove knives.

The panel groove is usually cut around the inside edge to receive the panel. The groove for most panel materials is cut to a depth of 3/8". (Solid wood panels require a deep groove [up to 1" deep] in the stiles to take care of the cross-grain expansion of the solid panel.) While most molded stickings are cut with a shaper or router, they can be formed on a table saw with a molding head if care is exercised.

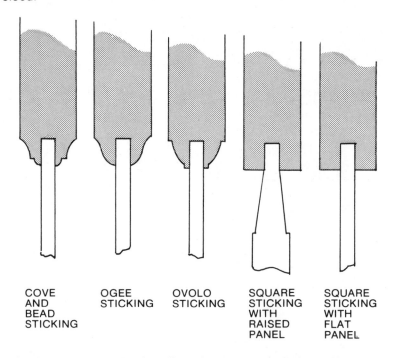

COVE AND BEAD STICKING   OGEE STICKING   OVOLO STICKING   SQUARE STICKING WITH RAISED PANEL   SQUARE STICKING WITH FLAT PANEL

Figure 11-31: Some common "stickings" used in frame-panel construction.

Chapter 12
Furniture Construction
and Your Table Saw

The true "magic of your table saw" is when you can put it to use in building something. This "something" can be any object, but for most woodworkers, it is a piece of furniture. With this in mind, we have devoted this chapter to going over the basics of good furniture construction and how your table saw can help you accomplish them.

BASIC CONSTRUCTION. There are three common methods of making large surfaces for furniture or cabinets: (1) by edge gluing solid stock; (2) by building a frame and panel; and (3) by employing plywood or other large sheet material. The first two methods will be covered in this chapter, while the use of plywood is detailed in Chapter 13.

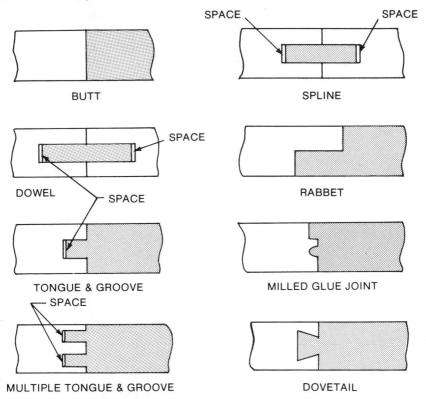

SPACE   SPACE

BUTT   SPLINE

SPACE

DOWEL   SPACE   RABBET

SPACE

TONGUE & GROOVE   MILLED GLUE JOINT

SPACE

MULTIPLE TONGUE & GROOVE   DOVETAIL

Figure 12-1: Joints suitable for edge-to-edge gluing of solid stock.

Solid Lumber Parts. In most furniture construction where wide pieces of solid lumber are needed, the boards are generally built up by gluing together comparatively narrow strips.

Figure 12-1 illustrates the various edge-to-edge glue joints that can be used effectively when building up solid lumber. The simplest is, of course, the butt joint. Both edges must be straight and square. It is ideal for stock less than 3/8" thick. The splined joint is a strong type of construction. For 3/4" material, the spline should be 1/4" thick by 1 to 1-1/2" wide. The groove in which the spline is fitted is cut with the dado head. It can be stopped short of the ends.

The dowel joint is easy to make and is quite sturdy when a number of pins are used. Three-eighth-inch dowels should be used for 3/4" or 7/8" material, while 1/4" dowels should be used for 1/2" stock.

The rabbet, tongue-and-groove, multiple tongue-and-groove, and the dovetail are other strong edge-to-edge joints. They also give extra glue area. Of course, one of the best is the milled glue joint which is made with special knives in the molding cutterhead. The same cut is run in on both edges of the work, the joint being fitted by reversing one of the pieces end for end.

The arrangement of the boards for assembly is most important in gluing edge-to-edge. If you place them with all the sap sides at the top, all will cup in the same direction as they shrink and the wide board will be a trough (Figure 12-2A). Alternate sap with heart sides produce a wavy board which will approximate flatness if warping has been slight or the pieces are narrow; here a little planing will take out the curl (Figure 12-2B). If, in addition, you arrange the boards with the grain running in the same direction, planing will be easy when the work is removed from the clamps. When edge gluing boards of different widths, place the narrower boards in the center of the panel, with the wider boards at the edge. It is important that the clamping pressure be uniform over the entire glued area.

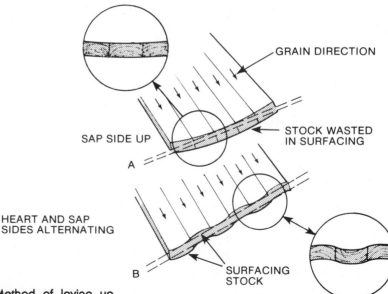

GRAIN DIRECTION

SAP SIDE UP

STOCK WASTED IN SURFACING

A

HEART AND SAP SIDES ALTERNATING

B

SURFACING STOCK

Figure 12-2: Method of laying up boards for edge-to-edge gluing.

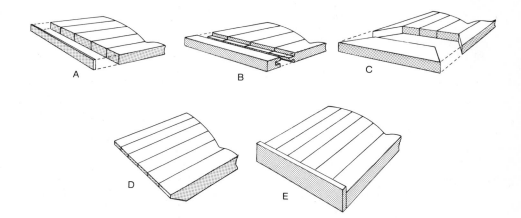

Figure 12-3: Methods of concealing ends of glued-up slabs: (A) banding; (B) tongue-and-groove joint; (C) wood insert; (D) beveled edge; and (E) raised lip. The latter is especially suitable for coffee tables.

For table and desk tops where the ends of the slab may be objectionable, use one of the methods shown in Figure 12-3 to conceal the ends.

Dovetail Tapers—A number of operations employing taper cutting have been discussed in Chapters 5 and 10. Taper cutting is also useful in a number of special cases. For example, it is often a standard practice to fit wide pieces of solid lumber with dovetail keys to prevent warping (Figure 12-4A). The tapering jig can be used to cut both the groove and the key. Make the taper about 3/8″ per foot. The taper can be as little as 1/16″ per foot if appearance is especially important. But keep in mind that some taper is always required. Otherwise it would be impossible to drive a straight key for any distance. Cut the groove by tilting the saw blade as shown in Figure 12-4B.

The setup for cutting dovetail tapers is illustrated in Figure 12-4C. To begin, open the taper jig to the required taper and tilt the saw blade about 10°. Now place the work against the end of the tapering jig. Set the miter gauge to the same angle to cut the tapered side of the keyway. A series of successive cuts across the work clean the slot on one side. The opposite, untapered edge will have been cleaned previously with the miter gauge in the zero position. Without changing the tilt of the saw blade, cut the keys using the tapering jig set at the angle previously set. Make the keys slightly longer than is necessary, and cut them off flush after fitting them into place. An extremely tight, driving fit is not wanted, since this in itself can cause warping.

Frame-and-Panel. Frame-and-panel construction is often used to make doors, form fronts and sides, and do interior casework. While solid wood slabs and man-made panels—plywood and particleboard—are becoming increasingly popular with the average home woodworker, the true craftsperson—either amateur or professional—still prefers frame-and-panel construction for the following good reasons:

1. It has good dimensional stability;

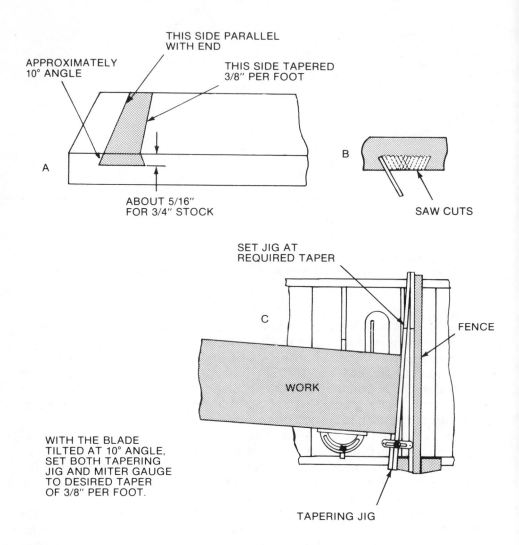

THIS SIDE PARALLEL
WITH END

APPROXIMATELY
10° ANGLE

THIS SIDE TAPERED
3/8" PER FOOT

A

ABOUT 5/16"
FOR 3/4" STOCK

B

SAW CUTS

SET JIG AT
REQUIRED TAPER

C

FENCE

WORK

WITH THE BLADE
TILTED AT 10° ANGLE,
SET BOTH TAPERING
JIG AND MITER GAUGE
TO DESIRED TAPER
OF 3/8" PER FOOT.

TAPERING JIG

Figure 12-4: Steps in making a dovetail taper.

2. It doesn't readily warp;
3. It provides strength to thin paneling material; and
4. It offers more interest to the final design than a simple flat surface.

Most frame-and-panel construction (often called an open or skeleton frame) consists of two horizontal members (called rails) and vertical members (called stiles) upon which is fastened the cover material. The members are usually joined with a butt joint with dowels, haunched mortise-and-tenon joint, open mortise-and-tenon joint, or an end half-lap joint (Figure 12-5). The panels can be made of joined (solid) wood boards, hardwood-veneered plywood, decorative hardboard, corrugated fiberglass, plate glass, or metal grille. For most furniture and cabinet frames, solid 3/4" wood is used.

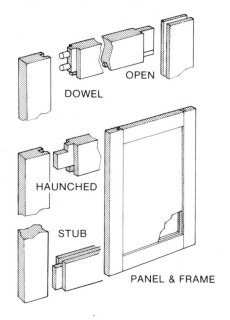

DOWEL

OPEN

HAUNCHED

STUB

PANEL & FRAME

Figure 12-5: Common joints used in frame-and-panel construction.

Figure 12-6 shows several ways in which panels can be secured to the frame. If plywood is used as the panel center, there is little problem from expansion and contraction or warpage. However, if a solid wood panel is employed, the groove or rabbet which holds it must be deep enough to allow for these natural occurrences. For details on cutting the standard molded stickings—bead and cove, ogee, and ovolo—see Chapter 11.

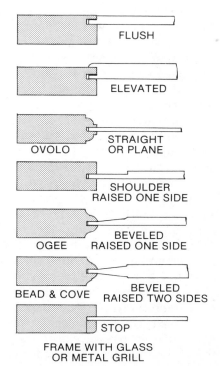

FLUSH

ELEVATED

OVOLO   STRAIGHT
           OR PLANE

SHOULDER
RAISED ONE SIDE

BEVELED
OGEE   RAISED ONE SIDE

BEVELED
BEAD & COVE   RAISED TWO SIDES

STOP

FRAME WITH GLASS
OR METAL GRILL

Figure 12-6: Common types of panels.

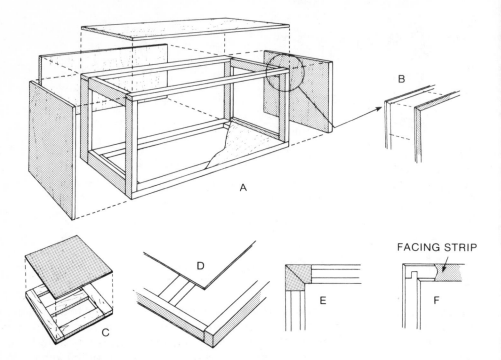

Figure 12-7: Thin slabs over a skeleton frame to form a case.

A skeleton frame can also be an economical method of construction since the frame pieces can be covered with thin panels or slabs. Figure 12-7 shows how the skeleton frame can be used in case goods work. This method of covering is more applicable in built-ins where an existing floor, wall, or ceiling is employed as a part of the project.

Solid Casework Frame. The base solid frame consists of top, bottom, and side slabs assembled like a box (Figure 12-8) and then fitted with frames, dividers, shelves, drawers, doors, and faceplates to complete the furniture unit. The solid frame requires no other joints than those which bond the parts together and which may be further strengthened by the addition of other components such as rails, dividers, shelves, and so on.

As shown in Figure 12-9, many different types of corner joints can be used, ranging from the simple doweled butt to the miter with rabbet joint. The advantages of the various types are given in Chapters 10 and 11; the best for plywood are the spline miter, the miter with rabbet, and the lock miter.

Frames are often installed in chests, desks, and cabinets to add stability to the unit and give horizontal support for the drawers (Figure 12-10). While an open frame is suitable for most units, better built furniture pieces usually feature a dust panel. This is a simple wood frame with a center panel of 1/4" hardboard and plywood. This panel keeps dust from seeping from one drawer to the next. When planning to use dust panels, a rabbet is cut around the inside edges of rails to receive the hardwood or plywood piece. Methods of attaching the rail assemblies to the sides of a case are illustrated in Figure 12-11.

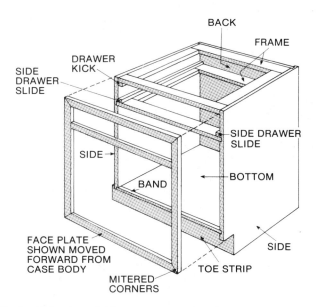

Figure 12-8: Parts of simple solid frame casework unit.

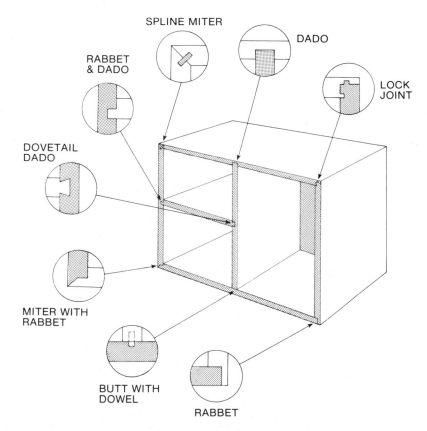

Figure 12-9: Joints used in solid frame casework.

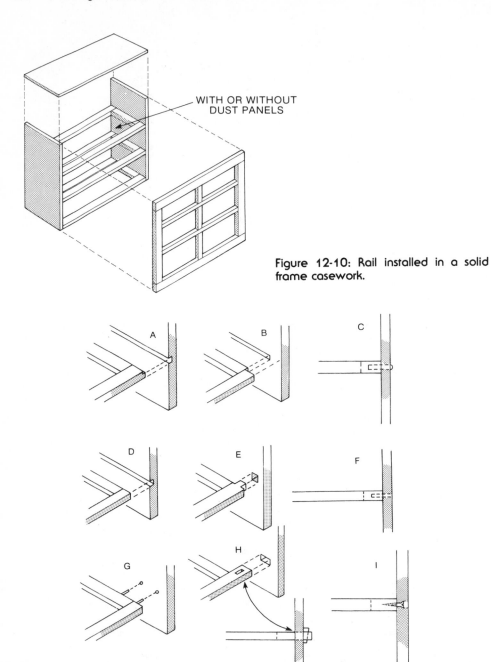

Figure 12-10: Rail installed in a solid frame casework.

Figure 12-11: (A) Rabbet and dado; (B) "stopped" or "blind" dado leaves no exposed cuts; (C) raised dowels for decorative effect; (D) the full length dado is simply made, but unless covered with molding, the cut is visible from the front; (E) mortise-and-tenon; (F) dowel joint with dowels passing through the panel, sanded flush on outer panel—ideal method for locating dowel holes in panel is to drive small brads into the dowel positions on rails, clip off brad heads, and push rail against panel so brads mark drilling points; (G) standard dowel joint; (H) stylish wedge-locked tenon joint; and (I) butt joint with securing screws concealed by dowel plugs.

Occasionally it is necessary to install a cross or middle rail and stile. The joints most commonly used for this purpose are shown in Figure 12-12.

When plywood or particleboard is used as a case, a faceplate is employed to cover the edges. This is made in the same manner as the frame in a skeleton frame and is joined with butt dowel joints, haunched mortise-and-tenon joints, open mortise-and-tenon joints, or spline-miter joints. While the faceplate may be fastened to the frame with screws and glue, it is joined with just glue under pressure in quality work.

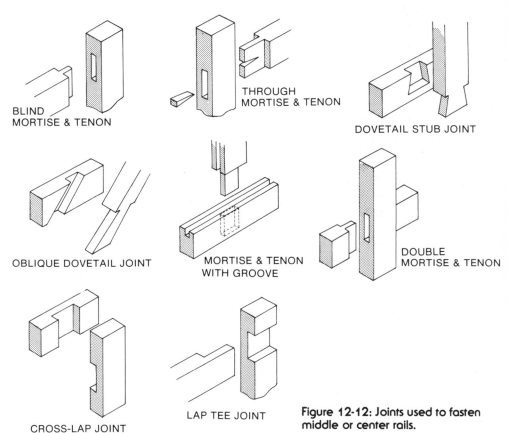

BLIND MORTISE & TENON

THROUGH MORTISE & TENON

DOVETAIL STUB JOINT

OBLIQUE DOVETAIL JOINT

MORTISE & TENON WITH GROOVE

DOUBLE MORTISE & TENON

CROSS-LAP JOINT

LAP TEE JOINT

Figure 12-12: Joints used to fasten middle or center rails.

CABINET BACKS AND DIVIDERS. While cabinet backs can be butted against the back edges of the case, a much neater job is achieved by cutting a rabbet around the inside of the unit's back edges. This cut usually should be just deep enough to hold the 1/4" plywood, hardboard, or particleboard panel (Figure 12-13A). If the cabinet is to fit against a wall, the rabbet should be cut deeper—1/2" to 3/4"—to leave a lip that can be trimmed to get a good fit against the wall.

Another method of installing a back is to set it in a groove cut about 1/2" to 3/4" from the back edges of the unit (Figure 12-13B). This arrangement requires that the back is assembled with the sides.

Dividers in cabinet and furniture pieces are usually set in dadoes cut in opposite case members. It is important to correctly lay out these dadoes—either

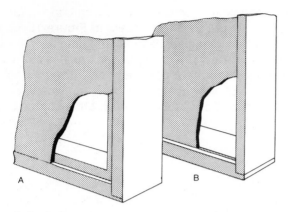

Figure 12-13: Two simple methods of attaching cabinet backs.

vertical or horizontal—before cutting so that the dividers will be straight. If the dividers will be visible from the front of the finished unit, it is a good idea to use a blind dado.

DOOR CONSTRUCTION. Doors for furniture pieces and cabinet goods can be swung on hinges or made to slide.
   Hinged Doors. There are two basic types of hinged doors, panel and solid. With either type, the edge of the door (Figure 12-14) may be set in flush with the case edges or butted against the case edges (flush overlay). The door edge may also "lip" over a portion of the case edges.

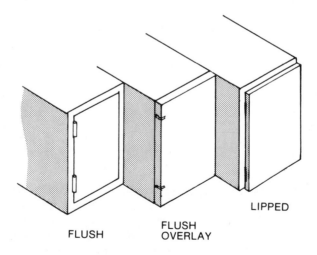

Figure 12-14: Methods of setting doors.

   While flush doors are the easiest to install, they have a tendency to sag; and when this occurs, the doors will jam against the cabinet form or show an open space along the door edges. Sometimes this problem can be minimized by recessing or attaching the doors so that they project slightly.

Lipped doors minimize sagging problems and therefore give a better appearance. The lip is nothing more than a 3/8″ or 1/2″ rabbet cut around the edge of the door. This lipped edge will completely cover the door opening at all times, and minor sags won't be noticed.

Panel hinged doors are constructed in the same manner as the frame-and-panel construction shown in Figure 12-5. The solid, hinged door consists of a simple slab of suitable material—solid lumber, plywood, or particleboard.

Hinges and Their Installation—The edge of the door, lipped or flush, will determine the type of hinge to use. In fact, there are many different styles and designs of hinges from which to select when you mount swinging doors on a cabinet. Usually, the better hinges come with mounting instructions, some even with templates or patterns, to make attaching the doors a simple job. Some of the more popular methods of hinging doors are shown in Figure 12-15.

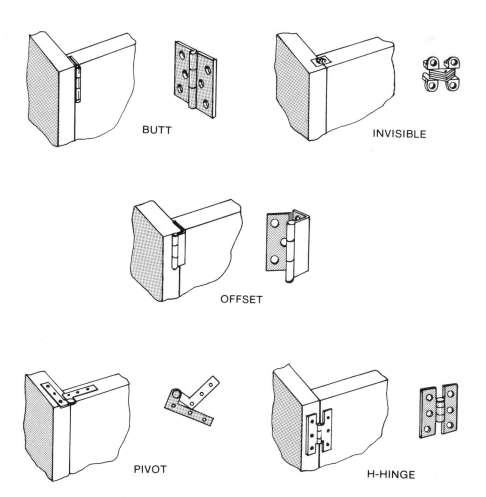

Figure 12-15: The more popular methods of hinging doors.

How to Add a Doorstop—The basic use of single or double doorstops is to seal a furniture compartment and so protect its contents from dust and other injury. Doorstops also help to mask the gaps that appear when the wood shrinks. Some ways of accomplishing doorstops are as follows:

1. **Butt Stop.** The easiest method is to have the side opposite the hinge act as the stop. The door fits over the side (Figure 12-16A). When closed, it can't go any further.

2. **Door Rabbet Stop.** By cutting a rabbet along the inside edge of one side of the door, it can overlap the side and thus it can be stopped when it is closed (Figure 12-16B). When cutting the rabbet, its width should be the thickness of the door if the remaining extending part of the door is thicker than 1/4".

3. **Side Rabbet Stop.** This is merely a modification of the door rabbet. In this instance, the rabbet is cut into the side rather than the door (Figure 12-16C).

4. **Miter Stop.** This type of stop is generally used in fine work (Figure 12-16D).

For double doorstops, using the rabbet is considered to be the best method (Figure 12-16E). The score line shown in Figure 12-16F helps to hide any movement or shrinking of the doors.

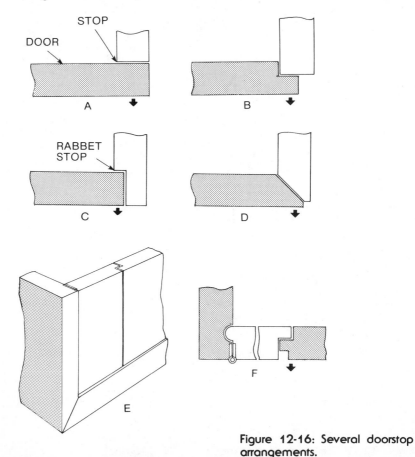

Figure 12-16: Several doorstop arrangements.

Sliding Doors. Sliding doors are very popular in contemporary furniture. The use of this type of door makes it possible to open a furniture unit without having the doors swing out where they may get in the way. You have a choice of many materials to use for sliding doors—tempered hardboard, perforated hardboard, plywood, flat, reinforced fiberglass, mirror, glass, and particleboard. One important point to remember about sliding doors is that you must use a material that won't warp.

Here are several ways in which you can install sliding doors in cabinets or built-ins. These methods can all be done with a table saw.

Double Dado—Two dadoes cut into the bottom surface of the cabinet top and two dadoes in the top surface of the cabinet base provide the grooves in which the doors will slide (Figure 12-17A). To make the sliding doors removable, follow this formula: W equals X minus the sum of Y and Z; Y equals 2Z.

Rabbet Dado—A modified method of the double dado, this is used when a faceplate trim is to be added to the outside of the unit (Figure 12-17B). In this way only one dado is cut, while a rabbet is cut along the edge.

Dado and Cleat—A single dado is cut into the top and bottom of the door itself rather than into the top and bottom of the unit. This groove in the door rides on a 1/2" by 1/2" cleat that is nailed and glued into the cabinet's top and bottom.

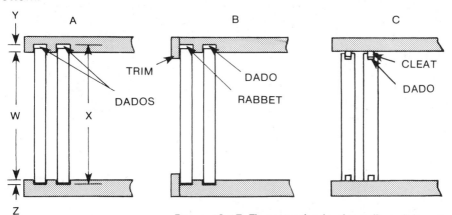

Figure 12-17: Three methods of installing sliding doors.

A variation of this technique is to cut dadoes in the underside of the cabinet top and the top surface of the cabinet base to provide tracks in which the door rides. Cut the top and bottom edges of the door with a tongue to fit into the dado grooves.

LEGS AND THEIR JOINERY. Furniture legs can be simple or complex. They can be straight, tapered, turned, or molded. The shapes shown in Figure 12-18 can be cut on the table saw. Full information on how to cut tapered legs is given in Chapter 5.

As shown in Figure 12-19, there are several ways of joining legs to transverse rails and of attaching legs and rails to the body of the piece of furniture. Great care should be taken in the selection and execution of such joints, so that they will be able to withstand strain.

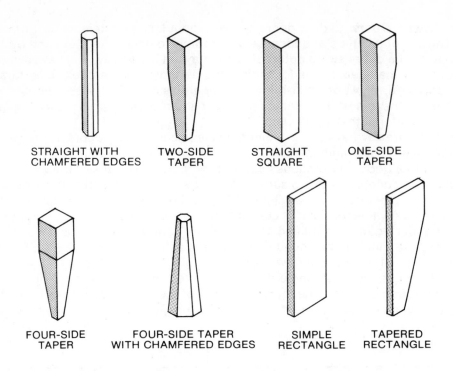

STRAIGHT WITH
CHAMFERED EDGES

TWO-SIDE
TAPER

STRAIGHT
SQUARE

ONE-SIDE
TAPER

FOUR-SIDE
TAPER

FOUR-SIDE TAPER
WITH CHAMFERED EDGES

SIMPLE
RECTANGLE

TAPERED
RECTANGLE

Figure 12-18: Leg designs that can be made on the table saw.

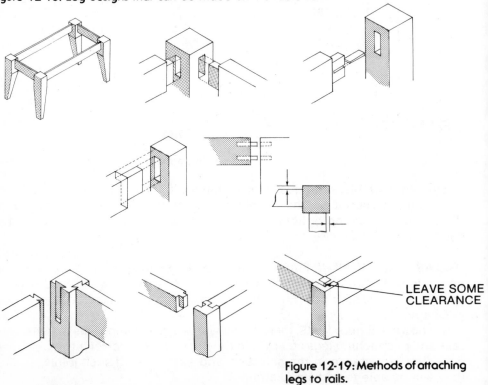

LEAVE SOME
CLEARANCE

Figure 12-19: Methods of attaching
legs to rails.

DRAWERS AND DRAWER GUIDES. Drawers come in handy for hundreds of uses in our everyday life. They are pulled out and pushed back many times a day in the office, shop, and home. Often they are treated carelessly. And yet if drawers are carefully built, they will stand up for years, never sticking, never giving trouble.

There are many forms of drawer construction that can be made on the table saw, and there are a variety of designs for a multitude of purposes and different kinds of furniture (Figure 12-20). It is practically essential that all woodworkers have an understanding of basic drawer construction as applied both to cabinetmaking and house carpentry.

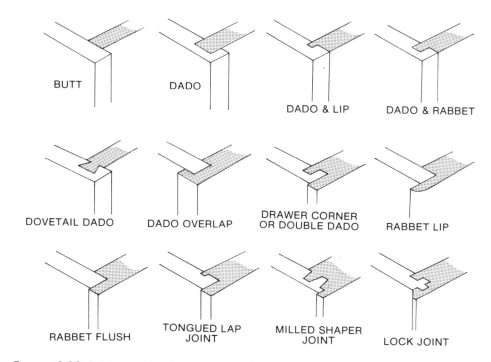

BUTT

DADO

DADO & LIP

DADO & RABBET

DOVETAIL DADO

DADO OVERLAP

DRAWER CORNER OR DOUBLE DADO

RABBET LIP

RABBET FLUSH

TONGUED LAP JOINT

MILLED SHAPER JOINT

LOCK JOINT

Figure 12-20: Joints used in drawer construction.

Any drawer is made to fit a definite opening of fixed dimensions (Figure 12-21), making due allowance for clearance to provide a sliding fit. The minimum amount of clearance through the body of the drawer is about 1/16" at the sides and top. The actual closing part of the drawer—the front—can be worked to a closer fit if desired, as shown in Nos. 2 and 3 construction of Figure 12-22, and by various other methods, but the body of the drawer should have ample clearance to prevent binding.

Average drawer stock will run to 3/4" for the front, 1/2" for the sides and back, and 1/4" or 3/16" plywood or hardboard for the bottom. Given these fixed wood sizes and a definite type of construction, the net width and length of each piece can be expressed in terms of the size of the opening, minus a

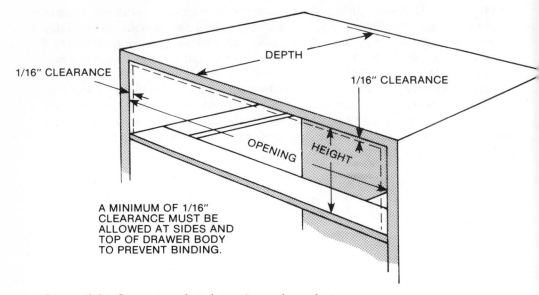

Figure 12-21: Dimensions that determine a drawer's size.

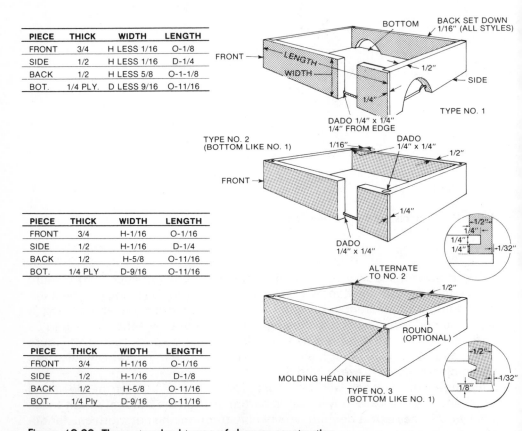

PIECE	THICK	WIDTH	LENGTH
FRONT	3/4	H LESS 1/16	O-1/8
SIDE	1/2	H LESS 1/16	D-1/4
BACK	1/2	H LESS 5/8	O-1-1/8
BOT.	1/4 PLY.	D LESS 9/16	O-11/16

PIECE	THICK	WIDTH	LENGTH
FRONT	3/4	H-1/16	O-1/16
SIDE	1/2	H-1/16	D-1/4
BACK	1/2	H-5/8	O-11/16
BOT.	1/4 PLY	D-9/16	O-11/16

PIECE	THICK	WIDTH	LENGTH
FRONT	3/4	H-1/16	O-1/16
SIDE	1/2	H-1/16	D-1/8
BACK	1/2	H-5/8	O-11/16
BOT.	1/4 Ply	D-9/16	O-11/16

Figure 12-22: Three standard types of drawer construction.

certain amount for clearance and construction. In No. 1 of Figure 12-22, for example, the width of the front will be the same as the height of the opening, minus 1/16" for clearance. Consulting the table, it can be seen that the width of the back is the same as the height of the opening, minus 5/8" (1/16" for clearance, 1/16" for set down, 1/4" for the bottom, and 1/4" for the wood below the bottom). All other net sizes are similarly expressed in terms of the size of the opening, minus a certain amount for clearance and construction. This method of charting a drawer speeds up the work considerably, insures uniformity, and eliminates errors. The tables can be adjusted to suit variations in construction or wood thickness. Once determined, the table is used as a standard in making drawers for any size of opening.

The wood stock is first ripped to width, using a hollow-ground blade. Fronts and sides are usually the same width and are cut at the same setting. Cutting to length makes use of a stop block on the fence, cutting all similar pieces at the same setting. The scale on the front rip fence guide should be used for all cuts. The stop for crosscutting should be exactly 1" wide to permit accurate use of the scale in cutting to length. Clearance is allowed in the table of dimensions so that the bottom will not crowd the bottom grooves. If more than one size of drawer is being worked at one time, the various pieces should be clearly marked with pencil to avoid confusion.

After cutting to net size, it will be apparent that the exact construction to match the table of dimensions being used must be followed since a fixed allowance for a certain type of joint or joints is made in each case. As already mentioned and illustrated in Figure 12-20, joints for fastening drawer parts together using a table saw are chosen primarily with regard to the quality of drawers, time available, and the quantity of drawers needed.

To detail the operations in drawer making, let's take a closer look at the standard construction No. 3 of Figure 12-22. After the drawer stock has been cut to the net width and length, there are about six operations required to fit the various parts. A regular routine should be followed. Figures 12-23 and 12-24 show the order of operations for a drawer with a milled drawer joint at the front edges. Where any other type of front joint is used, the schedule runs in the same order.

1. The front corner joints are cut first. The depth of the cut for the front is equal to the thickness of the side stock.

2. Rounding the side edges is an optional step. The first cut is stopped when the end of the work is in line with the table insert (Figure 12-24B). The cut on the opposite edge is made by dropping the workpiece over the cutter with the end of the stock in line with the far end of the insert.

3. The bottom grooves are run in with a 1/4" dado combination, 1/4" from the edge of the work. The depth of the cut is 1/4" or slightly less. Both the sides and front are cut at this setting.

4. Grooves in the side pieces to take the back are cut with the dado head and fence in the same position as for Step 3. The cut can be cleaned entirely, eliminating Step 5.

5. Tenons on the ends of the back piece are cut with a dado cutter combination at the same depth as before. The width of the cut is set by eye and should be slightly less than 1/4" (the depth of the groove).

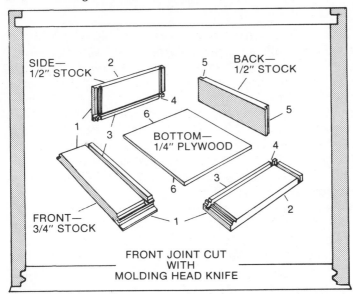

SIDE—
1/2" STOCK

BACK—
1/2" STOCK

BOTTOM—
1/4" PLYWOOD

FRONT—
3/4" STOCK

FRONT JOINT CUT
WITH
MOLDING HEAD KNIFE

Figure 12-23: Parts of a milled joint drawer. Numbers indicate order of the construction operation.

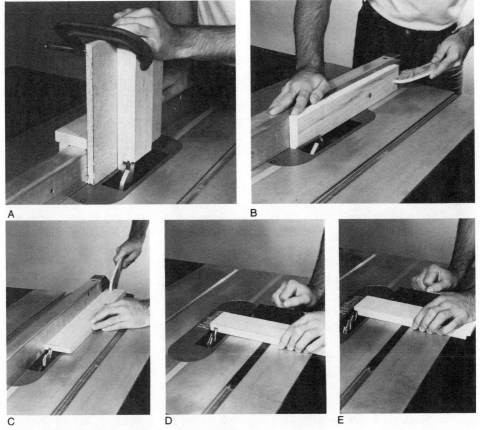

A   B   C   D   E

Figure 12-24: Steps in making milled joint drawer.

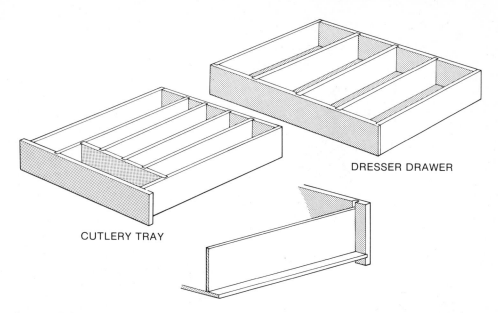

DRESSER DRAWER

CUTLERY TRAY

Figure 12-25: Typical uses for drawer dividers.

6. The front and side edges of the bottom are given a quick sweep over a belt sander to slightly bevel the edge, permitting an easy fit in the bottom grooves.

For greater convenience, a drawer is frequently divided into sections. The easiest way to do this is to cut dadoes in the sides or between the front and back so that dividers will slip into place (Figure 12-25).

Drawer Guides. Commercial drawer slides are available. These can be either bottom or side mounted guides. The latter slides come as a matching pair that fits against the inside of the case and along the outside of the drawer sides. The amount of clearance needed between the drawer sides and case varies with the size and kind of slides. Therefore, it is important to buy the slides before building the drawers. Drawer guides, of course, can be made on your table saw. The two most popular designs are side and center guides.

Center guides (Figure 12-26) extend between the front rail and back of the cabinet. Butt and dowel the ends, or notch the fronts over and into the rails. A toenailed butt is generally used in built-in cabinets. The front end acts as a drawer stop, while the lower edge is flush with the underside of the rail and serves as a hold-down for the drawer below it, keeping its front from dropping when the drawer is open. Top drawers, of course, need a separate hold-down.

Square each guide from the front rail and be sure it is parallel to the guides above and below. Insert a drawer and, using the sides of the guide as a gauge, scribe lines on the bottom for placing the strips. Little sliding clearance is needed. Construction is improved if slides or runs are installed at the sides of the cabinet to relieve the guides of most of the weight of the drawer.

Methods of installing side guides are also shown in Figure 12-26. If these guides are allowed to project 1/16" beyond the rails and stiles where this is possible, much wear will be prevented. Heavy drawers require a greater projection.

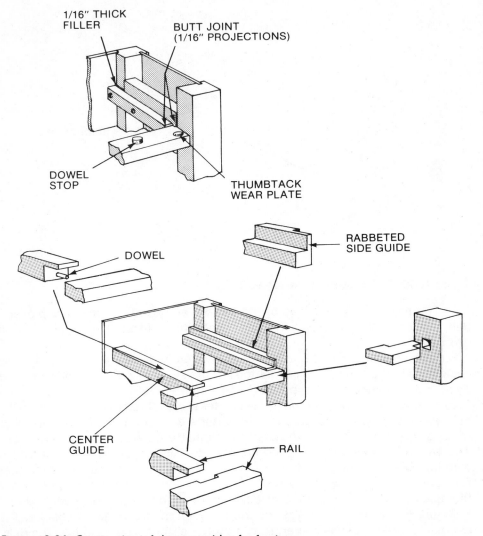

Figure 12-26: Construction of drawer guides for furniture.

Figure 12-27 shows several drawer guides cut with the dado head cutter. In Figure 12-27A, the extended bottom is set in a dado groove cut in the side panels. You can also cut a dado in the side of the drawer and add a cleat to each side of the cabinet (Figure 12-27B). This keeps the drawer bottom off of the shelf and puts all of the weight on the trim. When the added strips are made of hardwood, you should encounter little difficulty in opening and closing the drawer. Incidentally, the dado needn't be cut into the drawer front if the cleat doesn't extend all the way to the front of the unit. Even heavy drawers slide easily on guides like these if they have been waxed or lubricated with paraffin after finishing.

In Figure 12-27C, the procedure is reversed, and the cabinet side is dadoed before assembly. A matching strip is glued and screwed to the side drawer.

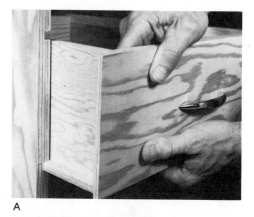

A

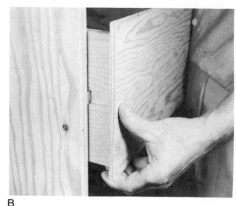

B

C

Figure 12-27: Drawer guides that can be cut with a dado cutter.

Fitting Drawer Fronts. After the guides have been installed and the drawer otherwise completed, insert it in its opening and dress the ends and top until the front will enter. Pull the drawer out again and bevel inward slightly, continuing the fitting until a uniform joint of about 1/16″ is obtained. This provides space for several coats of paint or varnish.

Fitting such as this requires the use of closing stops. Dowels inserted in the lower rail and filed or chiseled in front to allow the front to be pushed back into place are excellent for drawers having side guides. Hardwood strips tacked until adjusted and then nailed or screwed permanently are also good. If drawers are set back behind the edges of the rails, the stops must be set back correspondingly.

Lip drawers, having fronts with rabbeted top and side edges that lap over rail and stiles to conceal the joints, require little fitting. Side clearance is also less critical than with flush fronts. Close the drawers and lay a straightedge across the fronts to mark the ends for cutting to length. The lips customarily act as stops, but for drawers subjected to abuse, stops may be placed behind the drawers to take the shock of closing off the fronts.

If you wish to have dust panels for your drawers, groove the rails and slides to take the edges of the dust shelves, or rabbet them to hold the shelves flush with the lower edges (Figure 12-28). Flush shelves leave no projections to catch on contents of drawers beneath them.

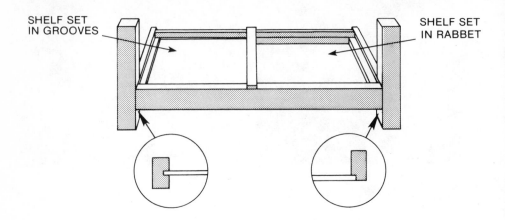

Figure 12-28: Fitting dust panels in drawer compartments.

Drawer Pulls. There are many different types of drawer pulls on the market. Usually, they are of some kind of plastic or metal hardware which is attached to the exterior of the drawer front. As shown in Figure 12-29, several decorative drawer pulls can be cut on your table saw. Strips are first cut to size and then beveled, rabbeted, or plowed to shape. After the strip has been shaped, it can be cut into individual pulls. The wood pulls can also be decorated with designs cut by a molding head cutter.

You can also make drawers with built-in pulls. That is, the bottom edge of the drawer front can be shaped for the fingers (Figure 12-30).

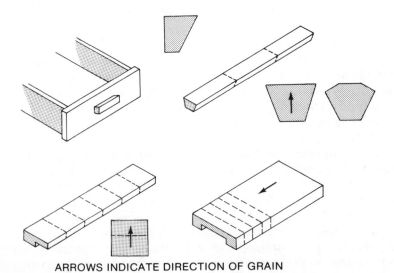

ARROWS INDICATE DIRECTION OF GRAIN

Figure 12-29: Drawer pulls that can be cut on your table saw.

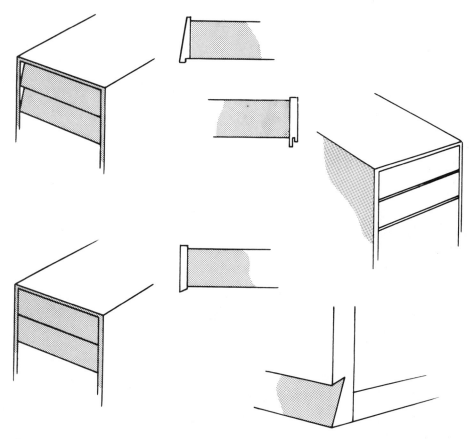

Figure 12-30: Drawer pulls shaped for your fingers.

SHELVES. In fitting shelves in furniture projects, you have a choice of several methods of construction. The simplest of all is the plain butted joint, either nailed or screwed. The most popular is the housed joint. Running the groove right through, as in Figure 12-31A, presents the simplest method of working, but exposes the joint. Half-round molding is often used to face the edges, as in Figure 12-31D, to cover the joint. The best housed joint is stopped a little short of the edges, as in Figure 12-31B. Vee jointing (Figure 12-31C) makes an attractive joint. The vee must be very blunt, since any angle of 45° or over would cut the work in two. A method of housing the shelf in a square-cut groove with only the exposed edge vee jointed is shown in Figure 12-31E.

Dovetail housed joints make excellent construction, as shown in Figure 12-32, but they take longer to construct than the other shelf fittings. In addition to being dovetailed, the joint must also be tapered so that it can be driven in from the back.

Where adjustable shelves are needed, it is best to use one of the metal adjustable shelving systems available from your local hardware store or home center dealer.

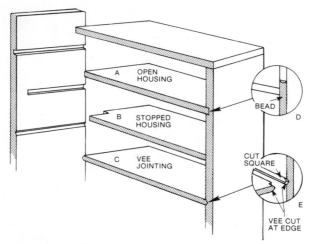

Figure 12-31: Various shelf joints.

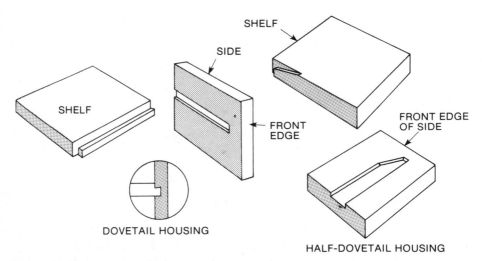

Figure 12-32: Two types of housed dovetail joints.

In this chapter we have attempted to show how the basic table saw techniques given in the previous chapters of this book can make furniture construction a great deal easier.

Chapter 13
Cutting Other Building Materials on Your Table Saw

The table saw can be used to perform many cutting tasks on the so-called new building materials such as plywood, particleboard, hardboard, asbestos-cement board, foam insulation board, marble, aluminum, etc. Some of these materials may be cut with the standard woodworking blades. However, for most cutting operations on harder surface materials, special blades such as the nonferrous and ferrous saw blades, carbide-tipped saw blades, and abrasive cut-off wheels must be employed.

PLYWOOD. While plywood is a wood product and has been shown in some of the illustrations in previous chapters, it has several working characteristics that should be fully discussed. Although it has been manufactured for some time, plywood did not become popular with home craftsmen until after World War II. Today, it is one of the most popular materials used.

Types of Plywood. Plywood is made of an odd number of thin sheets of wood glued together with the grain of the adjacent layers perpendicular. The grain of the two outside plies must be parallel to provide stability. This gives the panel nearly equalized strength and minimizes dimensional changes. The thin layers of wood, called plies, usually are "peeled" from a log as veneer. In some instances the veneer is sliced from the log. The veneer is cut into various lengths, dried, selected or graded, then glued together to make a sheet or panel of plywood.

Both softwood and hardwood plywoods are available. Softwood plywood is extensively used in building construction; hardwood plywood is used for cabinetwork and furniture; both are used for paneling. Softwood and hardwood plywood are classified by grade and type. Grade is determined by the quality or condition of the separate plies and the appearance of the face plies; type refers to the durability of the adhesive bond between the plies. A major difference in the manufacture of softwood and hardwood plywood is the use of a solid "core," or extra-thick middle ply, in some hardwood panels. As shown in Figure 13-1, there are three types of plywood cores:

Veneer-Core—Veneer-core plywood is manufactured with layers of wood veneer joined in the standard manner. It is intended for uses such as paneling, sheathing, and furniture parts, or when the plywood might be bent or curved.

Lumber-Core—Lumber-core plywood contains a thick core made by edge-gluing several narrow strips of solid wood. This core forms the middle section to which veneer crossbands and face plies are glued. Lumber-core plywood is manufactured for specific uses such as tabletops, built-in cabinets, and fixtures and doors where butt hinges are specified.

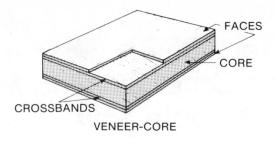

VENEER-CORE

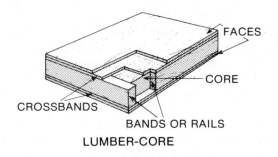

LUMBER-CORE

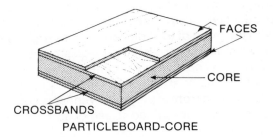

PARTICLEBOARD-CORE

Figure 13-1: Three major types of plywood construction: veneer, lumber, and particleboard.

Particleboard-Core—In this plywood, the core is an aggregate of wood particles bonded together with a resin binder. Face veneers are usually glued directly to the core, although crossbanding is sometimes used. Particleboard-core plywood is used in manufacturing furniture and is particularly adaptable for table, desk, and cabinet tops. In most instances, particleboard-core plywood has greater dimensional stability than the other types.

Working with Plywood. When you cut plywood on a table saw, the good face of the material should be up. The best saw blade to use is the special fine-tooth plywood type (see Chapter 2). This blade has a thin-rim taper, ground for clearance, and has little or no tooth set. It therefore makes cuts with a satin smooth finish ideal for glue joints. The table saw can rip 4' wide panels right down the middle with ease. It's easier to handle large panels alone if you build an extension support with a roller or rollers as described earlier in this book; such a support can also have a base of its own or it can be clamped to a saw horse (Figure 13-2). Other paneling cutting tips are given in Chapter 5.

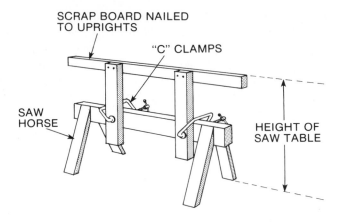

SCRAP BOARD NAILED
TO UPRIGHTS

"C" CLAMPS

SAW
HORSE

HEIGHT OF
SAW TABLE

Figure 13-2: Method of supporting large panels.

The plywood operations of the various other attachments for the table saw—the dado head, molding head, etc.—are handled in the same manner as regular wood. For 3/4" plywood, the dowel and spline joint is the most commonly used in joining panels. The spline, usually about 1/4" thick and 5/8" wide, is continuous and may be made from plywood. The dowels (usually No. 7 or 8 spiral) are on centers anywhere from 4 to 10" (Figure 13-3A). The tongue-and-groove (Figure 13-3B) and tongue-and-rabbet (Figure 13-3C) joints are also standard treatments. The tongue is usually 1/4" wide and approximately 5/16" deep. When bowing panels into place, the sides of the tongue are chamfered slightly. The groove is always made a little larger than the tongue. Dowels are also used to provide extra joint security. For thinner plywood, joint treatments recommended for wall paneling can be used. Reinforcement strips must be used behind the thinner materials (it is a good idea for thicker material, too). Glue should be used on all panel joints.

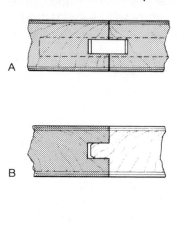

A

B

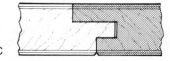

C

Figure 13-3: Methods of jointing thicker plywood panels.

Corner butt joints are the easiest to make and are suitable for 3/4" plywood. For thinner panels, use a reinforcing block or nailing strip to make a stronger joint. In all cases, glue will make the joint many times stronger than nails or screws alone. Frame construction makes it possible to reduce weight by using thinner plywood. As shown in Figure 13-4A, the corner posts can be dadoed to receive the plywood panels. A tongue-and-groove joint can also be used with a corner post to hold a panel (Figure 13-4B).

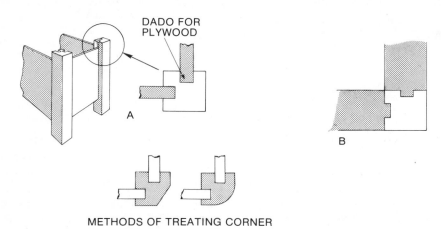

METHODS OF TREATING CORNER

Figure 13-4: Use of corner posts to conceal plywood edges.

Plywood edges can be a problem. If care is not exercised, the finished job will be bonded with raw edges that resemble half-healed scars. First, check the design of the piece to be built. Even with plain butt joints, there are an astonishing number of ways to assemble a simple box, and each one makes a difference in the number or position of visible edges. By using rabbets and miters or solid wood moldings (Figure 13-5), a little thought at the design stage can reduce the problem. Consider where the piece of furniture will be located, what surface will be exposed, and what finish you will use.

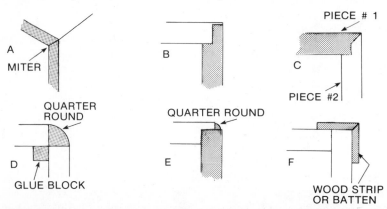

Figure 13-5: Methods of concealing the plywood edges in corner construction: (A) Miter; (B) rabbet; (C) rabbet-miter joint; (D) quarter-round molding and a glue block; (E) rabbet and quarter-round molding; and (F) wood strip or batten.

Possibly the best treatment for edge grain is shown here in Figure 13-6A. Two 45° cuts are made from the underside, completely through the wood, the small piece is removed, and the end is bent as shown. By this method a continuous grain is shown—even on the ends.

A solid piece of material—that is, solid hardwood—in the shape of a T in cross section can be glued to the piece of plywood so that, when the edge is viewed, it will appear as solid lumber (Figure 13-6B). The procedure shown in Figure 13-6C is the same, except that the piece of lumber is triangular in cross section. Cutting the edge at an angle, as shown in Figure 13-6D, is a neat and cheap method; the edge grain may be painted or stained to match the panel.

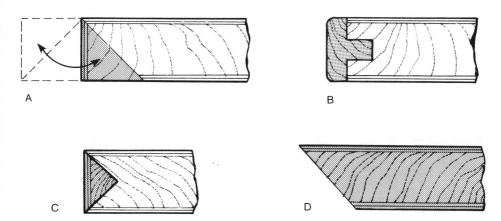

Figure 13-6: Popular ways of concealing plywood edge grain.

It is also possible to bead the edge with a table saw's molding head (Figure 13-7A) or to glue a beading strip or molding to the edge. A mitered framing strip, secured by glue and by brads that have been set and puttied, is a very effective treatment, especially for table and desk tops (Figure 13-7B). Solid-wood moldings, either purchased or made with the molding head attachment, are also good for the exposed top edges of tables and desks (Figures 13-7C to G). Do not overlook common half- or quarter-round molding (Figure 13-7H); its width may be greater than the edge width. Aluminum veneer cap molding (Figure 13-7I) may be used to cover edges with good results.

Thin strips of real wood edge-banding now are available, already coated with pressure-sensitive adhesive (Figure 13-8A). You need only peel off the backing paper and apply it to the edges according to the manufacturer's recommendations. These tapes are sold in several different kinds of wood by lumber dealers. You can apply laminated plastic-surface materials to table edges with the same contact cement used in applying them to the tops; apply first to the edges, then to the top (Figure 13-8B). A thicker effect can be secured by nailing or gluing a 1 or 1-1/2″ strip all around the under edge. You can also bulk a plywood edge and thus conceal the plies as shown in Figure 13-9. When bulking the edge, insert the slab in a dado cut in solid material or set the slab in a rabbet cut in solid wood.

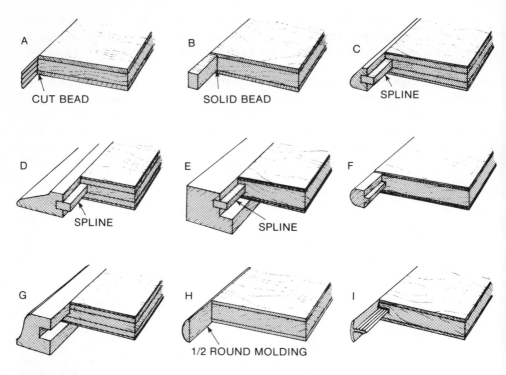

Figure 13-7: Other methods of concealing plywood edge grain.

Figure 13-8: Two other common edge grain treatments: (A) wood edge-banding and (B) laminated plastic.

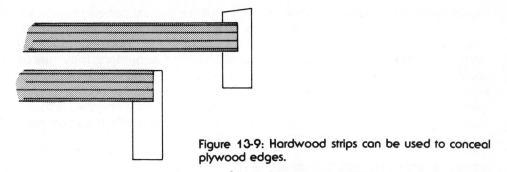

Figure 13-9: Hardwood strips can be used to conceal plywood edges.

Framed panels will help to eliminate the problem of plywood edges, too. The panel can be fitted to the solid-wood frame in several ways (Figure 13-10), and the frame can be treated decoratively with molding.

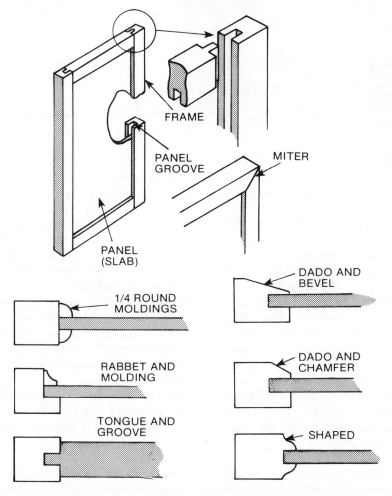

FRAME

PANEL
GROOVE

MITER

PANEL
(SLAB)

1/4 ROUND
MOLDINGS

DADO AND
BEVEL

RABBET AND
MOLDING

DADO AND
CHAMFER

TONGUE AND
GROOVE

SHAPED

Figure 13-10: Framed panels can also be used to eliminate the problem of plywood edges.

HARDBOARD. Properties and characteristics of hardboard panels (Figure 13-11) make them suitable for interior and exterior use in new construction or remodeling of residential, farm, commercial, and industrial buildings. Since hardboards are made of wood, with no artificial fillers or binders, they may be easily worked and applied by the usual carpentry methods. A wide variety of surface treatments is easy to produce. Simple bends and curves are easily formed. Finishing presents no special problems—paint, enamel, lacquer, stain, shellac, and varnish may be applied by ordinary methods. It is commonly supplied in 1/8 and 1/4" thick sheets of 4' by 8' size.

Figure 13-11: Hardboard sports several thicknesses, textures, and colors.

Fundamentally, there are two types of hardboards—standard and tempered. Both are available in various thicknesses and textures. However, as with any good product, the wrong usage can result in unsatisfactory results. Standard types do not have as high a water-resistant or wearing quality as tempered boards. They are more adaptable for interior walls, cabinets, and places where moisture or abrasion are no problem. The wearing and water-resistant qualities of the tempered variety make them an excellent flooring and siding material. They are satisfactory for exterior applications or wherever high or changing humidity may prevail as in bathrooms and basements.

Perforated hardboard or pegboard offers a completely new idea in wall surfacing. Both useful and decorative items may be arranged and rearranged on either smooth or embossed panels without in any way defacing the wall. There are over 60 metal hangers available which are instantly interchangeable and self-locking without the use of any tools and make perforated hardboard panels adaptable to an infinite variety of applications.

Hardboard can be cut with standard combination or plywood blades, but when extensive cutting is to be done, use a carbide-tipped blade, especially when using tempered hardboard. Like plywood, be sure to cut with the good or finished face up.

WALLBOARD. The range of materials classed as wallboard is wide. They include such products as asbestos-cement board, gypsum or plasterboard, fiberboard, and insulation board. They are all available in panel form and some come in predecorated finishes.

As a rule, you can cut asbestos-cement board, gypsum board, or plasterboard by first scoring the material, then snapping it off. But you can get accurate cuts on these materials by placing a silicon-carbide cutoff wheel on your table saw. Fiberboard and insulation boards—including foam insulation panels—are easy to cut with the standard combination blade (Figure 13-12), but the most accurate results can be obtained by employing a hollow-ground or a plywood type. When cut, the materials mentioned above produce large amounts of dust that could clog the saw motor. Be sure to vacuum and clean the saw frequently. Work in well ventilated areas and always wear a dust mask and eye protection.

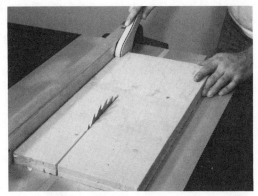

Figure 13-12: Cutting foam insulation with a standard combination blade.

PARTICLEBOARD. As previously mentioned, particleboard, often called "chipboard," is sheet material made up of resin-bonded wood particles and is most often used as an underlayment for resilient flooring. It is also adaptable as covering material for interior walls or other uses where it is not exposed to moisture. Particleboard is usually supplied in 4' by 8' sheets and in 3/8" thickness for paneling, in 5/8" thickness for underlayment, and in block form for flooring. It is also used for cabinet and closet doors and as core stock for tabletops and other built-in furniture.

Because it can dull a saw blade rather quickly, particleboard is best cut with a carbide-tipped blade (Figure 13-13). Most of the edge and joint treatments discussed for plywood hold good when working with particleboard.

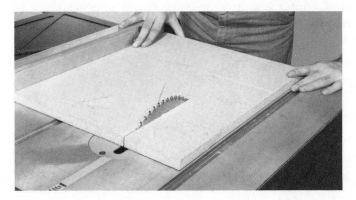

Figure 13-13: Cutting chipboard with a carbide-tipped blade.

ALUMINUM AND LIGHT METAL. Light metal, especially aluminum, is becoming more and more a home shop material. While all aluminums can be cut with either an aluminum oxide, silicon-carbide cutoff wheel, or a nonferrous metal cutting blade, one type—aptly called do-it-yourself aluminum—can be cut with any standard table saw blade. Always remember to advance the metal into the blade slowly and evenly. It is important to avoid continuous cutting with a heavy feed. This heats up the saw-blade tips and causes them to pick up aluminum particles which partially weld themselves to the blade. To prevent such metal pickup, stop the feed occasionally and allow the blade to run unloaded for a short time to keep it cool. Also, while the blade is at rest, lubricate it with a paraffin block or old candle to reduce friction (Figure 13-14). Check the set of your saw if it tends to bind after lubricating. If the saw drags when making a heavy cut, stop it and inspect the blade. Remove any aluminum particles sticking to the teeth by flipping them off with a knife or screwdriver. A wire brush is also excellent for cleaning saw teeth. Then, reduce your rate of feed to avoid "leading up" the teeth again and causing damage to the blade.

Figure 13-14: Lubricating a nonferrous metal blade with an old candle. Be sure the lubricant coats the teeth and the gullets.

To cut thin-wall tubing, it's wise to hold it in a V-block (Figure 13-15). The block can be clamped to the miter gauge and tubing permitted to project beyond the block, or the block may have a saw kerf to permit the passage of the blade. Various stop blocks and stop block arrangements can be used to accurately gauge the exact cutting length in the same way as when crosscutting (see Chapter 5).

As previously stated in Chapter 2, aluminum oxide cutoff wheels should be used on metals, especially the hard ones that take shallow cuts. Allow the work

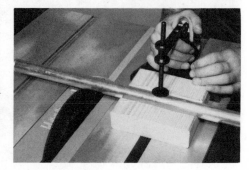

Figure 13-15: Cutting thin-wall tubing in a V-block.

to cool between cuts. When cutting metal—anytime you use the abrasive wheel —wear goggles to protect your eyes from flying sparks or particles.

BRICK, FLAGSTONE, AND OTHER MASONRY UNITS. Brick and flagstone can be cut by making several passes through the material with a silicon-carbide cutoff wheel (Figure 13-16) or other blades, raising the blade approximately 1/8″, until you're through. For rough cuts, you can score the stone or brick and then break it clean with a mason's hammer or a brick chisel. Since most masonry units—either cinder or concrete blocks—are too thick for passing the wheel through from one side, it must be turned over and cut from the other side or it can be scored on all four sides so it will break cleanly. When cutting these materials, be sure to use goggles and a face mask as there is a great amount of dust produced during this operation.

Figure 13-16: Cutting a brick with a silicon-carbide cutoff wheel.

Marble. In the last few years marble has made a comeback in our modern homes. It is employed in furniture which can be used for serving hot meals and in outdoor furniture which will withstand the weather.

While a few soft marbles can be cut with either carbide-tipped or nonferrous saw blades, the majority will require a cutoff wheel. It is usually better to make a number of very shallow cuts instead of one big one, to avoid straining the blade. You can also use the side of an abrasive wheel like a sanding disc to smooth the edges after cutting and to shape curves. When sawing, wear goggles to protect the eyes from flying particles.

Ceramic Tile. If you have ever attempted to get a straight break line on a ceramic tile after having scored it with a glass cutter, you know what a blessing it is to be able to cut the tiles on a table saw equipped with a silicon-carbide cutoff wheel. As with marble, take shallow cuts, say about 1/8″ deep on each pass. Curved shapes or smoothed edges may be obtained by using the side of the wheel. Cut the tile with the glazed surface down on the tabletop.

PLASTICS. Clear, glass-like acrylic plastics can also be cut on the table saw (Figure 13-17) using either a nonferrous saw blade, silicon-carbide abrasive wheel, or regular carbide blade. Keep the protective paper on the plastic until you're ready to buff. When cutting some thicker plastics of this type, there is a tendency for the waste material, heated by blade friction, to fuse in the kerf behind the blade. To prevent this, make shallow cuts, increasing the depth for each pass until the material is severed.

Figure 13-17: Cutting acrylic plastic with an abrasive wheel.

Fiberglass-reinforced plastic paneling makes a good roof for a patio, shower-door for your bathtub, screen for room divider, flower box and planter, and many other things around the home. They come in many attractive colors and designs in flat or corrugated sheet forms. It's easy to "do-it-yourself" with this material since plastic cuts well with a table saw and is simple to nail to framing. It requires only light framing because of its own rigidity. The panels can be cut to size with a silicon-carbide cutoff wheel (Figure 13-18), a metal cutting blade, or a regular carbide blade. Be sure to provide proper ventilation and use a face mask when cutting fiberglass reinforced panels as there are toxic fumes given off during this operation. If possible, perform the cutting tasks outdoors.

Figure 13-18: Cutting corrugated fiber-glass with a cutoff wheel.

The table saw equipped with cutoff wheel or carbide-tipped blade can be used to cut rigid and flexible plastic pipe. As when cutting thin-wall metal tubing, it is advisable to position the work in a V-block or use a clamping arrangement such as the one shown in Figure 13-19. The feed should always be slow, and side pressure should not be exerted against the wheel.

Figure 13-19: Clamping method of holding plastic pipe.

Laminated Plastics. Decorative laminated plastic materials are available in sheet form or come already glued to 3/4" plywood. Although laminated plastics are harder than marble, they are surprisingly easy to cut. As a general rule, carbide-tipped blades are the most durable, but they must be handled carefully because they tend to be brittle. The thin-rim combination or plywood blades are also good, but they dull rather quickly when cutting this material. When making any cuts, be sure the decorative face is up (Figure 13-20).

Figure 13-20: Cutting laminated plastic with thin-rim plywood blade.

CUTOFF OR ABRASIVE WHEELS. As described in Chapter 2 and mentioned several times in this chapter, silicon-carbide and aluminum oxide cutoff or abrasive wheels are excellent for cutting many hard surface materials. Although these wheels possess remarkable strength, they'll chip or break if improperly handled. The feed should be steady and even at all times and of sufficient pressure to prevent glazing of the wheel. Remember that an abrasive wheel cuts on its side as well as its edge. Try to keep the work as straight as possible or the discs may snow-plow, cutting a wide and sloppy groove. However, the work shouldn't be forced too much, since this will shorten the life of the wheel considerably. Because cutoff wheels are mounted on the motor arbor in the same manner as a saw blade, the safety guard should be used. Once mounted, you can make the same basic cuts with the cutoff wheels as those made with a saw blade in wood. Proper ventilation is essential whenever operating the cutoff wheel. Also, always use eye protection when working with abrasive wheels.

Successful cutting is dependent upon the wheel's being properly balanced and having a clean cutting edge. If the wheel should be knocked out of round, it will begin to vibrate. One result of this will be an increased width-of-cut—much wider than the thickness of the wheel. Wheel life is shortened and precise cutting becomes impossible. If the wheel should get out of round or chip, use a suitable abrasive stick like the one shown in Figure 13-21 to bring the wheel into round.

Figure 13-21: Method of truing a cutoff wheel.

Chapter 14
Table Saw and
Saw Blade Maintenance

The most important maintenance you can perform on your table saw is to keep it clean and free from sawdust build-up. In most cases, all bearings on the modern table saw have been permanently lubricated and require no maintenance on the part of the operator. There are, however, various sliding joints and other areas in which sawdust can accumulate (Figure 14-1). This accumulation could cause problems, such as difficulty of movement or even reduced movement of saw parts. The bottom folds of the front dust cover, the front and rear carriage mounts, and the front and rear end bells of the motor are areas which should be given particular attention in this regard.

Figure 14-1: Frequent use of a shop vacuum is the best way to keep your saw and work area clean.

An excess build-up of sawdust in the folds of the dust covers and/or carriage mounts may cause a loss of full travel of the bevel and elevation controls. Such a build-up at the motor end bells could affect cooling and motor performance.

Regular application of oil or grease to the moving parts of the table saw is not recommended. Too much oil or grease would only serve to catch sawdust and decrease the time interval between cleanings. Periodic, light applications of lubricants will not cause problems. For instance, after cleaning the sawdust out of the carriage mounts, apply a thin coat of grease to the mounts. Also, occasional application of a few drops of lightweight oil on the pivot points of the miter gauge, rip fence, blade guard, antikickback pawls, and the elevation pivot point will keep these areas trouble free and working smoothly (Figure 14-2). Remember, these applications should be light to avoid build-up. One of the available silicone products or powdered graphites is also excellent for the lubrication of moving parts.

Figure 14-2: Apply oil lightly to avoid build-ups.

MAINTENANCE ADJUSTMENTS AND CHECKS. The various types of blade, table, and guide adjustments are discussed in Chapter 3. These settings should be checked from time to time and any necessary adjustments made. Follow the procedures given in Chapter 3 or in the owner's manual of your table saw.

When compared to most other power tools, the table saw requires very little maintenance. The following checks should be made periodically to safeguard against more serious problems:

1. Check all safety devices and make sure they are operating properly. This is especially true of the blade guard.

2. Check all nuts, bolts, and screws for tightness. To check the arbor bearings, set the blade to its highest elevation, and then try to wiggle it. If there is play in the arbor, replace the arbor bearings. Check the elevation and tilt gears to make certain they are functioning properly.

3. Make sure the table insert plate is in good order. It should lie flush with the table surface. Replace it if necessary.

4. Inspect the belt and make sure it is in good working condition. Check for tightness. The belt should be snug enough to operate smoothly without any slippage.

5. Pitch, gum, and other deposits reduce the cutting efficiency of any blade. Remove pitch and gum from the sides of the blade with kerosene or gum solvent (Figure 14-3), then cover it with oil. A little kerosene wiped on a clean blade will help prevent the accumulation of pitch and gum.

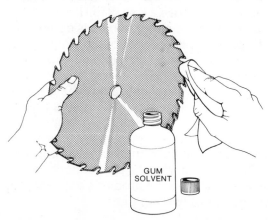

Figure 14-3: Cleaning saw blades with a solvent.

Figure 14-4: Use paste wax to protect the surface of the table.

6. Keep all surfaces, such as the tabletop, free of rust and corrosion. This, of course, would not apply to the aluminum and composition tabletops which are available. If a build-up of pitch forms on the tabletop, clean it off with a solvent, such as paint thinner. Apply a coat of wax to the surface of the table and to all other finished parts of the saw, including the miter gauge slots and rip fence. Automobile paste wax is especially good for this purpose (Figure 14-4). Buff this wax to a high gloss finish. The wax will fill the pores of the casting and prevent rust. It will also make the surfaces extra smooth, allowing the work to slide freely without jerking or sticking. This adds to the safe, easy operation of the machine.

7. Clean all plastic parts with a clean, damp cloth. Solvents should never be used to clean plastic parts. They could possibly dissolve or otherwise damage the material.

Troubleshooting Table Saw Problems. No matter how well a table saw is maintained, there is still the possibility of a problem occurring. The following troubleshooting charts list the probable causes and remedies for the most common problems. Before troubleshooting any problem, however, **always turn the power switch to the OFF position and remove the plug from the power source outlet.**

TROUBLESHOOTING CHART—GENERAL

Trouble	Probable Cause	Remedy
Excessive vibration.	Saw blade out of balance.	Replace blade.
	Saw not mounted securely on stand.	Tighten all mounting hardware.
	Damaged saw blade.	Replace blade.
	Machine positioned on uneven floor.	Position on flat, even surface.
	Bent motor or arbor pulley.	Check and replace pulley if necessary.
	Uneven belt.	Replace drive belt.
Saw does not make square, accurate crosscuts. Cut binds, burns, or stalls motor when ripping.	Miter gauge not adjusted properly.	Adjust miter gauge. See Chapter 3.
	Dull blade with improper tooth set.	Sharpen or replace blade.

TROUBLESHOOTING CHART—GENERAL

Trouble	Probable Cause	Remedy
Saw does not make square, accurate crosscuts. Cut binds. burns, or stalls motor when ripping.	Blade is heeling.	Correct heel condition. See Chapter 3.
	Warped board or workpiece.	Make sure concave or hollow side is facing up. Feed slowly. Replace board.
	Splitter out of alignment.	Realign splitter. See Chapter 3.
	Rip fence not parallel to saw blade.	Adjust fence. See Chapter 3.
Bevel cuts not true at 90° or 45°.	Stop screws not properly adjusted.	Reset screws. See Chapter 3.
Bevel hard to set.	Sawdust on threads of bevel screw.	Wipe off excess sawdust.
	Sawdust on carriage brackets.	Wipe off excess sawdust.
Stock kicked back from blade during ripping.	Rip fence misaligned.	Properly align fence. See Chapter 3.
	Splitter misaligned.	Properly align splitter. See Chapter 3.
	Feeding stock without rip fence.	Always use the rip fence for support.
	Dull antikickback fingers or pawls.	Sharpen pawls.
	Dull or resin-coated saw blade.	Sharpen and or clean saw blade.
	Releasing material before it fully passes the saw blade.	Push material all the way past the blade before releasing.
Saw blade cutting poorly.	Dull or dirty saw blade.	Sharpen, clean, or replace blade.
	Pitch or resins on table surface causing erratic feed.	Clean tabletop with a suitable solvent.
	Improper type blade for work being done.	Use blade that suits the job required.
	Blade improperly sharpened.	Use proper sharpening techniques. Have blade sharpened by professional. Replace badly damaged blades.

Troubleshooting Motor Problems—The motors used on all woodworking tools are particularly susceptible to the accumulation of sawdust and wood chips and should be blown out or "vacuumed" frequently to prevent interference with normal motor ventilation. The importance of properly matching the power supply with the needs of the table saw motor is discussed in detail in Chapter 3. When motor problems do occur, refer to Chapter 3 and/or the chart given below.

TROUBLESHOOTING CHART—MOTOR AND ELECTRICAL

Trouble	Probable Cause	Remedy
Excessive noise.	Motor.	Have motor checked by qualified service technician.
Motor will not run.	Protector open; circuit broken.	Reset protector by pushing on red button (indicated by audible click).
	Low voltage.	Check power line for proper voltage.
	Power cord not plugged in.	Plug in power cord of saw.
	Power cord damaged.	Have cord repaired or replaced by qualified service technician.
Motor will not run and fuses "blow" or circuit breakers "trip."	Short circuit in line cord or plug.	Inspect line cord and plug for damaged insulation or shorted wires.
	Short circuit in junction box, or loose connections.	Inspect all terminals in motor junction box for loose or shorted connections.
Motor fails to develop full power. (Power output of motor decreases rapidly with decrease in voltage at motor terminals.)	Power line overloaded with lights, appliances, and other motors.	Reduce line load.
	Undersize wires or circuit too long.	Increase wire sizes, or reduce length of wiring.
	General overloading of power company's facilities. (In many sections of the country, demand for electrical power exceeds the capacity of existing generating and distribution systems.)	Request a voltage check from the power company.
	Incorrect fuses in power line.	Install correct fuses.
Motor starts slowly or fails to come up to full speed.	Low voltage—will not trip starting relay.	Correct low voltage condition.

TROUBLESHOOTING CHART—MOTOR AND ELECTRICAL

Trouble	Probable Cause	Remedy
Motor starts slowly or fails to come up to full speed.	Starting relay not operating.	Replace relay.
Motor overheats.	Motor overloaded.	Correct overload condition.
	Improper cooling. (Air circulation restricted through motor due to sawdust, etc.)	Clean out sawdust to provide normal air circulation through motor.
Starting relay in motor will not operate.	Burned relay contacts (due to extended hold-in periods caused by low line voltage, etc.).	Replace relay and check line voltage.
	Open relay coil.	Replace relay.
	Loose or broken connections in motor terminal box.	Check and repair wiring.
Motor stalls (resulting in blown fuses or tripped circuit breakers).	Starting relay not operating.	Replace relay.
	Voltage too low to permit motor to reach operating speed.	Correct the low line voltage condition.
	Fuses or circuit breakers do not have sufficient capacity.	Replace fuses or circuit breakers with proper capacity units.
Frequent opening of fuses or circuit breakers.	Motor overloaded.	Reduce motor load.
	Fuses or circuit breakers do not have sufficient capacity.	Replace fuses or circuit breakers.
	Starting relay not operating (motor does not reach normal speed).	Replace relay.
Overload kicking out frequently.	Feeding stock too fast.	Feed into blade slower.
	Blade dull, warped, or gummed.	Sharpen, clean, or replace saw blade.
	Blade binding due to rip fence misalignment.	Properly align rip fence. See Chapter 3.
	Extension cord too light or too long.	Use adequately sized extension cord.
	Low voltage supply.	Request a voltage check from power supplier.

SAW BLADE MAINTENANCE. All types of wood contain certain resins and pitches which have a tendency to accumulate on saw blades. Certain species of wood, such as pine and fir, contain unusually large amounts of resins. Saw blades used to cut these high resin woods will have their gullets and sides of their teeth filled with sawdust and resin mixture that clings tenaciously to the metal. Using blades in this condition can result in dangerous motor overloads. The blade surface can also burn, drastically shortening the life of the blade.

This build-up of pitch can easily be removed by submerging the blade in a container of solvent, such as kerosene or turpentine. Soak the blade for a few hours. This will soften the sawdust so it can easily be removed with firm brushing. This treatment can be repeated several times for the most stubborn build-up problems. Remember, whenever solvents are used, adequate ventilation is absolutely essential.

SHARPENING SAW BLADES. The practice of sharpening saw blades in the home workshop has dropped off drastically in recent years. The reason for this is obvious. Professional sharpeners offer precision sharpening jobs at reasonable prices. Yet for those who have both the time and the inclination, sharpening your own saw blades can be an enjoyable and satisfying job.

This sharpening procedure is usually broken down into four distinct parts—jointing, gumming, setting, and filing. Some of these procedures, jointing for example, need not be done every time a saw blade is sharpened. One thing to keep in mind is that since all the teeth on the saw blade are subject to the same amount of wear, a worn blade will have no teeth to serve as an original pattern. So, if you plan on doing your own sharpening, it is essential to make a pattern of each new saw blade you acquire. A typical pattern complete with the necessary length and angle data is shown in Figure 14-5.

Figure 14-5: Trace the pattern of your saw blades and record the necessary information.

CUTTING TEETH

RAKER TOOTH

60°

1/32"

12°

18°

HOOK TO CENTER

Jointing. Bringing the point of every saw tooth to exactly the same distance from the center of the arbor hole in the blade is known as jointing. In most cases, jointing is only necessary after the blade has been sharpened several times and the length of the teeth have become unequal.

The first step in jointing is to reverse the saw blade on the arbor so that it runs backwards. Lower the blade until its teeth barely project above the saw table. They should project just enough to score a piece of wood held flat on the table. Start the saw, and pass a medium-grit oilstone over the table above it (Figure 14-6). A lot of sparks will now fly, so be sure to wear protective eye gear. When they diminish, stop the saw, unplug the cord from its electrical source, and examine every tooth by revolving the blade by hand. If some of the teeth haven't been touched by the stone, raise the blade slightly, install the electrical plug, start the saw, and continue jointing until **every** tooth has a bright point. The saw is then perfectly round.

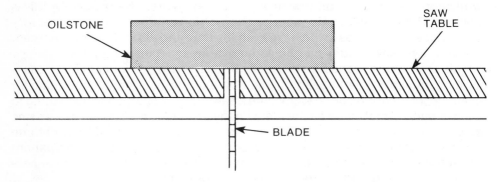

Figure 14-6: Jointing with an oilstone.

Gumming. The function of the gullets between the saw teeth is to carry away sawdust from the cutting teeth as the cut is being made. The depth of these gullets must be kept constant for optimum operation. The process of increasing the depth of the gullets is known as gumming. It is usually necessary to gum a saw blade after it has been jointed, because jointing shortens the teeth and decreases gullet depth. Normal wear can also decrease gullet depth to a point where gumming is necessary. Periodically check the blade against its original pattern. If the gullets have decreased in depth more than 1/16", gumming is in order. Remember that a shallow, poorly shaped gullet can quickly cause a blade to crack (Figure 14-7).

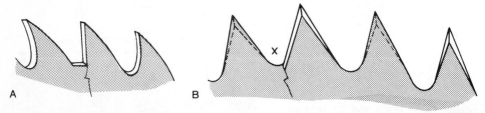

Figure 14-7: (A) Crack caused by a square gullet on ripsaw blade. (B) Wrong shape of the bevel and gullet at X on a crosscut blade.

Figure 14-8: Marking the saw blade during the gumming process.

The first step in the gumming process is to mark a pencil line on the saw blade so that all the gullets will be filed to the same depth. To do this, mount the blade on the saw arbor and rotate it by hand, holding the pencil as shown in Figure 14-8. The blade is then removed from the arbor and placed on a special saw vise (Figure 14-9).

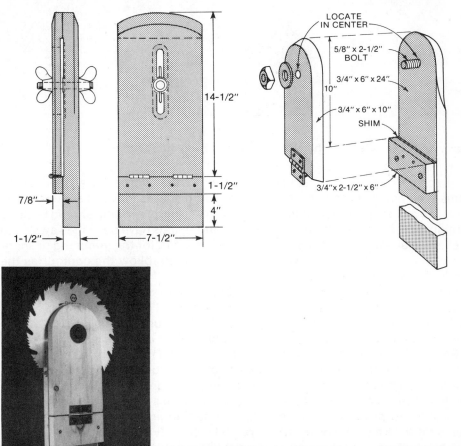

Figure 14-9: Construction details for a saw-filing vise and how the vise is used.

To make this vise, use a 1" by 6" board rounded at one end and bored to accommodate a 5/8" bolt. Make a short front jaw, boring it to match and hinging it to the first board. Position the blade so it is held between the jaws by the bolt, and clamp the vise against any suitable support. The saw vise can also be held in a bench vise while the blade is being filed. It should be held firmly enough to prevent chatter during filing.

Clean the gullets with a rattail file or the tang of another file (Figure 14-10A). Now, holding the rounded edge of the file down, file the gullets to the depth of the line. Proceed for each gullet, filing it to the depth indicated in the original pattern (Figure 14-10B). Be certain to maintain the original angle of the front of each tooth. This angle, known as the rake, is essential for the proper cutting action. To determine the rake of a particular saw blade, mark a circle on the saw blade halfway between its center and its edge. Then, draw a line from the front of any one of the teeth tangent to this circle.

A   B

Figure 14-10: (A) Cleaning the blade gullets. (B) Filing the saw teeth.

Shape corresponding teeth in sequence. In other words, file all teeth of the same type before proceeding to the next tooth shape. Filing in sequence will equalize any stresses set up in the blade during filing. All filing should be done straight across (no beveling) until all the jointing flats have been filed away and the teeth have their correct shape. The best method for the gumming or shaping of round gullets is to rotate the file slightly to follow the contour as the stroke is being made.

For the best results, use a 6" to 8" fine-slim, extra-slim, or double extra-slim taper file on crosscut teeth. (The type of file should depend on the size of the teeth.) Use a 6" to 10" fine round or rattail file for round gullets. A 7" to 12" fine mill file is a good general purpose file suitable for all other filing needs.

Setting. Bending some saw teeth to one side and the others to the opposite side is called setting. Setting is necessary for all saw blades except those which are hollow-ground or those which are swaged. A proper set assures the saw blade will cut a kerf wide enough for the blade to pass through without binding.

In order to properly set a saw blade, a setting jig should be constructed. Plans for such a jig are given in Figure 14-11. Use a 5/8" bolt to fasten the blade to a block of wood screwed to a base block that holds the "anvil." This anvil is a bolt with half of its head beveled to the angle of the set. When setting a ripsaw

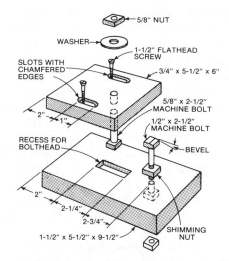

Figure 14-11: Plans for a setting jig.

blade, for instance, adjust it so that each tooth projects one-third over the beveled part on the anvil. Mark a tooth that has been bent away from you with a piece of chalk. Place the tooth on the anvil, hold a flat ended punch on it, and strike the punch a solid blow with a hammer to bend the tooth (Figure 14-12).

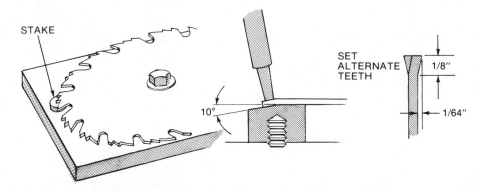

Figure 14-12: The correct method of setting a saw blade.

Skip the next tooth, but set the following one as before. Alternate setting the teeth in this manner until the tooth with the chalk mark has been reached. Reverse the saw blade on the setting jig and set those teeth which were skipped before. Because a saw can only cut itself free with the points of its teeth, the teeth should not be set more than one-half their length or thickness. It is also true that if the teeth are set too much, the saw produces an added cutting resistance and does not operate as well. Saw blades used for cutting soft, resinous woods or for fast or rough cutting should have the maximum working set possible. The minimal set should be used on blades which cut hard, dry woods or for blades used for extra-fine cutting. Thin-rim blades are a good example of those with minimal set. They are used for making extra-smooth and waste-free cuts. As mentioned before, hollow-ground blade teeth have no set whatsoever.

Filing. This is the final step in the sharpening operation. All filing should be done with the saw blade held in the saw vise (see the gumming section of this chapter). The same files used for gumming are also used in the final filing operation. To file the various blades, proceed as follows:

Rip Blades—To file a rip blade, start by filing the front edge of each tooth square to its sides with a flat mill file with rounded ends. (**Note:** If the saw blade has just been gummed, this step will have been done during the gumming process.) After the edge has been squared to its sides, file the top edges of the teeth, using only light strokes. Begin on a tooth set away from you and file it so the top edge is in line with the original pattern (Figure 14-13A). The teeth should be filed straight across. When a good amount of material must be filed away, go over the saw blade twice to make certain all the flat points have been removed. The rounded edges of the file will keep the gullets round. As previously mentioned, square gullets (see Figure 14-7A) often cause a rip blade to crack.

Crosscut Blades—The table saw crosscut blade has beveled edges like those of a handsaw. These bevels shouldn't extend all the way down to the gullets, as these should be round. File the bevels on those teeth that are set away from you, then reverse the saw and file the remaining half of the teeth (Figure 14-13B).

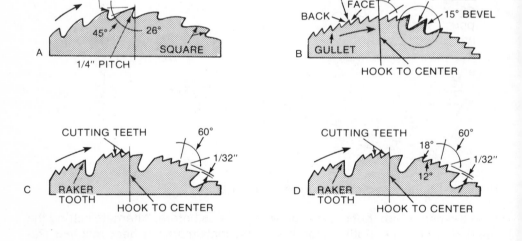

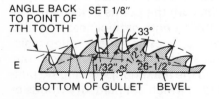

Figure 14-13: Typical tooth patterns of the more common blades: (A) Ripsaw blade; (B) crosscut blade; (C) planer blade; (D) novelty tooth combination blade; and (E) chisel-tooth combination blade.

Planer or Miter Blades—This blade has groups of four crosscut teeth with a rip or raker tooth separating each group (Figure 14-13C). File the crosscut teeth of these blades in the same way as the regular crosscut blades. Usually there are no gullets between the crosscut teeth, and the bevel extends all the way down. Follow these bevels as closely as possible, using either a flat or a triangular file.

The rip or raker teeth are filed straight across as in a rip blade, but they should be a trifle lower (1/64" to 1/32") than the crosscut teeth. Test them by taking a shallow cut in a piece of wood. If the bottom of the saw cut is flat, the raker teeth are too high and must be filed a little more, but if too sharp lines are scored in each side of the saw cut, it shows that the crosscut teeth are a trifle longer than the raker teeth. When the crosscut teeth are a little longer, a smoother cut will result.

Combination Blades—A novelty tooth combination blade is filed in the same manner as a hollow-ground blade with one exception. The crosscut teeth are beveled on alternate sides, the fronts 18° and the backs 12°, with the front radial (Figure 14-13D).

The chisel-tooth combination blade is filed as shown in Figure 14-13E.

Carbide-Tipped Blades—All types of carbide-tipped saw blades should be resharpened only by properly equipped professionals. When your blade first shows signs of dullness, it should be resharpened for best service and added life. If the blade is used when dull, cutting pressure increases and costly damage to the teeth will result. If you accidently chip or lose a tooth, have your blade repaired immediately. It is **extremely** dangerous to run a blade with chipped or fractured teeth. Missing teeth cause the blade to be out of balance, which causes vibration.

Sharpening Dado Heads. The points listed below should always be followed when sharpening a dado head:

1. When the spurs (or crosscut teeth) are in need of jointing, place the two outside cutters on the arbor as shown in Figure 14-14A. Locate an oilstone over the dado table insert (Figure 14-14B). Hold the stone in place and joint the spurs by turning the arbor by hand. **Caution**: Be sure the machine is disconnected from its power source during this operation.

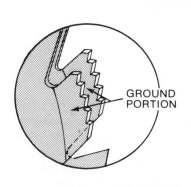

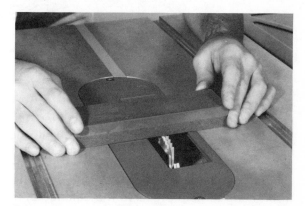

A   B

Figure 14-14: Jointing the spurs of outside cutters of a dado head.

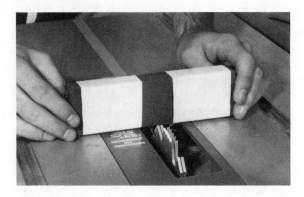

Figure 14-15: Jointing the rakers.

2. The rakers are jointed by a crosswise motion after the arbor has been raised an additional 1/64" (Figure 14-15). The inside cutters are jointed at the same setting as the rakers.

3. When setting spurs, always use the setting stake. Set all spurs in one group in the same direction as shown in Figure 14-16. Set the next group in the opposite direction.

Figure 14-16: Setting the spurs.   SETTING STAKE

4. As the outside cutters are being filed, file the crosscut teeth to the same bevel set originally by the manufacturer. File the raker teeth (those larger teeth) square across their faces. Keep them 1/64" lower than the crosscut teeth (Figure 14-17A). Use a square file to work the spurs, being careful to maintain the original angle (Figure 14-17B). Always take the same amount off of each tooth when filing to help preserve the balance of the saw blade. This is best done by counting the number of filing strokes and using the same number on each cutter.

A   B

Figure 14-17: Filing the raker and spurs of the outside saw blades.

5. When working the dado head's inside cutters, file the top of the teeth only (Figure 14-18). Do not touch the face of the teeth, except to remove the burr left when the tops are filed. When placed on the saw arbor, the inside cutters should be the same length as the raker teeth on the outside cutter—1/64" shorter than the cutter teeth. As with the outside cutters, use the same number of filing strokes on each cutter to assure proper blade balance and uniform cutter diameter. Examples of both a good and bad dado cut are shown in Figure 14-19.

Figure 14-18: Filing the dado's inside cutters.

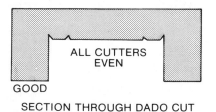 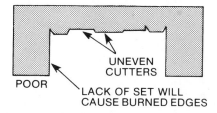

GOOD
SECTION THROUGH DADO CUT

ALL CUTTERS
EVEN

POOR

UNEVEN
CUTTERS

LACK OF SET WILL
CAUSE BURNED EDGES

Figure 14-19: Cross-sectional view of a good and bad dado cut.

SHARPENING MOLDING CUTTERHEAD KNIVES. Molding knives must be kept as sharp as possible to assure safe, accurate cutting. Proper sharpening requires a number of sharpening stones. The first should be a flat, Arkansas oilstone approximately 2" by 6" in size. (A slipstone with rounded edges made of the same material is a suitable alternative. It should be roughly 4" long and taper in thickness from 1/8" to 3/8".) Also, an oilstone or a slipstone roughly 4" long and 1/4" square and another 4" long, 2" wide, and 3/8" or 1/2" thick should be kept on hand. A triangular sectional oilstone is another convenient sharpening aid. It is possible to sharpen almost any type of cutting knife with this basic collection of stones.

The knives are ground in such a way that sharpening is easily done by whetting the flat side and removing the burr formed from the beveled edge. To preserve the shape of knives with involute bevels, grind them on their flat side only. When the knives are in overall good shape and are only in need of a slight touch-up, sharpen them by hand. This can be done with any oilstone. If the knives have nicks in them and are in overall poor condition, grind the blades on the front surface only. As shown in Figure 14-20, grind the cutterhead knife in the cross-section portion only.

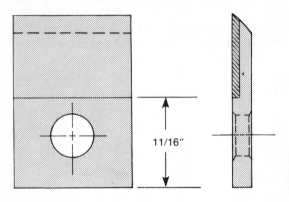

11/16"

Figure 14-20: Grind molding knives on the cross-section area as shown here.

In most cases, the high speed cutter knives are made in sets of three for use on the table saw. It is obvious that each set must be kept together to assure even cutting. Each member of the set must match the others in shape and in the extent to which it has been filed. It is necessary to purchase a new set of knives if one is broken or lost, so proper care of your molding cutters makes good sense.

Appendix A
Woodworking Terms

Across the grain. At right angles to the run of the wood grain.

Adhesive. A medium, such as glue or cement, by which surfaces or objects are held together.

Apron. A strip of wood at the base of cabinets, table tops, and chair seats, sometimes called a **rail** or **skirt.**

Band. Any flat, decorative or protective strip set flush with or projecting above a surface.

Batten. A narrow strip of wood nailed over joints of boards or plywood panels.

Bead. A rounded decorative molding with a small groove.

Beading. Small wooden molding used for decorative purposes.

Bevel. To cut on a slant so the angle formed is not a right angle.

Board. Sawed thin lumber, longer than it is wide.

Board foot. A unit of measurement. It refers to a piece of lumber measuring 1 square foot on the surface and 1″ in thickness.

Brad. A thin wire nail with a small head.

Butt. To join end to end without overlapping.

Butt joint. A joint formed by fastening parts together end to end without overlapping.

Butt miter. A surface beveled at an angle of 45°, joined with a similar surface and not overlapping.

C-clamps. A hand clamp, shaped like the letter C, by which pressure is applied with a thumb screw.

Chamfer. A sloping or beveled edge.

Channel. A shape which is like a **dado** or **groove**.

Cleat. A piece of wood or metal screwed or nailed across the back of a panel to brace it against buckling; a short piece of wood fastened to a wall to support the end of a shelf.

Compound miter. A cut made by combining a blade tilt (bevel) with a miter angle. Usually done to form a structure with sloping sides.

Corner block. A wooden block which reinforces the corners of a frame assembly.

Counterbore. To recess the head of a screw or other fastener below the surface of the wood in order to conceal it with a dowel plug.

Countersink. To drive nail heads below a surface or make depressions for screw heads, so that they will be below the surface of the wood in which they are inserted.

Cove. Concave molding.

Crosscutting. Sawing wood across the grain.

Cross lap joint. A method of joining wooden members, at an angle, usually 90°, by removing half the thickness of each member so that the members lie in the same plane.

Cross miter. Called a bevel or simply a miter, but specifically a bevel cut made across the grain.

Dado. A rectangular, flat-bottomed groove cut in wood.

Dado joint. A joint made where one member fits into a dado cut in the other member.

Dentil. A classic design which is actually a series of equally spaced rectangular blocks.

Depth of cut. A saw's capacity is often called out as "maximum depth of cut." Depth of cut may also mean how far into the work the saw or other tool should penetrate.

Direction of rotation. How a tool or blade turns on the arbor.

Dovetail. A flaring-shaped tenon.

Dovetail joint. A method of fastening together, especially in cabinet work, by a system of interlocking tenons cut in dovetail form.

Dowel. Pin which fits into a hole in an abutting piece and prevents slipping.

Dowel joint. A joint made by gluing a dowel into two pieces of wood.

Dressing. The operation of squaring and smoothing lumber.

Edge-glue. To glue two or more boards edge-to-edge to make a broad panel.

Edge grain. Lumber sawed so that the wide surfaces extend approximately at right angles to the rings of growth.

Edging. The decoration forming an edge or border.

End-match lumber. Boards having the ends as well as the sides tongued and grooved.

Face. The front or principal side of a building; surface of an object, a working face from which other surfaces or faces are trued.

Face mold. A pattern for making the board from which ornamental hand railings and other works are to be cut.

Fastening. Anything used in making an object secure, such as nails, screws, bolts, rivets, or adhesive.

Feed direction. The direction in which wood is moved past a saw blade or other cutting tool; or the direction in which the cutting tool is moved.

Feed speed. Refers to how fast the work is moved.

Flute. A channel or curved portion forming one of the several grooves in classical decoration.

Fluting. A series of decorative flutes.

Gain. A notch or groove made across the grain in a piece of lumber to receive a second member.

Gang cutting. Holding several pieces so all can be cut at the same time.

Glue. An adhesive material.

Glue block. A square or triangular block of wood glued and set into the interior angle formed by two boards to strengthen the joint.

Glue joint. A joint formed by two boards to which glue has been applied to hold them together.

Grain. The pattern or direction of the fibers in a piece of wood, such as straight, open, close, cross, curly, or short grain.

Groove. A term used to signify a sunken channel whose section is rectangular. It is usually used on the edge of a molding, stile, or rail, etc., into which a tongue corresponding to its section, and in the substance of the wood to which it is joined, is inserted.

Half lap joint. A joint used in splicing boards in which one half the thickness of each board is removed, permitting the boards to fit closely and to be firmly joined.

Hardboard. Panel building material made by pressing wood fibers into thin (1/8 or 1/4") sheets.

Heeling. The action of saw blade teeth when they are not cutting in a true plane. In effect, the back teeth of the cutting blade are not following the plane (kerf) of the front teeth.

Inlay. To cut out a surface to a desired pattern and insert a different material for ornamental purposes.

Jig. A device employed to simplify the operation of a power tool; a template used in producing numerous shapes of the same kind.

Joinery. Skilled work in wood, such as cabinet work, furniture, building, etc.

Joint. The point at which two pieces of material are joined to one another.

Kerf. A cut or groove made by the saw blade in sawing.

Kerfing. Sawing a series of cuts in a piece of wood so it can be bent or rounded.

Knot. A hard section interrupting the grain of a piece of wood.

Laminated construction. Any working member built up in layers to secure greater strength.

Laminated plastic. Hard surface decorative material used for counter tops, table tops, etc.

Lap dovetail. A joint used in drawer fronts in which the dovetail is not exposed on the front of the drawers.

Lap joint. A joint made by cutting away half the thickness from the face of one piece and half the thickness from the back of another, thus making the surfaces flush when joined.

Lumber. Sawed parts of a log such as boards, planks, scantling, and timber

Marble. A type of crystalline limestone capable of taking a high polish, found in various colors caused by impurities.

Matched boards. Boards cut with tongue and groove.

Miter. To fit together at an angle to form a miter joint.

Miter joint. A joint made by cutting two members at an angle and fitting them together, generally forming a 90° angle.

Molding. A narrow decorative strip applied to a surface.

Mortise. A hole cut into a piece of wood to receive a tenon or tongue shaped at the end of another piece of wood. The resulting fit is called a mortise-and-tenon joint.

Mortise-and-tenon joint. A furniture joint accomplished by fitting a tenon on one member into a mortise in the other.

Notch. A groove cut in a board into which another board may be inserted.

Notched joint. A joint in which two boards crossing at right angles are gained or notched to prevent lateral movements.

Panel. A finished board enclosed in a frame; a decorative design on a wall or paper to represent a panel; a sheet of plywood, fiberboard, insulation board, hardboard, etc.; a raised or sunken section in a wall, ceiling, wainscoting, or door.

Particleboard. A hard, durable panel of pressed wood chips or other materials which has many structural uses.

Pass. The action of moving work past a saw blade or other cutting tool.

Pivot. A central point established so a piece of work can be rotated against a cutting tool.

Plough. To cut a groove running in the same direction as the grain of the wood.

Plywood. A piece of wood made of three or more layers of thin sheets of wood or veneer joined with glue and usually laid with the grain of adjoining plies at right angles.

Pusher. A special device used to move material past a cutting tool. The idea is to keep hands away from danger areas. Especially important when doing ripping operations.

Quarter-round. A plain molding showing a quarter circle in section.

Rabbet. A rectangular recess cut on the face or edge of any material so that it may receive another member. Also, to break or cover a joint, as in rabbeted doors, door jambs, etc.

Rabbeted joint. A joint formed by two boards, rabbeted on opposite sides.

Raised panel. The face of the panel is above the face of the framing.

Re-saw. To saw a piece of timber already cut to dimensions, as in cutting boards from a squared timber.

Reeding. Raised parallel lines of convex or beaded form on the surface of wood, usually on molding. The reverse of **fluting**.

Rip miter. Actually a bevel but often identified as a miter especially when two such cuts are joined to form a 90° corner.

Ripping. Sawing wood with the grain or along the length of the wood.

Rpms. The number of revolutions a tool makes in a minute.

Scarfing. Joining and bolting two pieces of lumber together transversely so that the two appear to be one.

Score. To make notches or incisions along a cutting line.

Shim. A strip of material used to fill a small space.

Slot. A long narrow groove or opening, as a mortise.

Softwood. The wood obtained from needle-leaved (coniferous) trees such as redwood, tamarack, spruce, fir, cypress, cedar, larch, etc.

Spiral. A twisting form; same effect obtained by twisting together several strands of wire or string.

Splice. To join two pieces of wood or other material lengthwise by beveling, scarfing, overlapping, or entwining.

Spliced joint. A joint that has been formed by lapping materials at the corners or end.

Spline. A thin piece of wood placed in a miter joint after the miters have been grooved in order to strengthen the joint.

Splined joint. A tongued and grooved joint formed by placing a loose strip of wood or metal in the grooves formed on the edge of adjoining boards.

Stop (stop block). A device used to control the length of a cut or to position work so the same cut can be made on many pieces.

Strip cut. To cut slim strips from the edge of a board.

Template. A thin piece of metal or board used as a pattern.

Tenon. A projection on the end of a piece of wood which is fitted into a mortise.

Thickness. The distance between the two broad surfaces.

Timber. Lumber with a cross section over 4″ by 6″, such as posts, sills, and girders.

Tongue. A rib on the edge of a board that fits into a groove on the edge of another board to make a flush joint.

True. To make even; to level.

Veneer. A thin layer of wood glued to a base made of a cheaper or inferior wood.

Wall board. Wood pulp, gypsum, or similar materials made into large, rigid sheets that may be fastened to the frame of a building to provide a surface finish.

Width. The distance across the grain on the broadest surface.

Appendix B
Valuable Information
for the Home Shop

All dimensions in this book are given in English measurement. The following chart is arranged to make conversion to the metric system an easy matter:

INCH/MILLIMETER CONVERSIONS

INCHES TO MILLIMETERS Multiply inches by 25.4				MILLIMETERS TO INCHES Multiply millimeters by 0.03937	
INCHES	**MILLIMETERS**	**INCHES**	**MILLIMETERS**	**MILLIMETERS**	**INCHES**
.001	.025	17/32	13.4938	.001	.00004
.01	.254	35/64	13.8906	.01	.00039
1/64	.3969	9/16	14.2875	.02	.00079
.02	.508	37/64	14.6844	.03	.00118
.03	.762	19/32	15.0812	.04	.00157
1/32	.7938	.6	15.24	.05	.00196
.04	1.016	39/64	15.4781	.06	.00236
3/64	1.191	5/8	15.875	.07	.00276
.05	1.27	41/64	16.2719	.08	.00315
.06	1.524	21/32	16.6688	.09	.00354
1/16	1.5875	43/64	17.0656	.1	.00394
.07	1.778	11/16	17.4625	.2	.00787
5/64	1.9844	.7	17.78	.3	.01181
.08	2.032	45/64	17.8594	.4	.01575
.09	2.286	23/32	18.2562	.5	.01969
3/32	2.3812	47/64	18.6531	.6	.02362
.1	2.54	3/4	19.050	.7	.02756
7/64	2.7781	49/64	19.4469	.8	.0315
1/8	3.175	25/32	19.8438	.9	.03543
9/64	3.5719	51/64	20.2406	1.0	.03937
5/32	3.9688	.8	20.32	2.0	.07874
11/64	4.3656	13/16	20.6375	3.0	.11811
3/16	4.7625	53/64	21.0344	4.0	.15748
.2	5.08	27/32	21.4312	5.0	.19685
13/64	5.1594	55/64	21.8281	6.0	.23622
7/32	5.5562	7/8	22.225	7.0	.27559
15/64	5.9531	57/64	22.6219	8.0	.31496
1/4	6.35	.9	22.86	9.0	.35433
17/64	6.7469	29/32	23.0188	1 CM	.3937
9/32	7.1438	59/64	23.4156	2 CM	.7874
19/64	7.5406	15/16	23.8125	3 CM	1.1811
.3	7.62	61/64	24.2094	4 CM	1.5748
5/16	7.9375	31/32	24.6062	5 CM	1.9685
21/64	8.3344	63/64	25.0031	6 CM	2.3622
11/32	8.7312	1.0	25.4	7 CM	2.7559
23/64	9.1281	2.0	50.8	8 CM	3.1496
3/8	9.525	3.0	76.2	9 CM	3.5433
25/64	9.9219	4.0	101.6	1 DM	3.937
.4	10.16	5.0	127.0	2 DM	7.874
13/32	10.3188	6.0	152.4	3 DM	11.811
27/64	10.7156	7.0	177.8	4 DM	1 Ft., 3.748
7/16	11.1125	8.0	203.2		
29/64	11.5094	9.0	228.6	ABBREVIATIONS	
15/32	11.9062	10.0	254.0	MM-Millimeter(1/1000)	
31/64	12.3031	11.0	279.4	CM-Centimeter(1/100)	
1/2	12.7	1 Ft.	304.8	DM-Decimeter(1/10)	
33/64	13.0969				

WOOD GRADES

Boards refer to stock less than 2" thick and usually more than 6" wide. Narrower boards are **strips**. **Dimension** lumber, also called **framing** lumber, includes structural pieces from 2 to 5" thick used for studs, joists, and rafters. Lumber 5" thick or more is **timber**. Each type is sold in various grades according to the size, number, and kind of defects found in them. Softwoods and hardwoods are graded differently; there is no relation between softwood and hardwood grades.

SOFTWOOD LUMBER GRADES

SELECT
(Lumber of good appearance and finishing qualities.)

Suitable for Natural Finishes

GRADE A (also called No. 1 Clear). Free of defects. Because of cost, this grade is not stocked in all lumberyards.

GRADE B (also called No. 2 Clear). Allows a few small defects and blemishes. (A slightly higher category—B & Better—is sold by lumberyards. While not an "official" grade, it contains a few pieces of Grade A, but the majority is Grade B. This is slightly more expensive than Grade B itself.)

Suitable for Paint Finishes

GRADE C. Allows a limited number of small defects or blemishes that can be covered with paint. Some pieces can even take a natural finish.

GRADE D. Allows any number of defects or blemishes that do not detract from a finish appearance, especially when painted.

COMMON
(Lumber containing defects or blemishes which detract from a finish appearance, but which is suitable for general utility and construction use.)

Lumber Suitable for Use Without Waste

NO. 1 COMMON (also called Construction Grade). Good, sound, watertight lumber with tight knots (none larger than 2" and rarely on edges) and limited blemishes. No warp, splits, checks, or decay.

NO. 2 COMMON (also called Standard Grade). Allows larger and coarser defects than No. 1, but is considered graintight lumber.

Lumber Permitting Waste

NO. 3 COMMON (Also called Utility Grade). Allows larger and coarser defects than No. 2 and occasional knotholes.

NO. 4 COMMON (also called Economy Grade). Low-quality lumber admitting the coarsest defects, such as decay and knotholes.

NO. 5 COMMON. Practically waste lumber, good only for use as a filler, and then with considerable waste.

HARDWOOD LUMBER GRADES

Hardwood grading is not consistent for all trees, nor in all parts of the country. On the whole, however, the grades are as follows:

FIRSTS: Lumber that is 91-2/3% clear on both sides; considered the best possible for cabinetwork.

SECONDS: Lumber that is 83-1/3% clear on both sides; still very good for most cabinetwork.

FIRSTS & SECONDS: A selection that must contain not less than 20% firsts.

SELECTS (in alder, ash, beech, birch, cherry, chestnut, mahogany, maple, sycamore, and walnut only): Lumber that is 90% clear on one side only (other side not graded). Good for most cabinetwork, with some waste.

SAPS (in poplar only): Approximately the same as select above.

NO. 1 COMMON: One side only, 66-2/3% clear. With waste, good for interior and less demanding cabinetwork.

NO. 2 COMMON: One side only, 50% clear. Okay for painting, some paneling and flooring.

STAINED SAPS (in poplar only): Equivalent to No. 2 common, above.

NO. 3A COMMON: One side only, 33-1/3% clear.

NO. 3B COMMON: One side only, 25% clear.

SOUND-WORMY (in chestnut only): A No. 1 above but with wormholes.

Notes: Hardwoods are supposed to be free of warp, wind, bad splits, and checks. "Clear" refers to the number of clear cuttings that can be obtained.

AVERAGE FURNITURE, DIMENSIONS

Item	Length, Inches	Depth-Width, Inches	Height, Inches
Dining table	60	42	29
Kitchen table	42	30	30
Card table	36	36	30
Coffee table	36-60	18-24	14-18
End table	24	15	24
Lamp table	24 diam.		30
Desk	48	24	30
Secretary	36	24	84
Lowboy	30	18	30
Highboy	36	18	60-84
Breakfront	48-60	18	78-84
Sofa	72	30	36
Love seat	48	30	36
Occasional chair	27	30	36
Occasional chair (armless)	24	30	30
Dining, desk, folding chair	15-18	15-18	30-36*
Twin bed	78	39	20-24
Double bed	78	54	20-24
Dresser	42-60	22	32-36

*Seat Height 16-18 inches

HOW LUMBER IS SOLD

Lumber is sold by the board-foot measure. A board foot is equal to a piece 1" thick and 12" square. If you know the board-foot price, you can find the cost of any size or shape of lumber by using this formula (thickness and width are in inches and length is in feet):

$$\frac{\text{Thickness x width x length}}{12} = \text{board feet.}$$

Or, the number of board feet in lumber of various sizes and lengths is given in the following lumber calculator chart:

LUMBER CALCULATOR

Size in inches	8-foot	10-foot	12-foot	14-foot	16-foot
1 x 2	1-1/3	1-2/3	2	2-1/3	2-2/3
1 x 3	2	2-1/2	3	3-1/2	4
1 x 4	2-2/3	3-1/3	4	4-2/3	5-1/3
1 x 5	3-1/3	4-1/6	5	5-5/6	6-2/3
1 x 6	4	5	6	7	8
1 x 8	5-1/3	6-2/3	8	9-1/3	10-2/3
1 x 10	6-2/3	8-1/2	10	11-2/3	13-1/3
1 x 12	8	10	12	14	16
1-1/4 x 4	3-1/3	4-1/6	5	5-5/6	6-2/3
1-1/4 x 6	5	6-1/4	7-1/2	8-3/4	10
1-1/4 x 8	6-2/3	8-1/3	10	11-2/3	13-1/3
1-1/4 x 10	8-1/3	10-5/12	12-1/2	14-7/12	16-2/3
1-1/4 x 12	10	12-1/2	15	17-1/2	20
2 x 4	5-1/3	6-2/3	8	9-1/3	10-2/3
2 x 6	8	10	12	14	16
2 x 8	10-2/3	13-1/3	16	18-2/3	21-1/3
2 x 10	13-1/3	16-2/3	20	23-1/3	26-2/3
2 x 12	16	20	24	28	32
4 x 4	10-2/3	13-1/3	16	18-2/3	21-1/3
4 x 6	16	20	24	28	32
4 x 8	21-1/3	26-2/3	32	37-1/2	42-2/3
4 x 10	26-2/3	33-1/3	40	46-2/3	53-1/3
4 x 12	32	40	48	56	64
6 x 6	24	30	36	42	48
6 x 8	32	40	48	56	64

The prices of lumber are based on **nominal** or original rough sizes rather than **actual** dimensions as sold. In the case of softwoods, the actual thickness and width depend upon whether the pieces are rough-sawed or planed smooth, green or dry. For instance, a green, rough-sawed board 1″ thick is actually 3/4″ thick if dry and dressed; it is 25/32″ thick if it is green (above 19% moisture content) and dressed. If the lumber is grade-marked, the stamp will indicate whether the piece was green or dry when it was dressed to size.

NOMINAL AND ACTUAL SIZES OF SOFTWOODS

THICKNESSES Actual (inches)			FACE WIDTHS Actual (inches)		
Nominal (rough) size*	Minimum dry**	Dressed green	Nominal (rough) size*	Minimum dry**	Dressed green
1	3/4	25/32	2	1-1/2	1-9/16
1-1/4	1	1- 1/32	3	2-1/2	2-9/16
1-1/2	1-1/4	1- 9/32	4	3-1/2	3-9/16
2	1-1/2	1- 9/16	6	5-1/2	5-5/8
3	2-1/2	2- 9/16	8	7-1/4	7-1/2
4	3-1/2	3- 9/16	10	9-1/4	9-1/2
			12	11-1/4	11-1/2

*Thickness sometimes is expressed as 4/4, 5/4, etc.
**Dry lumber has been seasoned to a moisture content of 19% or less.

In softwoods, thickness less than 1″ is charged as a full inch, though in hardwoods the prices vary. The amount of size reduction of hardwoods depends partly on the standards used by the planing mill and partly on the amount of finishing (also called "dressing"). A piece may be dressed on one side only (S1S) or on both sides (S2S) and/or on one edge (S1E) or both edges (S2E). In the accompanying table, it should be kept in mind that the widths of hardwoods vary with various grades.

NOMINAL AND ACTUAL SIZES OF HARDWOODS

Nominal (rough) size	Surfaced 1 Side (S1S)	Surfaced 2 Sides (S2S)
3/8″	1/4″	3/16″
1/2″	3/8″	5/16″
5/8″	1/2″	7/16″
3/4″	5/8″	9/16″
1″	7/8″	1-13/16″
1-1/4″	1- 1/8″	1- 1/16″
1-1/2″	1- 3/8″	1- 5/16″
2″	1-13/16″	1- 3/4″
3″	2-13/16″	2- 3/4″
4″	3-13/16″	3- 3/4″

COMMON HOME-WORKSHOP WOODS

Name of Wood	Hardness	Strength	Stability	Weight	Rot resistance	Split resistance	Working quality for hand tools	Shaping	Turning	Mortising	Planing and jointing	Nailing	Gluing	Sanding	Cost
Alder	medium	weak	G	light	F	F	F	F	F	G	G	G	G	F	medium
Ash, white	medium	medium	E	medium heavy	F	G	E	F	F	G	G	G	F	E	medium
Balsa	soft	weak	G	light	P	E	P	P	P	G	G	E	E	P	low
Basswood	soft	weak	G	light	P	E	P	P	F	G	E	E	E	P	medium
Beech	hard	medium	P	heavy	P	F	F	F	G	F	P	G	G	G	medium
Birch	hard	strong	G	heavy	P	G	E	G	E	G	G	F	F	F	high
Butternut	soft	weak	E	light	F	F	F	G	F	G	G	G	G	F	medium
Cedar, red	soft	weak	G	medium	E	P	F	P	F	G	F	G	G	P	medium
Cherry	medium	medium	G	heavy	F	P	E	E	E	E	P	E	E	E	high
Chestnut	soft	weak	E	light	E	P	G	E	G	G	F	E	E	E	high
Cottonwood	soft	weak	G	light	P	E	P	P	P	G	G	E	E	P	low
Cypress	soft	medium	G	light	E	F	P	P	P	G	F	F	F	F	medium
Elm	medium	medium	P	medium heavy	F	G	P	P	G	P	E	F	G	G	medium
Fir, Douglas	medium	medium	F	medium heavy	G	F	G	P	G	G	G	G	G	F	medium
Fir, white		low	G	light	G	G	G	P	G	G	G	G	G	G	low
Gum, red	medium	medium	P	medium	F	G	P	F	E	F	F	P	G	F	medium
Hickory	hard	strong	G	heavy	P	F	F	G	E	G	P	G	G	E	medium

Wood														
Lauan	medium	medium	E	medium	G	P	G	F	G	F	G	E	P	medium
Magnolia	soft	weak	F	medium	F	G	G	G	F	P	E	E	G	medium
Mahogany	medium	medium	E	medium heavy	F	P	G	E	E	E	G	E	G	high
Maple, hard	hard	strong	G	heavy	P	P	P	E	E	E	P	F	G	high
Maple, soft	medium	medium	F	medium	F	G	G	F	F	P	F	G	G	medium
Oak, red	hard	strong	E	heavy	P	F	P	F	G	E	G	G	E	medium
Oak, white	hard	strong	E	heavy	F	F	P	G	G	E	G	G	E	high
Pine, ponderosa	soft	weak	G	light	F	P	E	G	G	F	E	E	F	low
Pine, sugar	soft	weak	G	light	F	P	E	G	G	F	E	E	P	low
Pine, white	soft	weak	G	light	F	P	E	G	G	F	E	E	G	low
Pine, yellow	hard	strong	F	heavy	G	P	F	G	P	G	F	F	F	medium
Poplar	soft	weak	G	medium	P	G	E	G	G	F	E	E	P	medium
Redwood	soft	medium	E	medium	E	G	G	P	F	P	G	E	P	medium
Spruce	soft	weak	G	light	F	F	G	G	G	F	G	G	G	medium
Sycamore	medium	medium	P	heavy	F	G	G	P	E	E	P	G	P	medium
Walnut	medium	strong	E	heavy	G	G	G	G	F	E	G	E	E	high
Willow	soft	weak	G	light	G	G	G	F	F	F	F	G	G	low

(E = Excellent, G = Good, F = Fair, P = Poor)

SOFTWOOD PLYWOOD

Softwood plywood is manufactured from several species of wood, of which Douglas fir is the most common. Some of the other species used in significant quantity include Southern yellow pine, Western larch, Western hemlock, Sitka spruce, commercial white firs, Alaska and Port Orford cedar, and California redwood.

Size. Plywood is most readily available in sheets or panels 4' wide by 8' long. Lengths up to 16' are available, but not always stocked. Widths range from 24 to 60", with 48" being most common.

Thickness. Plywood is manufactured in thicknesses of 1/4" to 1-1/8". A special 1/8" plywood is also available for model making and similar uses. There always will be an odd number of plies, the minimum number being three.

Product Standard. Construction and industrial plywood is manufactured in accordance with U.S. Product Standard PS 1. American Plywood Association grade-trademarks (shown here) are positive identification of plywood manufactured in conformance with PS 1 and with rigid quality standards of the Association.

Types. Two types of softwood plywood are available: exterior (waterproof) and interior (moisture-resistant); within each type there are several grades.

Exterior-type plywood is used when the wood will come into contact with excessive moisture and water, such as in boats, outdoor fences, combination sheathing and siding for houses, and outdoor furniture. This type of plywood is manufactured with phenolic or resorcinol-type adhesives that are insoluble in water.

Interior-type plywood will withstand occasional wetting during construction, but should not be permanently exposed to the elements. Within the interior-type classification there are two levels of adhesive durability: (1) interior with interior glue, which may be used where the plywood will not be subject to prolonged moisture conditions or extreme humidity and (2) interior with exterior waterproof glue for use where prolonged but temporary exposures to moisture are expected. Because lower veneer grades are permitted for inner plies of interior plywood, however, these panels are not equal in durability to fully exterior plywood and should not be exposed to continuous moisture conditions.

Group. All appearance grades are identified in the APA grade-trademark with a group number that refers to species. Plywood is manufactured from over 70 wood species of varying strength that have been classified under PS 1 into five groups (see table below). Each species within a given group meets a common criterion for that group. The strongest woods are found in Group 1 (the lower the group number, the greater the stiffness and strength). The group number in APA grade-trademarks is based on the species used for the face or back of the panel. Where face and back veneers are not from the same species, the number is based on the weaker group, except for decorative and sanded panels 3/8" or less, which are identified by face-species group.

CLASSIFICATION OF SPECIES (Softwood and Hardwood)

Group 1	Group 2	Group 3	Group 4	Group 5
Apitong (a), (b)	Cedar, Port Orford	Alder, Red	Aspen	Basswood
Beech	Cypress	Birch, Paper	Bigtooth	Fir, Balsam
American	Douglas Fir 2 (c)	Cedar, Alaska	Quaking	Poplar, Balsam
Birch	Fir	Fir, Subalpine	Cativo	
Sweet	California Red	Hemlock, Eastern	Cedar	
Yellow	Grand	Maple, Bigleaf	Incense	
Douglas Fir 1 (c)	Noble	Pine	Western Red	
Kapur	Pacific Silver	Jack	Cottonwood	
Keruing (a), (b)	White	Lodgepole	Eastern	
Larch, Western	Hemlock, Western	Ponderosa	Black (Western	
			Poplar)	
Maple, Sugar	Maple, Black	Spruce	Pine	
Pine	Mengkulang (a)	Redwood	Eastern white	
Caribbean	Meranti, Red (a), (b)	Spruce	Sugar	
Ocote	Mersawa (a)	Black		
Pine, Southern	Pine	Engelmann		
Loblolly	Pond	White		
Longleaf	Red			
Shortleaf	Virginia			
Slash	Western White			
Tanoak	Spruce			
Lauan	Red			
Almon	Sitka			
Bagtikan	Sweetgum			
Mayapis	Tamarack			
Red Lauan	Yellow-poplar			
Tangile				
White Lauan				

KEY TO SYMBOLS
(a) Each of these names represents a trade group of woods consisting of a number of closely related species.
(b) Species from the genus Dipterocarpus are marketed collectively, Apitong if originating in the Philippines, Keruing if originating in Malaysia or Indonesia.
(c) Douglas fir from trees grown in the states of Washington, Oregon, California, Idaho, Montana, Wyoming, and the Canadian provinces of Alberta and British Columbia shall be classed as Douglas fir No. 1. Douglas fir from trees grown in the states of Nevada, Utah, Colorado, Arizona, and New Mexico shall be classed as Douglas fir No. 2.
(d) Red Meranti shall be limited to species having a specific gravity of 0.41 or more based on green volume and oven dry weight.

Grades. The presence or absence of defects in the face or surface plies determines the grade of the plywood. The quality of the veneer is graded N (best), A, B, C, and D (poorest). N grade is a special-order veneer for use as a natural finish. In A-A grade plywood, for instance, both faces are of A quality; in C-D grade, one face is of C quality and the other of D quality. Only minor surface defects and limited patches are permitted in Grade A quality, and the face must be sanded. Grade B allows some appearance defects and permits more patching than Grade A as long as the surface is sanded smooth. Grades C and D permit knots, knotholes, and some splits, with larger defects permitted in the D grade. Some manufacturers produce plywood with an improved C veneer called C-plugged. A special grade of plywood, which usually has the second ply repaired, is used for underlayment. Only plywood bearing the "underlayment" or "Sturd-I-Floor" grade stamps should be used for that purpose. The inner plies may be of any grade, although D is commonly used interior type plywood. C is the lowest-grade veneer permitted for exterior type, and defects in the inner plies of marine plywood for boat hulls must be patched and repaired.

COMMON GRADES OF PLYWOOD

EXTERIOR

Grade (exterior)	Face	Back	Inner plies	Uses
A-A	A	A	C	Outdoors, where appearance of both sides is important.
A-B	A	B	C	Alternate for A-A, where appearance of one side is less important; face is finish grade.
A-C	A	C	C	Soffits, fences, base for coatings.
B-C	B	C	C	For utility uses such as farm buildings, some kinds of fences, etc., base for coatings.
303 Siding	C (or better)	C	C	Panels with variety of surface texture and grooving patterns; for siding, fences, paneling, screens, etc.
T1-11	C	C	C	Special 5/8" siding panel with deep parallel grooves; available unsanded, textured, or MDO surface.
C-C (plugged)	C (plugged)	C	C	Excellent base for tile and linoleum, backing for wall coverings, high-performance coatings.

COMMON GRADES OF PLYWOOD

EXTERIOR

Grade (exterior)	Face	Back	Inner plies	Uses
C-C	C	C	C	Unsanded, for backing and rough construction exposed to weather.
B-B Plyform	B	B	C	Concrete forms; reuse until wood literally wears out.
MDO	B	B or C	C	Medium Density Overlay— ideal base for paint; for siding, built-ins, signs, displays.
HDO	A or B	A or B	C-plugged or C	High Density Overlay—hard surface; no paint needed; for concrete forms, cabinets, counter tops, tanks.
A-A	A	A	D	Cabinet doors, built-ins, furniture where both sides will show.
A-B	A	B	D	Alternate of A-A, face is finish grade, back is solid and smooth.
A-D	A	D	D	Finish grade face for paneling, built-ins, backing.
B-D	B	D	D	Utility grade; for backing, cabinet sides, etc.
C-D	C	D	D	Sheathing and structural uses such as temporary enclosures, subfloor; unsanded.
Underlayment	C-plugged	D	C[1] and D	For separate underlayment under tile, carpeting.
Sturd-I-Floor	C-plugged	D	C[1] and D	For combination subfloor-underlayment under tile, carpeting.

[1] Special construction to resist indentation from concentrated loads.

HARDWOOD PLYWOOD

The species used in the face plies identifies hardwood plywood—that is, black walnut plywood would have one or both face plies of black walnut. Some of the more common species used in hardwood plywood are cherry, oak, birch, black walnut, maple, and gum among the native woods; mahogany, lauan, and teak in the imported category. A major difference in the manufacture of softwood and hardwood plywood is the use of a solid "core" or extra-thick middle ply in some hardwood panels.

Veneer-Core. Veneer-core plywood is manufactured with layers of wood veneer joined in the standard manner. It is intended for such uses as paneling, sheathing, and furniture parts, or when the plywood might be bent or curved.

Lumber-Core. Lumber-core plywood contains a thick core made by edge-gluing several narrow strips of solid wood. This core forms the middle section to which veneer crossbands and face plies are glued. Lumber-core plywood is manufactured for specific uses such as tabletops, built-in cabinets, and fixtures and doors where butt hinges are specified.

Particleboard-Core. In this plywood the core is an aggregate of wood particles bonded together with a resin binder. Face veneers are usually glued directly to the core, although crossbanding is sometimes used. Particleboard-core plywood is used in manufacturing furniture and is particularly adaptable for table, desk, and cabinet tops.

Size. Hardwood plywood is most commonly sold in panels 4' by 8', although it is possible to have plywood made in almost any desired size.

Thickness. Hardwood plywood is manufactured in three, five, seven, and nine plies with thicknesses ranging from 1/8" to 1". The table shows the most common thickness dimensions for the different number of plies.

Number of plies	Plywood thickness (inches)			
3	1/8	3/16	1/4	
5	1/4	3/8	1/2	5/8
7	5/8	3/4		
9	3/4	1		

Types. The following four types of hardwood plywood are available:

1. Type I is manufactured with waterproof adhesives and is used in areas where it will come in contact with water.

2. Type II is manufactured with water-resistant adhesives and is used in areas where it will not ordinarily be subjected to contact with water. However, it can be used in areas of continued dampness and excessive humidity.

3. Type III is manufactured with moisture-resistant adhesives and is intended for use in areas where it will not come in contact with any water. It can be subjected to some dampness and excessive humidity.

4. Technical has the same adhesive specifications as Type I but varies in thickness and arrangement of plies.

Grades. Hardwood plywood is manufactured in six specific grades. As in softwood plywood, each face must be specified.

Specialty Grade (SP)—This is a plywood made to order to meet the specific requirements of a particular buyer. Plywood of this grade usually entails special matching of the face veneers.

Premium Grade (#1)—The veneer on the face is fabricated for matched joints, and contrast in color and grain is avoided.

Good Grade (#1)—The veneer on the face is fabricated to avoid sharp contrasts in color and grain.

Sound Grade (# 2)—The veneer on the face is not matched for color or grain. Some defects are permissible, but the face is free of open defects and is sanded and smooth. It is usually used for surfaces to be painted.

Utility Grade (#3)—Tight knots, discoloration, stain, wormholes, mineral streaks, and some slight splits are permitted in this grade. Decay is not permitted.

Backing Grade (#4)—This grade permits larger defects. Grain and color are not matched, and the veneer is used primarily as the concealed face. Defects must not affect strength or serviceability of the panel made from it. At the manufacturer's option, this face can be of some species other than the exposed face.

Plywood, particleboard, and other sheet stock used in construction has been based traditionally on the 4' by 8' module. A soft conversion to metric dimensions would be 1220 by 2440 mm, or 1.22 by 2.44 m. However, construction in metric dimensions is expected to be based on a 100 mm building module. Therefore, the basic size of panel stock will be 1200 by 2400 mm or 1.2 by 2.4 m, a close approximation of the 4' by 8' panel. Traditional paneling dimensions and metric approximations are given here:

TRADITIONAL PANELING
(DIMENSIONS AND METRIC APPROXIMATIONS)

Paneling Widths/Lengths	Thicknesses
4 ft. = 1200 mm	1/8 in. = 3 mm
8 ft. = 2400 mm	1/4 in. = 6 mm
9 ft. = 2700 mm	3/8 in. = 9 mm
10 ft. = 3000 mm	1/2 in. = 12 mm
12 ft. = 3600 mm	5/8 in. = 15 mm
14 ft. = 4200 mm	3/4 in. = 18 mm
	1 in. = 25 mm

Veneers. Finished veneers have been sold traditionally in strips 1/28" thick. In metric, veneers will be sold per square meter (m²) in thicknesses of 1.5 mm or 3 mm.

GRADE AND GRIT NUMBERS OF ABRASIVES

	Aluminum oxide or silicon oxide	Garnet	Flint
Super fine	12/0 — 600 11/0 — 500 10/0 — 400	10/0 — 400 9/0 — 320 8/0 — 280	
Extra fine	9/0 — 320 8/0 — 280 7/0 — 240	7/0 — 240	
Very fine	6/0 — 220 5/0 — 180	6/0 — 220 5/0 — 180	4/0 3/0
Fine	4/0 — 150 3/0 — 120 2/0 — 100	4/0 — 150 3/0 — 120 1/0 — 100	0
Medium	1/0 — 80 1/2 — 60	1/0 — 80 1/2 — 60	1/2 1
Coarse	1 — 50 1-1/2 — 40	1 — 50 1-1/2 — 40	1-1/2 2
Very coarse	2 — 36 2-1/2 — 30 3 — 24	2 — 36 2-1/2 — 30 3 — 24	2-1/2 3

RECOMMENDED GRADES OF PAPER

Handwork	Backing	Grit number	Grade number	Word description
Rough sanding and shaping	D	60 or 80	1/2 or 1/0	medium
Preparatory sanding on softwood	A	100 to 150	2/0 to 4/0	fine
Preparatory sanding on hardwood	A	120 or 150	3/0 or 4/0	fine
Finish sanding on softwood	A	180 or 220	5/0 or 6/0	very fine
Finish sanding on hardwood	A	220 to 280	6/0 to 8/0	very fine to extra fine
Dry-sanding sealers and finishes between coats	A	220 to 280	6/0 to 8/0	very fine to extra fine
Wet-sanding sealers and finishes between coats	J or X	220 to 280	6/0 to 8/0	very fine to extra fine
Rubbing down after finish coat	J	280 to 400	8/0 to 10/0	extra fine to super fine

ABRASIVE SELECTION CHART FOR POWER SANDERS

Abrasive	Use	Grit		
		Rough	Medium	Fine
Aluminum oxide	Hardwood	2-1/2—1-1/2	1/2—1/0	2/0—3/0
	Aluminum	1-1/2	1/2—0	2/0
	Copper	1-1/2—1	0—2/0	2/0—3/0
	Steel	3—2-1/2	1/2—0	2/0
	Ivory	1/2—0	2/0—3/0	2/0—8/0
	Plastics	1—0	3/0—5/0	7/0
Garnet	Hardwood	2-1/2—1-1/2	1/2—1/0	2/0—3/0
	Softwood	1-1/2—1	1/0	2/0
	Composition board	1-1/2—1	1/2	1/0
	Plastics	1—0	3/0—5/0	7/0
	Horn	1-1/2	1/2—0	2/0—3/0
Silicon carbide	Glass	1—1/2	2/0—3/0	4/0—8/0
	Cast iron	3—2-1/2	1/2—0	2/0
	Ceramics	1/2	3/0	4/0—8/0
	Gemstones	1—1/2	0—3/0	4/0—8/0
	Steel	3—2-1/2	1/2—0	2/0
	Plastics	1—0	3/0—5/0	7/0
Flint	Removing paint or old finishes	3—1-1/2	1/2—1/0	

COVERING-CAPACITY SPECIFICATIONS*

Material	Square feet per gallon	Material	Square feet per gallon
Bleaching solutions	250—300	Spirit stain	250—300
Lacquer	200—300	Shellac	300—350
Lacquer sealer	250—300	Rubbing varnish	450—500
Paste wood filler	36—50 (per pound)	Flat varnish	300—350
Liquid filler	250—400	Paste wax	125—175
Water stain	350—400	Liquid wax	600—700
Oil stain	300—350	Non-grain-raising stain	275—325
Pigment oil stain	350—400	Paint	650—750

* General average—will vary considerably, depending on thickness of coat application to porous or nonporous surface, etc.

COMPARISON OF WOOD TYPE ADHESIVES

TYPICAL READY-USE WOOD ADHESIVES

	Aliphatic Resin Glue	Polyvinyl Acetate Glue	Liquid Hide Glue
Appearance	Cream	Clear white	Clear amber
Viscosity (poises at 83°F)	30-35	30-35	45-55
pH*	4.5-5.0	4.5-5.0	7.0
Speed of Set	Very fast	Fast	Slow
Strength (ASTM# Test)	All three easily exceed government specifications of 2800 pounds per square inch on hard maple. On basis of percent wood failure, aliphatic best, liquid hide next, polyvinyl acetate third.		
Stress Resistance†	Good	Fair	Good
Moisture Resistance	Fair	Fair	Poor
Heat Resistance	Good	Poor	Excellent
Solvent Resistance‡	Good	Poor	Good
Gap Filling	Fair	Fair	Fair
Wet Tack	High	None	High
Working Temperature	45°-110°F	60°-90°F	70°-90°F
Film Clarity	Translucent but not clear	Very clear	Clear but amber
Film Flexibility	Moderate	Flexible	Brittle
Sandability	Good	Fair (will soften)	Excellent
Storage (shelf life)	Excellent	Excellent	Good

TYPICAL WATER-MIXED AND TWO-PART WOOD ADHESIVES

	Casein	Plastic Resin	Resorcinol
Appearance	Cream	Tan	Dark reddish brown
Viscosity	35-45,000 cps	25-35,000 cps	30-40,000 cps
Speed of Set	Slow	Slow	Medium
Strength (ASTM# Test)	2,800 plus psi	2,800 plus psi	2,800 plus psi
Stress Resistance	Good	Good	Good
Moisture Resistance	Good	Good	Waterproof
Heat Resistance	Good	Good	Good
Solvent Resistance	Good	Good	Good
Gap Filling Ability	Fair to good	Fair	Fair
Wet Tack	Poor	Poor	Poor
Working Temperature	32°-110°F	70°-100°F	70°-120°F
Film Clarity	Opaque	Opaque	Opaque
Film Flexibility	Tough	Brittle	Brittle
Sandability	Good	Good	Good
Storage (shelf life)	1 year	1 year	1 year

*pH—glues with a pH of less than 6 are considered acidic and thus could stain acid woods such as cedar, walnut, oak, cherry, and mahogany.

#ASTM—American Society of Testing Materials.

†Stress resistance (cold flow)—refers to the tendency of a product to give way under constant pressure.

‡Solvent resistance—ability of finishing materials such as varnishes, lacquers, and stains to take over a glued joint.

COMMON NAILS

Size	Length	Diameter Gauge No.	Diameter Of Head	Approx. No. Per Pound
2d	1"	15	11/64"	830
3d	1-1/4"	14	13/64"	528
4d	1-1/2"	12-1/2	1/4"	316
5d	1-3/4"	12-1/2	1/4"	271
6d	2"	11-1/2	17/64"	168
7d	2-1/4"	11-1/2	17/64"	150
8d	2-1/2"	10-1/4	9/32"	106
9d	2-3/4"	10-1/4	9/32"	96
10d	3"	9	5/16"	69
12d	3-1/4"	9	5/16"	63
16d	3-1/2"	8	11/32"	49
20d	4"	6	13/32"	31
30d	4-1/2"	5	7/16"	24
40d	5"	4	15/32"	18
50d	5-1/2"	3	1/2"	14
60d	6"	2	17/32"	11

FINISHING NAILS

Size	Length	Diameter Gauge No.	Diameter Of Head Gauge No.	Approx. No. Per Pound
2d	1"	16-1/2	13-1/2	1351
3d	1-1/4"	15-1/2	12-1/2	807
4d	1-1/2"	15	12	584
5d	1-3/4"	15	12	500
6d	2"	13	10	309
8d	2-1/2"	12-1/2	9-1/2	189
10d	3"	11-1/2	8-1/2	121
16d	3-1/2"	11	8	90
20d	4"	10	7	62

DRYING-TIME SPECIFICATIONS*

Material	Touch	Recoat	Rub
Lacquer	1—10 minutes	1-1/2—3 hours	16—24 hours
Lacquer sealer	1—10 minutes	30—45 minutes	1 hour
Paste wood filler		24—48 hours	
Paste wood filler (quick dry)		3—4 hours	
Water stain	1 hour	12 hours	
Oil stain	1 hour	24 hours	
Spirit stain	zero	10 minutes	
NGR stain	2 minutes	15 minutes	
Penetrating resin finishes	15—45 minutes	3—4 hours	4 hours
Pigment oil stain	1 hour	12 hours	
Pigment oil stain (quick dry)	1 hour	3 hours	
Shellac	15 minutes	2 hours	12—18 hours
Shellac (wash coat)	2 minutes	30 minutes	
Varnish (spar)	1-1/2 hours	18—24 hours	24—48 hours
Varnish (synthetic)	1/2 hour	4 hours	12—48 hours

* Average time. Different products will vary.

GENERAL WOOD-CHARACTERISTIC AND FINISHING TABLE

Wood	Natural color	Grain figure	Stain Type	Stain Color	Filler Weight +	Filler Color	Natural finish	Bleach	Paint
Alder	pink to brown	plain or figured	oil or water	red or brown	none	none	yes	yes	yes
Amaranth	purple	plain or stripe	none	none	8	match wood	yes	no	no
Ash	white to brown	plain	any	any	1.5 to 2	white or brown	yes	yes	yes
Aspen	light straw	plain or stripe	water	amber	none	none	yes	no	yes
Avodire	white to cream	stripe	none	none	8	match wood	yes	yes*	no
Basswood	cream	mild	water	red or brown	none	none	no	yes*	yes
Beech	white to brown	mild	water	red or brown	8	red or brown	no	yes	yes
Birch	cream	mild	any	walnut or mahogany	none or 7	natural or brown	yes	yes	yes
Bubinga	pale red to flesh red	plain to figured	water	red or brown	12 to 14	red or brown	yes	no	no
Butternut	amber and cream	like walnut	water	walnut or oak	12 to 14	medium brown	yes	yes	no
Cedar	red and cream	knotty or stripe	none	none	none	none	yes	no	no
Cherry	red to brown	fine	water	red or brown	6 to 8	brown, red, or black	yes	no	no
Chestnut	gray-brown	heavy grain	oil‡	red or brown	15	red or brown	yes	yes	yes

Wood	Color	Grain	Stain	Stain color	Filler (lbs)†	Filler color			
Cypress	brown and cream	plain or figured	water or oil‡	red or brown	none	none	yes	no	yes
Ebony	dark brown to black	plain or stripe	water	red or brown	none	none	yes	no	no
Elm	cream to brown	heavy grain	water	red or brown	12 to 14	dark brown	yes	no	yes
Fir (Douglas)	cream	wild	oil‡	brown	none	none	no	no	yes
Gaboon	golden to pinkish tan	plain or stripe	water	red or brown	none	none	yes	no	no
Gum (red)	cream and red	plain or figured	any	red or brown	none or 4 to 6	match wood	yes	yes	yes
Hemlock	light reddish brown	plain	water or oil‡	red or brown	none	none	no	no	yes
Hickory	white to cream	straight	water	red or brown	15	brown	yes	yes	no
Holly	white	mild	water	amber	none	none	yes	yes*	yes
Kelobra	brown	plain or stripe	water	dark brown	12 to 14	dark brown	yes	yes	no
Korina	creamy gray	plain or stripe	water	red or brown	12 to 14	red or brown	yes	yes	no
Lacewood	light brown	flake	water	oak	12 to 14	dark brown	yes	yes	no

† Weight designates number of pounds of filler plastic per gallon of thinner.
* Generally not necessary because of the light color of the wood.
‡ Penetrating oil stain may also be used. Non-grain-raising stains may be substituted for water stains throughout.

GENERAL WOOD-CHARACTERISTIC AND FINISHING TABLE

Wood	Natural color	Grain figure	Stain Type	Stain Color	Filler Weight +	Filler Color	Natural finish	Bleach	Paint
Lauan	brown to red-brown	stripe	water or oil‡	red or brown	18	red, brown, or black	yes	yes	no
Locust	golden brown	wild	water or oil‡	brown	12 to 16	brown	yes	no	yes
Magnolia	light to dark yellowish brown	plain	water or oil‡	brown	none	none	yes	yes	yes
Mahogany	brown to red-brown	stripe	water	red or brown	12	red, brown, or black	yes	yes	no
Maple	cream	varied	water or oil‡	maple	none	none	yes	yes	yes
Oak (red)	red to brown	plain or flake	water	light green	15	brown	no	yes	yes
Oak (white)	white to pale brown	plain or flake	water	brown	15	brown	yes	yes	yes
Orientalwood	light brown	stripe	water	amber or brown	12	brown	yes	no	no
Padauk	golden red to crimson	stripe or mottle	none	none	14 to 16	red or brown	yes	no	no
Pine (white)	white to cream	very mild	water or oil	brown	none	none	no	no	yes
Pine (yellow)	cream to yellow	mild	water or oil	brown	none	none	yes	no	yes

Wood	Color	Figure	Stain base	Stain color	Filler	Finish color			
Poplar	white	mild	water or oil	red or brown	none	none	no	no	yes
Primavera	white to yellow	stripe	water	amber	12	natural	yes	yes	no
Redwood	red	mild	oil	red	none	none	yes	no	yes
Rosewood	red to brown	stripe to varied	water	red	12 to 15	dark red to black	yes	no	no
Sapeli	medium brown	stripe	water	red or brown	10	dark brown	yes	yes	no
Spruce	white	plain	water or oil	amber or brown	none	none	no	no	yes
Sycamore	white to pink	flake	water	amber or brown	none	none	yes	yes*	yes
Teakwood	golden brown	plain or figured	water or oil	brown	16	natural or brown	yes	yes	no
Tigerwood	golden brown	stripe	water	dark brown	8 to 12	dark brown	yes	yes	no
Tupelo	pale to brownish gray	plain	water	brown	none to 7	brown	yes	yes	yes
Walnut	cream and dark brown	varied	water	dark brown	12 to 15	brown to black	yes	yes	no
Zebrawood	tan with brown stripe	heavy stripe	water	light oak	12	natural	yes	no	no

+ Weight designates number of pounds of filler plastic per gallon of thinner.
* Generally not necessary because of the light color of the wood.
‡ Penetrating oil stain may also be used. Non-grain-raising stains may be substituted for water stains throughout.

BIT OR DRILL SIZES

| Size Of Screw | Shank Holes | | Pilot Holes | | | | Auger Bit For Countersink (By 16ths) |
| | Drill Number Or Letter | Drill Size Nearest Fraction | Hardwood | | Softwood | | |
			Drill Number Or Letter	Drill Size Nearest Fraction	Drill Number Or Letter	Drill Size Nearest Fraction	
0	52	1/16"	70	1/32"	75	1/64"	—
1	47	5/64"	66	1/32"	71	1/32"	—
2	42	3/32"	56	3/64"	65	1/32"	3
3	37	7/64"	54	1/16"	58	3/64"	4
4	32	7/64"	52	1/16"	55	3/64"	4
5	30	1/8"	49	5/64"	53	1/16"	4
6	27	9/64"	47	5/64"	52	1/16"	5
7	22	5/32"	44	3/32"	51	1/16"	5
8	18	11/64"	40	3/32"	48	5/64"	6
9	14	3/16"	37	7/64"	45	5/64"	6
10	10	3/16"	33	7/64"	43	3/32"	6
11	4	13/64"	31	1/8"	40	3/32"	7
12	2	7/32"	30	1/8"	38	7/64"	7
14	D	1/4"	25	9/64"	32	7/64"	8
16	I	17/64"	18	5/32"	29	9/64"	9
18	N	19/64"	13	3/16"	26	9/64"	10
20	P	21/64"	4	13/64"	19	11/64"	11
24	V	3/8"	1	7/32"	15	3/16"	12

Index